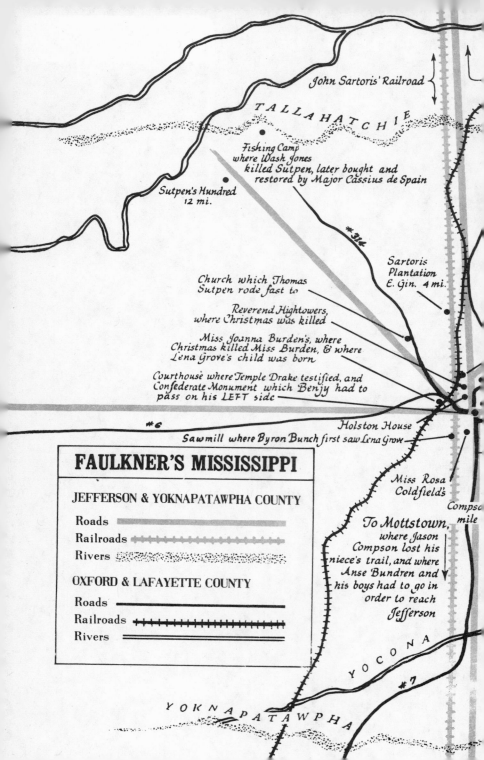

John Sartoris' Railroad

TALLAHATCHIE

Fishing Camp
where Wash Jones
killed Sutpen, later bought and
restored by Major Cassius de Spain

Sutpen's Hundred
12 mi.

#314

Sartoris
Plantation
E. Gin. 4 mi.

Church which Thomas
Sutpen rode fast to

Reverend Hightowers,
where Christmas was killed

Miss Joanna Burden's, where
Christmas killed Miss Burden, & where
Lena Grove's child was born

Courthouse where Temple Drake testified, and
Confederate Monument which Benjy had to
pass on his LEFT side

#6

Holston House

Sawmill where Byron Bunch first saw Lena Grove

Miss Rosa
Coldfield's

FAULKNER'S MISSISSIPPI

JEFFERSON & YOKNAPATAWPHA COUNTY

Roads
Railroads
Rivers

OXFORD & LAFAYETTE COUNTY

Roads
Railroads
Rivers

Compso
mile

To Mottstown,
where Jason
Compson lost his
niece's trail, and where
Anse Bundren and
his boys had to go in
order to reach
Jefferson

YOCONA

#7

YOKNAPATAWPHA

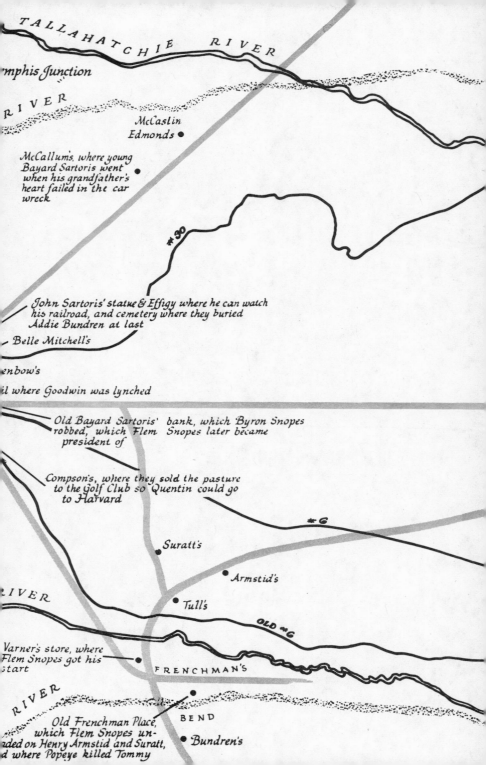

TALLAHATCHIE   RIVER

[Me]mphis Junction

[ ] RIVER

McCaslin
Edmonds •

McCallum's, where young
Bayard Sartoris went •
when his grandfather's
heart failed in the car
wreck

#30

John Sartoris' statue & Effigy where he can watch
his railroad, and cemetery where they buried
Addie Bundren at last

Belle Mitchell's

[ ]enbow's

[ ]l where Goodwin was lynched

Old Bayard Sartoris' bank, which Byron Snopes
robbed, which Flem Snopes later became
president of

Compson's, where they sold the pasture
to the Golf Club so Quentin could go
to Harvard

#6

Suratt's •

Armstid's •

RIVER

Tull's •

OLD #6

Varner's store, where
Flem Snopes got his
start

FRENCHMAN'S

RIVER

Old Frenchman Place,
which Flem Snopes un-
[lo]aded on Henry Armstid and Suratt,
[an]d where Popeye killed Tommy

BEND

• Bundren's

YOKNAPATAWPHA

WILLIAM FAULKNER, THE GRANDFATHER

J. R. Cofiel

"I'm sure you have often noticed how ignorant people beyond thirty
or forty are" (*The Reivers*, p. 5).

YOKNAPATAWPHA

Faulkner's "Little Postage Stamp of Native Soil"

Elizabeth M. Kerr

New York
FORDHAM UNIVERSITY PRESS

Printed in the United States of America

ACKNOWLEDGMENTS

To Doubleday for *Killers of the Dream* by Lillian Smith. Copyright © 1949, 1961 by Lillian Smith. Reprinted by permission of Doubleday & Company, Inc.

To Harcourt, Brace & World, Inc. for *Mississippi: The Closed Society* by James W. Silver.

To Harper & Row, Publishers, Inc. for *An American Dilemma* by Gunnar Myrdal.

To Kenkyusha Ltd., Publishers, for *Faulkner at Nagano* edited by Robert A. Jelliffe.

To Alfred A. Knopf, Inc. (Random House, Inc.—Vintage Books) for *The Mind of the South* by Wilbur J. Cash.

To Random House, Inc. for the map from *Absalom, Absalom!*; for Faulkner, *Absalom, Absalom!*, copyright © 1936 by William Faulkner, renewed 1964 by Estelle Faulkner and Jill Faulkner Summers; for Faulkner, *Go Down, Moses*, copyright © 1942 by William Faulkner; for Faulkner, *Intruder in the Dust*, copyright © 1948 by Random House, Inc. and by William Faulkner; for Faulkner, *The Mansion*, copyright © 1955, 1959 by William Faulkner; for Faulkner, *Sartoris*, copyright © 1929 by Harcourt, Brace and Co., Inc., copyright © renewed 1956 by William Faulkner; for Faulkner, *Requiem for a Nun*, copyright © 1950, 1951 by William Faulkner; for Faulkner, *The Town*, copyright © 1957 by William Faulkner and by the Curtis Publishing Co.

To The University Press of Virginia for *Faulkner in the University* edited by Frederick L. Gwynn and Joseph L. Blotner.

Permission to reprint has also been obtained from Chatto and Windus, Ltd., for the Faulkner works listed under Random House, Inc., excluding *Absalom, Absalom!* for which permission has been received from Curtis Brown, Ltd.

I wish to acknowledge the generous help the following people gave me in gathering material and preparing this volume:

Professor Ralph M. Aderman, University of Wisconsin–Milwaukee, Milwaukee, Wisconsin; Professor Maurice L. Beebe, Temple University, Philadelphia, Pennsylvania; Miss Mary Louise Bell, University of Wisconsin–Milwaukee, Milwaukee, Wisconsin; Professor Joseph L. Blotner, University of North Carolina, Chapel Hill, North Carolina; Professor Enola M. Borgh, University of Wisconsin–Milwaukee, Milwaukee, Wisconsin; Mr. J. R. Cofield, Oxford, Mississippi; Professor Carvel Collins, University of Notre Dame, Notre Dame, Indiana; Mr. Albert Erskine, Random House, New York; Professor Melvin J. Friedman, University of Wisconsin–Milwaukee, Milwaukee, Wisconsin; Professor Evans Harrington, University of Mississippi, University, Mississippi; Professor Robert B. Holland, Mississippi State University, State College, Mississippi; Professor Anita Hutcherson, University of Mississippi, University, Mississippi; Mrs. Louise Meadow, Oxford, Mississippi; Professor Emeritus Verna L. Newsome, University of Wisconsin–Milwaukee, Milwaukee, Wisconsin; Miss Dorothy Z. Oldham, University of Mississippi, University, Mississippi; Professor John Pilkington, University of Mississippi, University, Mississippi; Mr. Clark Porteous, Memphis *Press-Scimitar*, Memphis, Tennessee; Mr. W. McNeill Reed, Oxford, Mississippi; Professor James Silver, University of Notre Dame, Notre Dame, Indiana; Mr. Thomas W. Tullos, University of Mississippi, University, Mississippi; Professor Florence L. Walzl, University of Wisconsin–Milwaukee, Milwaukee, Wisconsin;

Professor James W. Webb, University of Mississippi, University, Mississippi.

I wish also to express appreciation to Rev. Edwin A. Quain, s.j., and Mr. H. George Fletcher, of Fordham University Press, for their expert assistance, to the Graduate School Research Committee of the University of Wisconsin for research grants, and to Miss Lisa McGaw, for preparing the index.

ELIZABETH M. KERR

Milwaukee, Wisconsin
October, 1968

PREFACE
TO THE SECOND EDITION

In preparing *Yoknapatawpha* for its new edition, I was able to make a modest number of corrections and revisions, but I was also convinced anew of the lack of need for general revision, and the work now appears again essentially unchanged from its original version. Because Yoknapatawpha County and Jefferson are based on Lafayette County and Oxford as Faulkner knew them, changes which have taken place there since 1962 are irrelevant to the purpose of this study and are not dealt with. The reader is urged to remember that time has marched on in Mississippi and that since 1965 the racial situation, in particular, has changed remarkably. The mythic world of Yoknapatawpha endures, but the physical world Faulkner dwelt in—"Was."

ELIZABETH M. KERR

Milwaukee, Wisconsin
June, 1976

CONTENTS

YOKNAPATAWPHA

INTRODUCTION

The Reivers, published a few months before the death of William Faulkner, marks the end of the Yoknapatawpha chronicles, a body of fiction unique in American literature. The creative genius of Faulkner brought Yoknapatawpha into being over a period of more than thirty years, from the beginning to the end of his successful literary career. During this period, critical evaluation of the chief Yoknapatawpha novels has ranged from bitter denunciation to extravagant praise. The final evaluation of Faulkner's literary achievement will rest upon this unified body of fiction dealing with Yoknapatawpha County and its people; none of his other novels and few of his short stories dealing with other scenes are of comparable quality. The annals of Yoknapatawpha are so long and complex, however, and often so difficult in technique that most readers and many critics can not take time to become acquainted with the whole. Yet a part may be misleading, and the whole adds new dimensions to the separate parts.

The purpose of this study is to provide the comprehensive view of Yoknapatawpha County that throws light upon any specific part and to furnish such aids to the reader as may increase his enjoyment and appreciation by facilitating his understanding. Behind the world of Yoknapatawpha lies the world of Lafayette County. To keep the two worlds distinct but still to show the relationship between them, the factual parallels to the fiction have generally been limited to footnotes, a method which not only suggests the double vision of the mind's eye and the physical eye but also keeps the emphasis where it should be, on the fiction. Like the map of Yoknapatawpha County superimposed on that of Lafayette County,*

* See endpaper map.

this study is intended to help the reader to find his way
wherever he may wish to go and to distinguish between the
domain of William Faulkner, "Sole Owner and Proprietor,"
and its geographical, historical, and social prototype.

Yoknapatawpha County is a triumph of the creative imagination. But it is not a mere figment of the imagination. The
parallels between the realities of Lafayette County and the
fictions of Yoknapatawpha County are traced in this study,
not primarily to prove that Faulkner was a realist but to show
ultimately that his imagination, working with the land, the
people, and the way of life he knew, brought forth a realism
of the spirit. It is to deny Faulkner's greatness to deny that
Yoknapatawpha bears resemblance in essentials to his South; it
is equally to deny his greatness to assert that Yoknapatawpha
County and Jefferson are merely Lafayette County and Oxford, thinly disguised.

To orient the reader in the land and the society, it is necessary to begin with the more factual and objective aspects of
Yoknapatawpha and their basis in reality. To those unfamiliar
with the area and the culture, some of the realities may seem
fantastic and some things which are typical may seem unique.
To distinguish between the idiosyncratic and the customary,
between the negligible and the significant in words, gestures,
and actions, one needs to know what details in Faulkner are
confirmed by observation and by authorities on the South.
Both imaginative realization and critical appreciation are
heightened by viewing specific scenes in Yoknapatawpha in
their larger context. There is no substitute, however, for im-
mersion in the world of Yoknapatawpha by reading and re-
reading the major novels and stories. Although this study may
aid the reader and increase his initial appreciation by providing
maps and signposts, as it were, he must be prepared to dwell
in imagination in Yoknapatawpha County if he would know it
and its creator.

ELIZABETH M. KERR

The University of Wisconsin—Milwaukee

I

THE CREATION OF THE
WORLD OF YOKNAPATAWPHA

1. *The Yoknapatawpha Fiction as an Organic Sequence*

BECAUSE William Faulkner's world of Yoknapatawpha took shape gradually, critics were slow in realizing that an evaluation of Faulkner's work should include not only critical analysis of the individual works but also consideration of the whole body of fiction and its extra dimension owing to recurrent characters and scenes, retelling of events, and repetition of unifying themes. The completion of the Yoknapatawpha fiction by the publication of *The Reivers* in 1962, shortly before the death of William Faulkner, has had little effect on critical approaches to the Yoknapatawpha novels and stories. But in order that Faulkner's creation may be appreciated for what it is, it must be viewed in its entirety, not merely in its parts, and the view must be unobscured by misleading analogies with other series of fictitious studies of a society. The genesis of the Yoknapatawpha fiction, the nature of Faulkner's genius, and the distinctive characteristics of his study of Yoknapatawpha should be understood before specific aspects are examined.

3

Faulkner made no claim to take all society or even all of Mississippi to be his province: he modestly reiterated that he wrote about what he knew.[1] He was content to spend the greater part of his life in the region where he was born, going deeply into the life and history of one county. He stated a modest and humanistic aim:

I was trying to talk about people, using the only tool I knew . . . .
No, I . . . wasn't writing sociology at all. I was just trying to write about people, which to me are the important thing. Just the human heart, it's not ideas. I don't know anything about ideas, don't have much confidence in them [*Faulkner in the University,* p. 10].

Furthermore, Faulkner wrote as a native of a rural and small-town environment who, according to the self-image which he chose to present to the public, remained a countryman first, a writer second, and a literary man not at all:

. . . my life was established before I began to write. I'm a country-man. My life is farmland and horses and the raising of grain and feed. I took up writing simply because I liked it—it was something very fine, and so I have no plans—I look after my farm and my horses and then when there is time I write, or if I have something I want to write, I will find time to write it, but just to be a writer is not my life . . . . I always find time to do the writing, but I do other things also [*Faulkner at Nagano,* p. 142].

Because, as he said, he lacked the formal education of such men as Edmund Wilson and Malcolm Cowley and did not associate much with writers and critics, Faulkner did not consider himself a literary man (*Faulkner in the University,*

[1] The chief sources in this chapter for the ideas of Faulkner are two volumes of recorded interviews with Faulkner: *Faulkner at Nagano,* A. Jelliffe, ed. (Tokyo: Kenkyusha, 1956); *Faulkner in the University,* Frederick L. Gwynn and Joseph L. Blotner, eds. (Charlottesville: University of Virginia Press, 1959). *Faulkner at West Point,* Joseph L. Fant III and Robert Ashley, eds. (New York: Random House, 1964), adds little that is new but is useful as confirmation of ideas and attitudes expressed in the earlier works and as Faulkner's last comments on himself and his art; p. 51 repeats the point in the quotation following, that sociology is "coincidental to the story."

p. 23). With all due allowance for Faulkner's probable under-
emphasis on the writing and overemphasis on the farming, one
can still accept Faulkner's image of himself as essentially true
in that he lived in order to write, rather than wrote to live.
He acted in accordance with his conviction that a writer must
"get down in the market place and stay there" and that a
writer should have some other job than writing so that he "can
remain an amateur all the time" (*Faulkner at West Point*, pp.
55, 98). The term *amateur* implies no lack of either skill or
serious purpose, but satisfaction in the activity for its own
sake rather than for profit.

Faulkner's concept of his role as a writer suggests that,
although the familiar comparison of the Yoknapatawpha
fiction with Balzac's *Comédie humaine* may be relevant to the
genesis of Yoknapatawpha, in view of Faulkner's frequent
references to Balzac, such a comparison must be made with
critical caution. Since Balzac and Zola were the founders of
the social history type of sequence novel to which Faulkner's
Yoknapatawpha fiction bears some resemblance, the genesis
of the two French fictional series may be enlightening.[2] A
sharp contrast is apparent between Balzac's and Zola's deliberate, premeditated approach and Faulkner's intuitive, imaginative inspiration.

With no precedent to follow, Balzac had written a number
of novels and stories before he gave up the idea of a series of
historical novels in the tradition of Scott and instead formulated
his plan for a history of French society in the nineteenth century, in which he would apply to human life Saint-Hilaire's
theory of the influence of environment on animals (Preface,
La Comédie humaine). By 1834, impelled by a temperament

[2] The origin of the social history sequence novel in the works of Balzac and Zola was dealt with by this writer in an unpublished Ph.D.
dissertation at the University of Minnesota (1941) and in the Preface
to *Bibliography of the Sequence Novel* (1950; rpt. New York: Octagon
Books, 1973). The sequence novel may be defined as a series of novels,
like the Yoknapatawpha fiction, unified by such linking devices as
recurrent scenes, characters, and themes, and together constituting a
whole with a logical or natural order and an aesthetic effect and inherent significance greater that the sum of its parts, the individual
novels, or novels and stories.

described by Philippe Bertault as "innately systematic,"[3] Balzac outlined the elaborate scheme into which his previous and succeeding fiction would fit, proceeding from the first stage, cause, to the second, effects, and the third, principles. Thus the *Comédie humaine* grew out of one coherent, schematized conception, arrived at some fifteen years after Balzac began writing but followed until his death. Martin Turnell shows how Balzac's method reflected the basic concept: "Balzac himself worked from outside and believed that once he had 'observed' externals he had arrived at a comprehension of the interior. This explains the technique of the novels, which scarcely varies from one book to another." This weakness had its source "partly in the theory outlined in the Foreword, that just as there are 'zoological species,' so there are 'social species.' "[4]

Following the example of Balzac, Zola planned his Rougon-Macquart series before he began to write it. According to the principles set forth in his *Roman expérimental*, Zola worked out an elaborate scheme, like Balzac's based on an analogy between natural and human history and inspired by a specific scientific work, Claude Bernard's *Introduction to the Study of Experimental Medicine*.

Thus the novels of Balzac and Zola represent those social history sequence novels which are based on abstract concepts and carefully formulated plans; in this respect Balzac's and Zola's series differ chiefly in the tardy formulation of Balzac's plans. But Faulkner's Yoknapatawpha County fiction did not originate in an intellectual concept of an integrated series following a preconceived scheme and based on scientific principles. Faulkner's sequence is inherent in the subject and the author's nature, like the piece of sculpture inherent in the

[3] Philippe Bertault, *Balzac and the Human Comedy,* English version by Richard Monges (New York: New York University Press, 1963), p. 130.
[4] Martin Turnell, *The Novel in France* (New York: Vintage Books, 1958), pp. 226–227, 228. Bertault expresses much the same idea: "The type is formed, the idea individualized" (p. 138). "The characters of *La Comédie Humaine,* like the novels themselves, are the habiliments of a general idea" (p. 145).

chunk of wood or block of stone, ready to be released if the sculptor studies his material and works with its grain and contours, finding them congenial to his tastes and skills. As Hawthorne says in *The Marble Faun*: "the outer marble was not merely an extraneous environment: the human countenance within its embrace must have existed there since the limestone ridges of Carrara were first made." Malcolm Cowley, who uses the same wood-stone analogy, points out that Faulkner could have divided his work into "Scenes" like Balzac's or into family sagas.[5] The fact remains that Faulkner did not choose to do so and did not give external clues to the relationships between his works except by his map of Yoknapatawpha County and by the explicit trilogy form of *Snopes*. He remained an amateur in his unrestrictive approach to his writing and allowed free scope to his imagination.

The three sources from which a writer draws his material are, according to Faulkner, experience, observation, and imagination (*Faulkner in the University*, pp. 78, 116–117). Although his own experience and observation extended beyond Lafayette County, Mississippi, Faulkner's best work deals with the imaginary domain which has roughly the same boundaries as the real county; here his imagination was most fully creative in working with what he had observed and experienced. Experience, he made clear, includes reading: "you can learn about people that way, to match against your own experience with living people" (*Faulkner in the University*, p. 117). He did not do research but read and reread whatever appealed to him and helped him to learn his craft. Neither did he keep a systematic file from which to draw material but rather a "junk box." His own life in Oxford and the traditions of his family and community, supplemented by reading and imagination, furnished what he knew.

The development of Faulkner as a creative artist dealing with the tradition of his own region strikingly illustrates Otto Rank's analysis of the stages in the growth of an artist, in

[5] Introduction, *The Portable Faulkner* (New York: Viking, 1967), pp. xi–xv.

Art and Artist, V. In the first stage Faulkner was imitative. In the second stage he was liberated from imitation of literary men or cliques and produced some of his best works, such as *The Sound and the Fury* and *As I Lay Dying,* but failed to establish himself as a major novelist in the eyes of the reading public and of most critics. The struggle between loyalty to his personal and literary past and loyalty to his own development was intensified for Faulkner by the fact that he remained a resident of the community from the traditions of which, in his concepts of man and society, he was breaking away. He seems to have been impelled by his own personal and artistic integrity to explore his world. Albert J. Guerard, using parallels between Faulkner and Conrad to illuminate the latter, outlines the same stages in purely literary terms relevant to Faulkner's discovery of the matter and method in the Yoknapatawpha fiction: the first period, of both learning and unlearning or rejecting what seemed suitable, is that of *Soldier's Pay* and *Mosquitoes,* in which Faulkner dealt with what he knew well but imitated such writers as Sherwood Anderson and Aldous Huxley. Guerard continues:

But we do not hear a true and sustained Faulknerian voice until we are well into *Sartoris.* Faulkner had first to discover the congenial material of ordinary life in a small town impinged upon and distorted by a romantic past and the congenial material of masculine comradeship in the "big woods." So too he had to discover a method that would permit exaggeration, and a nameless narrator free to meditate on the action.[6]

"The congenial material of ordinary life in a small town" centered on Oxford, Mississippi, with its surrounding county, Lafayette. This natural limitation in subject was essential to the kind of creative imagination Faulkner possessed, which could work best with familiar scenes and with a society which he could both identify himself with and view with critical detachment. Instead of imitating Sherwood Anderson, he was

[6] *Conrad the Novelist* (Cambridge: Harvard University Press, 1958), p. 61.

now discovering the validity of Anderson's advice to start from the "little patch" of Mississippi he knew, an essential building block in the foundation of the America which is still being built.[7]

The social history of Yoknapatawpha County is limited, chronologically and geographically, and exhibits a natural pattern. Those limits are modest, compared with Balzac's achievement and his original plan for a series covering France from the Middle Ages to his own time. In Yoknapatawpha County, one hundred and seventy years cover the period from the establishment of the trading post at what was to be Jefferson until old Lucius Priest tells his story to his grandson in *The Reivers*. The county is sparsely populated. Having staked his literary claim on such a modest, Johnny-come-lately piece of real estate, Faulkner found himself, when the idea of inter-related works of fiction occurred to him, already possessed of a suitable subject for comprehensive treatment.

The social heritage of the people increased the isolation caused by such geographical and economic factors as poor transportation and roads and lack of industries. In self-defense after the Civil War Southerners had to be clannish, "each springing to defend his own blood whether it be right or wrong" (*Faulkner at Nagano*, p. 192). The clannish tendency natural to those of Scottish extraction was thus encouraged by circumstances. Consequently Lafayette-Yoknapatawpha County became a homogeneous province, self-centered and self-absorbed.

This province had passed through distinct stages in its development which lend a clearly discernible pattern to its history: the coming of the first explorers, the period of the pioneer woodsmen, the establishment of plantations and the building of towns, and the vicissitudes resulting from the impact of events in the nation and the world—the Civil War, Reconstruction, twentieth-century commercialism, and world wars. Moreover, this pattern describes a dramatic rise and fall,

[7] Faulkner, "A Note on Sherwood Anderson," in *Essays, Speeches, and Public Letters*, James B. Meriwether, ed. (New York: Random House, 1965), p. 8.

with the climax in the flowering of the aristocratic tradition just before the Civil War and the fall in the defeat of the South and the collapse of the old tradition. The pattern lends itself naturally to both social realism and mythological implications, even as the society had created its own myth. Faulkner's search for the meaning latent in the history, not a premeditated interpretation and conceptual scheme, was the dynamic impulse behind the building of Yoknapatawpha.

The historical pattern inherent in Faulkner's chosen material was bound to manifest itself to a writer imaginatively recreating the tradition of his people. Similarly, when a novelist brings the life-history of a hero down to the present, he may find that the subject has its own inner shape and logic and as time passes demands continuation. Although this realization is rather often the genesis of a biographical or autobiographical sequence, rarely does a society fall as neatly into shape as does Faulkner's. Hardy, with great feeling for place and for native inhabitants, never discerned in Wessex the essentials of a social microcosm, to be created in a clearly related series.

Faulkner's perception of the potentialities of his material may be due to the reinforcement by literary "experience" of his tendency to explore exhaustively one locality and to embrace the "human comedy" therein represented. Among the authors whom he regularly reread were Balzac and Dickens. Balzac's "concept of a cosmos in miniature" profoundly appealed to him (*Faulkner in the University,* pp. 50, 232). His reason he stated more fully in an earlier interview:

I like the fact that in Balzac there is an intact world of his own. His people don't just move from page one to page 320 of one book. There is continuity between them all like a blood-stream which flows from page one through to page 20,000 of one book. The same blood, muscle and tissue binds the characters together.[8]

Faulkner's "intact world" is smaller than Balzac's, more adapted to the comprehension of the reader, with greater continuity and concentration.

[8] Cynthia Grenier, "The Art of Fiction: An Interview with William Faulkner—September, 1955," *Accent,* XVI (Summer, 1956), 168.

The combination of Balzac's intact but varied world with concentration upon a restricted setting, as in Dickens's use of London,[9] contained the essentials of Faulkner's method: recurrent characters in a limited setting. In the quality of imagination which created a world, rather than in schematization, Faulkner resembled Balzac; in the quality of imagination which created characters and in identification with place, different as are Yoknapatawpha County and London, he resembled Dickens.

But both Balzac and Dickens differed from Faulkner in one particular which explains why Faulkner did not proceed in the more deliberate, theoretical fashion of Balzac. The Bergsonian concept of time which underlies Faulkner's fusion of past and present prevented him from conceiving of different periods as discrete units. The tendency of the South to live in the past and to be preoccupied with family and tradition may have predisposed Faulkner to feel that "no man is himself, he is the sum of his past. There is no such thing really as was because the past is" (*Faulkner in the University,* p. 84). Thus even the story of an individual does not have a clear-cut beginning and end: continuity of consciousness of the past and effect of the past flow into the present and color the future: "A man's future is inherent in that man." Faulkner continues in this passage to explain his "mystical belief that there is no such thing as *was*":

That time *is,* and if there's no such thing as *was,* then there is no such thing as *will be.* That time is not a fixed condition, time is in a way the sum of the combined intelligences of all men who breathe at that moment [*Faulkner in the University,* p. 139].

[9] Although Paris was the heart of the *Comédie humaine,* Balzac remained a bourgeois provincial but lacked closeness to the land and the peasants, thus differing from both Dickens and Faulkner (Bertault, pp. 9, 6; Turnell, p. 229). J. Hillis Miller's premise concerning Dickens's London is true to a lesser degree of the relatively small and simple Yoknapatawpha: "Dickens wanted to absorb the city into his imagination and present it again in the persons and events of his novels" (*Charles Dickens: The World of his Novels* [Cambridge: Harvard University Press, 1959], p. xvi).

This theory he had expressed earlier in the *Paris Review* interview with Jean Stein: "time is a fluid condition which has no existence except in the momentary avatars of individual people."[10] The Bergsonian aspect of his concept and its implications for him as an artist Faulkner expressed in another interview:

In fact I agree pretty much with Bergson's theory of the fluidity of time. There is only the present moment, in which I include both the past and the future, and that is eternity. In my opinion time can be shaped quite a bit by the artist; after all, man is never time's slave.[11]

Time as experienced by individuals could not be represented by simple chronological order of events; the past as it existed in the consciousness of Faulkner could not be recreated in a series of works in which the history of Yoknapatawpha County was composed and presented in chronological sequence. Olga Vickery's comment on the implications of Faulkner's concept of time illuminates the way in which Yoknapatawpha grew out of Faulkner's sense of time and his concept of man:

When man realizes that *the* past and *the* future alike are unattainable fictions, he is disenchanted of his mania for linear time. . . . The communal and anonymous brotherhood of man can be reestablished if each man individually cherishes not his social but his human identity and accepts responsibility for all time as well as for the particular time into which he is born.[12]

Because of this concept of time, Faulkner could move his characters back and forth in time. He obviously did not feel that his characters were bound to any point in time, an at-

[10] Jean Stein, "William Faulkner," reprinted in *Writers at Work*, Malcolm Cowley, ed. (New York: Viking, 1958), p. 141.

[11] Loïc Bouvard, "Conversation with William Faulkner," *Modern Fiction Studies*, V (Winter, 1959–1960), 362.

[12] *The Novels of William Faulkner* (Baton Rouge: Louisiana State University Press, 1964), pp. 264–265.

titude which may be explained in part by Faulkner's fondness for the word *avatar* and the concept it expresses. When a character in real life had a fictional counterpart, that counterpart might play a role in both an earlier generation and his own, as Boon Hogganbeck did in "The Bear" and *The Reivers*. Faulkner also moved freely in his imagination through all of the history of Yoknapatawpha County. This practice is best exemplified in the combination of the early history of Jefferson and the state with the story of Temple and Nancy in *Requiem for a Nun,* not only in the juxtaposition of events more than a century apart but also in the sense of the mythic present and in Faulkner's delay in introducing into his chronicles the detailed account of the earliest events in Jefferson. In *Time and Reality,* Margaret Church observes, "Fusion and then transcendence of past, present, and future shape Faulkner's time pattern."[13] Faulkner's imaginative freedom in time and in creation and recreation of characters worked against logical and chronological consistency in characters and events in the Yoknapatawpha fiction but did not, of course, detract from the effect of individual works individually considered.

Faulkner's characteristic time-sense explains why he did not follow a chronological plan in dealing with his given body of material. Like the real county, the imaginary one seemed to offer a wealth of material from which he could choose as inspiration moved him. Another characteristic explains why he became a sequence novelist in spite of himself— why he did not, like Hardy, people his county with characters confined within single novels. In this second mental trait, Faulkner resembled Thomas Wolfe, another inadvertent sequence novelist. A remark Faulkner once made about Wolfe, which he had to explain repeatedly, is of more significance in this context than as representing Faulkner's critical estimate of Wolfe's achievement. He ranked Wolfe and himself above Dos Passos, Caldwell, and Hemingway on the basis of the

[13] Margaret Church, *Time and Reality: Studies in Contemporary Fiction* (Chapel Hill: The University of North Carolina Press, 1963), p. 228.

gallantry of their failures (*Faulkner in the University*, pp. 143, 206). The resemblance Faulkner noted between his style and Wolfe's, in contrast to Hemingway's control of his method, may be owing to a similarity in creative impulse:

Wolfe . . . and myself, . . . we didn't have the instinct, or the preceptors, or whatever it was, anyway. We tried to crowd and cram everything, all experience, into each paragraph, to get the whole nuance of the moment's experience, of all the recaptured light rays, into each paragraph. That's why it's clumsy and hard to read [*Faulkner at Nagano*, p. 37].

Faulkner and Wolfe had in common a romantic rejection of a limited intention which might make possible a perfect achievement, in favor of "splendid failure to do the impossible."[14]

As Southern writers whose material for fiction necessitated sequence relationships between their major novels and stories, Faulkner and Wolfe show significant similarities and differences. They shared not only the romantic attitude noted above, which is closer to impulse and instinct than to the rational, but also qualities more essential to the creative writer than are intellectual concepts: keen sense-perceptions and sensitivity to language, in its poetic qualities or colloquial aspects. But difference in personalities and in reactions to personal situations caused Wolfe and Faulkner to make completely different use of material which bore regional and historical similarities. Wolfe, with a strong sense of the past—individual, family, regional—was driven to seek self-fulfillment away from the family and the community in which he found no acceptable status or identity. For *his* microcosm, he took himself. Like Otto Rank's Romantic type, to whom "experience of his own appears to be an essential preliminary to productivity," Wolfe could "create only by perpetually sacrificing his own life." Despite his eventual realization that, like Antaeus, he derived his strength from the earth, his native soil, he spent little of his adult life in North

14 Stein, "William Faulkner," p. 123.

Carolina. In dealing with his mythical Altamont or Catawba, Wolfe showed some of the feeling for the land that distinguishes Faulkner, but since Wolfe was his own hero, the center of his sequence, the scene must change as he moves. Faulkner, however, in one respect is like Rank's Classical type, who "constantly makes use of other life than his own—in fact, nature—for the purpose of creating."[15] More fortunate than Wolfe in his sense of identification with the society into which he was born and in his secure position in that society, Faulkner subordinated self to place and people and remained a countryman, not seeking self-aggrandizement in the literary world. Therefore he could turn outward and make society *his* microcosm, with himself as author for the most part invisible. Faulkner illustrates the artist who uses private feelings chiefly as they illuminate human nature and may be projected in characters essentially unlike himself. As Faulkner put it, in one of his last statements of a reiterated idea, the writer "was simply writing about people involved in the passion and hope of the human dilemma" (*Faulkner at West Point,* p. 82). Wolfe observed himself first, and people and places in relation to himself; Faulkner observed the world around him, himself a spectator.

But despite these radical differences in relationship to and use of their Southern experience, Wolfe and Faulkner adopted significantly analogous solutions to their problems of dealing with closely connected material which far exceeded the bounds of single novels. Wolfe's two cycles were inherent in his material, although the inspired editorial work of Maxwell Perkins helped Wolfe to give form and unity to his first two novels, the only ones published during his life. Both Wolfe and Faulkner, therefore, show how authors gradually develop sequence form to accommodate material that inherently de-

[15] Otto Rank, *The Myth of the Birth of the Hero and Other Writings,* Philip Freund, ed. (New York: Vintage Books, 1959), p. 149. Rank's analysis of the psychology of the artist is particularly useful in explaining Faulkner's personal and artistic nature and his fairly unusual combination of Classical and Romantic qualities and of unliterary life and literary creation.

mands such handling, the history of an individual or the history of a self-contained society.

The failure of either author to anticipate his problem or, having found a solution, to proceed thereafter according to an orderly plan is due to the most significant similarity between them. A main theme throughout Wolfe's novels, dominant in *Of Time and the River* in "Orestes, Flight before Fury," is the fury that drove him to seek experience and to preserve it, a fury that involved a sense of guilt, as the allusion to Orestes suggests. This fury and the Faustian thirst for knowledge resulted in Wolfe's long-sustained periods of composition in solitude, recalling the writing habits of Balzac.[16] Although apparently Faulkner was able to intersperse writing with other activity and both live and write, his many references to being demon-driven reveal a compulsion to preserve his imaginative experience and visions, a compulsion which did not involve a craving for money and fame equal to Balzac's or for self-revelation like Wolfe's. In this demonic fury Wolfe and Faulkner seem very similar, as Faulkner recognized when he said that unlike himself, by implication, and Wolfe, Hemingway "wasn't driven by his private demon to waste himself in trying to do" what exceeded his control as a craftsman (*Faulkner in the University*, p. 143). Otto Rank's comments on *daimon* and *Genius* are relevant to the artist and to his "dualistic struggle" between "individuality and collectivity," and are an aid in distinguishing between Faulkner's choice of collectivity and Wolfe's of individuality:

. . . the Roman idea of Genius contains from the beginning, in addition to the individual urge to reproduction, a collective element which points beyond the individual, in a way that is not true of the Egyptian ka and the Greek daimon, both of which are purely personal.[17]

[16] Stefan Zweig speaks of Balzac's "demonic energy and creative willpower," *Balzac* (New York: Viking, 1946), p. 150.
[17] Rank, *The Myth of the Birth of the Hero*, p. 125.

That the urge to write is analogous to the reproductive urge is clear in Faulkner's explanations of the demon that drives the writer to work "in a kind of insane fury":

It could be . . . a desire to leave some mark on the world so that people after you will know that for a little while Smith was here, he made this scratch. . . . I don't think it's for glory, it's certainly not for profit, because there are many more profitable things than being a writer . . . it's certainly not to change man's condition. If anything, I would say that's what it is, it's simply to leave a scratch on the earth that showed that you were here for a little while.[18]

The impingement upon Faulkner's demon-driven creative impulses of communal and personal experience within chronological and geographical limits resulted, not in a schematic sequence, but in an organic one, shaped by the author's concept of human time.

II. *The Unifying Concept*

Driven by his demon to continue his chronicles of Yoknapatawpha County, Faulkner as a craftsman realized what, given his subject, artistic economy demanded that he do. Having tried his hand in *Soldier's Pay* and *Mosquitoes* at imitation of other writers, using Southern locales, Faulkner discovered that his strength lay in the country and tradition closest to his own experience. Charles Mallison's vision of his native locality suggests the imaginative boundaries which circumscribed Faulkner's vision of the human drama, his intense

[18] *Faulkner in the University,* pp. 194, 195–196. A similar statement, in *Faulkner at West Point* (p. 119), stresses "the pleasure of creation," in which a writer affirms his immortality. An example of "demon-possessed" writing is given by Andrew Lytle in his account of writing the last pages of *The Velvet Horn* as if he were "merely an instrument." "The Working Novelist and the Mythmaking Process," *Daedalus,* LXXXVIII (Spring, 1959), 337–338.

identification with his country and people, "one unalterable durable impregnable one: one people one heart one land" enclosed by the "green ridge" of Alabama and the "long wall of the levee and the great River itself" and "the North: not north but North, outland and circumscribing, and not even a geographical place but an emotional idea."[19] Having discovered his true subject and accordingly narrowed his range to Yoknapatawpha County, Faulkner at first had no "intention to write a pageant of a county" (*Faulkner in the University*, p. 3). He was simply using "the quickest tool to hand." But when he came to realize that he was creating such a pageant, he found his buried treasure:

Beginning with *Sartoris* I discovered that my own little postage stamp of native soil was worth writing about and that I would never live long enough to exhaust it, and that by sublimating the actual into the apocryphal I would have complete liberty to use whatever talent I might have to its absolute top. It opened up a gold mine of other people, so I created a cosmos of my own.[20]

Faulkner's first conscious recognition of what Brewster Ghiselin terms the "meaning, force, or importance implicit in his [the novelist's] material and his feeling for their possibilities" and his initial concept, in *Sartoris*, of major families, individuals, and episodes, including the whole Snopes story (pp. 172–173), were part of "the process of discovering the 'hidden meaning'" but did not serve to make the specific development of the Yoknapatawpha fiction premeditated or predictable. The organic nature of the material, intuitively perceived, was the determining factor in the evolution of Yoknapatawpha.[21] The full realization of the value of his "gold mine" came to Faulkner only after he had written *Sanctuary, The Sound and the Fury,* and *As I Lay Dying*:

---

[19] *Intruder in the Dust,* pp. 210, 151–153.
[20] Quoted in Stein, "William Faulkner," p. 141.
[21] Brewster Ghiselin, "Automatism, Intention, and Autonomy in the Novelist's Production," *Daedalus,* XCII (Spring, 1963), 302. Ghiselin's analysis of the roles of conscious intention and of spontaneity in the novelist's art is particularly applicable to Faulkner's writing.

. . . about that time I realized there was a great deal of writing I wanted to do, had to do, and I could simplify, economize, by picking out one country and putting enough people in it to keep me busy. And save myself trouble, time—that was probably the reason. . . . I was still trying to reduce my one individual experience of the world into one compact thing which could be picked up and held in the hands at one time [*Faulkner at Nagano,* pp. 80–81].

To Faulkner's readers, the publication of the map of Yoknapatawpha County in *Absalom, Absalom!* (1936) marked Faulkner's explicit recognition of the interrelationship of his novels, and of Yoknapatawpha County as the geographical scene of his comedies and tragedies.

The enlargement in scope and concept beyond single works introduced into the Yoknapatawpha stories and novels a new dimension, presenting characters and events from diverse points of view and over a much longer period than is covered in any one work. To develop the myth of the South demands an amplitude that casts the setting and customs into perspective, diminishing but not obliterating those aspects peculiar to one time and place and highlighting the universal aspect. Although fidelity to social background is observed, Faulkner used it as a means rather than an end and disavowed any intention to make merely a sociological study of Yoknapatawpha County and its people. He explained how the novelist uses social background in fiction:

. . . It's the story of human beings in conflict with their nature, their character, their souls, with others, or with their environment. He's got to tell that story in the only terms he knows, the familiar terms, which could be colored, shaped by his environment. He's not really writing about his environment, he's simply telling a story about human beings in the terms of environment, and I agree that any work of art, any book, reflects its social background, but I doubt if that were the primary consideration of that writer . . . . If he is merely telling a story to show a symptom of sociological background then he is first a propagandist rather than a novelist [*Faulkner at Nagano,* pp. 156–157].

Faulkner's selection of characters in Yoknapatawpha County, in conflict "with their environment," was usually based upon his needs for a single work and not upon premeditated plans for further development of Yoknapatawpha. Within the chronicles, however, there is a sequence novel conceived as a whole which shows that, for Faulkner, the more flexible and indeterminate approach was the more successful. *Snopes,* the trilogy made up of *The Hamlet, The Town,* and *The Mansion,* was conceived in an instant but took more than thirty years to complete:

I thought of the whole story at once like a bolt of lightning lights up a landscape and you see everything but it takes time to write it, and this story I had in my mind for about thirty years, and the one which I will do next—it happened at that same moment, thirty years ago . . . [*Faulkner at the University,* p. 90].

Whatever falling off of interest and force there may be in *Snopes,* Faulkner attributed to his feeling that "it's more fun doing a single piece which has unity and coherence, the proper emphasis and integration, which a long chronicle doesn't have" (*Faulkner at the University,* p. 108). Faulkner worked best when his only restriction was to his "own little postage stamp of native soil."

III. *The Scope of the Yoknapatawpha Fiction*

That restriction, however, is relative; it seems a real limitation only in comparison with a gigantic undertaking like Balzac's. Faulkner's personal feeling and his vision necessitated inclusion of the whole span of white civilization in the area. A boy growing up in that environment, surrounded by those to whom the past was still alive and who lived in it more than in the present, listening to the "unvanquished," the "maiden spinster aunts which had never surrendered" (*Faulkner in the University*, p. 249), was steeped in the tales of the Civil War and of the golden ante-bellum days. Faulkner, one feels, speaks through Gavin Stevens to Charles Mallison, who may resemble the boy Faulkner had been:

It's all *now* you see. Yesterday wont be over until tomorrow and tomorrow began ten thousand years ago. For every Southern boy fourteen years old, not once but whenever he wants it, there is the instant when it's still not yet two oclock on that July afternoon in 1863, the brigades are in position behind the rail fence, the guns are laid and ready in the woods and the furled flags are already loosened to break out and Pickett himself with his long oiled ringlets and his hat in one hand probably and his sword in the other looking up the hill waiting for Longstreet to give the word and it's all in the balance, it hasn't happened yet, it hasn't even begun yet, . . . but there is still time for it not to begin against that position and those circumstances . . . yet it's going to begin, . . . we have come too far with too much at stake and that moment doesn't need even a fourteen-year-old boy to think *This time.* *Maybe this time* with all this much to lose and all this much to gain: Pennsylvania, Maryland, the world, the golden dome of Washington itself to crown with desperate and unbelievable victory the desperate gamble, the cast made two years ago; or to anyone who ever sailed even a skiff under a quilt sail, the moment in 1492 when somebody thought *This is it*: the absolute edge of no return, to turn back now and make home or sail irrevocably on and either find land or plunge over the world's roaring rim [*Intruder in the Dust*, pp. 194–195].

From single sentences like this to the whole body of fiction, Faulkner's work is dominated by his sense of the continuity of human history in a given society intimately identified with its physical environment.

The chronological limits of Faulkner's subject, however, were not determined merely by this sense of the past or by the concept of time underlying it; those limits were set by Faulkner's vision of the moral implications of cultural patterns and changes. Therefore he must include the whole span of white occupation of the territory, because the exploitation

of the land began when the white man bought from the
Indians land which was not the Indians' to sell. That exploitation continues to the present; it is represented in *The Mansion*
in the post-World-War-II development of the Compson Mile
into Eula Acres, "a subdivision of standardised Veterans'
Housing matchboxes" (p. 332). The ineradicable effects of
the past still are evident. The myths and legends by which
the Southern aristocrats seek consolation and compensation
for the loss of their prestige and prosperity paralyze them and
leave the initiative in modern society to the Snopeses. These
myths and legends also preserve concepts of social classes and
castes which prevent the South from recognizing and admitting the moral guilt underlying present social and economic
problems. Faulkner's vision encompassed this whole sweep
of time: to communicate his vision, he had to begin with
the uncorrupted Indians and come down to the present. In
viewing this large, complex creation, the reader may find
helpful some understanding of the process by which it came
into being and some knowledge of the geography and history
of the County and of the society in which the human comedy
and the human tragedy are enacted.

2

YOKNAPATAWPHA COUNTY

1. *Lafayette and Yoknapatawpha Counties*

FAULKNER'S world of Yoknapatawpha exerts over the imagination a power which transcends the regional quality and the national significance of Yoknapatawpha and establishes it in the mind of Western man as a spiritual province. To the critic of Faulkner, all roads seem to lead to Yoknapatawpha County, from the legendary trail of the American myth to the actual riot-filled streets of Oxford, Mississippi. Viewed in quite a different perspective, however, Yoknapatawpha still exerts its centripetal force. Concerned with the Christian tradition in Western literature, Gabriel Vahanian accords to Yoknapatawpha a significance equalled in the past only by Dante's infernal and purgatorial territory:

No Western man today can know where he stands if he has not gone through Yoknapatawpha County at least once. . . . Faulkner's world is a historical map of the Christian tradition and its concomitant culture . . . . And Yoknapatawpha County is also a spiritual geography of Christendom, that of a land that lies more desolate with each generation of lost men, of renegade Westerners.[1]

[1] Gabriel Vahanian, *Wait Without Idols* (New York: Braziller, 1964), p. 93.

23

To perceive Yoknapatawpha County as "a spiritual geography" it may be helpful first to realize imaginatively its physical geography and that of its prototype, Lafayette County.

The maps of Yoknapatawpha County which William Faulkner drew named the creator of Yoknapatawpha County its "Sole Owner and Proprietor."[2] Only Faulkner could reduce the land of his imagination to a map and show with authority locations and distances, at times himself resolving discrepancies between details in different stories. Neither map, however, will be an infallible guide to every Yoknapatawpha story or novel. Faulkner never let himself be bound in his geography by a foolish consistency. To envision the land in its entirety, the reader must read all that Faulkner wrote about the county and assemble the mental pictures of scenes in their proper spatial relationships. Until he can achieve that happy orientation, some commentary—based on the fiction, on Faulkner's articles about Mississippi, on the geography of Oxford and Lafayette County, and on personal observation— may serve as an introduction to the limited but varied land where successive generations of Faulkner's characters gained their living and acted out the dramas that make up the Yoknapatawpha world. Faulkner constructed his scenes so carefully, repeating and varying them according to point of view and circumstances, that clearly he sought to share with the reader his own love of the land. And he would no doubt have agreed with Dante that knowledge is the necessary prelude to love: we cannot love what we do not know. Furthermore, as we must know the land to love it, we must also know the land to love the people, so intimate is the relation between them. Yoknapatawpha County, despite its changes, serves, like Thomas Wolfe's earth and rivers, as "time immutable": "A kind of eternal and unchanging universe of time

[2] *Absalom, Absalom!* (New York: Random House, 1936): fold-out map. This map, later redrawn for the Modern Library Edition (1951), is larger and more detailed than that in *The Portable Faulkner* (New York: Viking, 1946, 1967) and gives locations of more scenes of action; the ridges indicated on this first map suggest, as the *Portable Faulkner* map does not, the hills which are characteristic of Lafayette County.

against which would be projected the transience of man's life."[3]

This country is not only a country of Faulkner's imagination, but it is also very close to what either a comparative stranger or a native Southerner and authority on the South may observe. Howard Washington Odum was a student at the University of Mississippi in 1906 during Faulkner's boyhood. His impressions, as he recalled them, convinced him that Faulkner achieved an "unequaled combination of blending what is usually called an 'imaginary locale' with a powerful reality of situation":

. . . I myself have known Yoknapatawpha and it is no purely imaginary fantasy. Once when a son of the first and noblest families of 'Jefferson,' weakened by frustration and conflict between aspiration and reality, had gone off the deep end, I remember riding an unbroken colt from Toccopola to Pontotoc, to Tupelo to New Albany in and out across swollen streams and backwoods and pine hills, often reflecting physical reality stranger than fiction. I have been close enough to Faulkner's quicksands to sense something of its terrors and have often imagined, behind the cedars and columned houses, that anything could happen there. Faulkner's Yoknapatawpha was symbol of frontier, a frontier echoing both primitive and civilized heritage . . . .[4]

Odum's observations were ante-Faulkner and were not conditioned by the fictitious County. Moreover, he had the advantage of a Young-Bayard-Sartoris context. Present-day strangers, more conventional in mode of travel and more prepared by fiction for observing fact, may well find that Odum's impressions seem wholly authentic. Life-long residents of Lafayette County confirm the realistic aspect of Faulkner's settings. John Cullen, one of Faulkner's hunting companions, testifies

[3] Thomas Wolfe, *The Story of a Novel* (New York: Scribner, 1936), p. 52.
[4] "On Southern Literature and Southern Culture," in *Southern Renascence: The Literature of the Modern South,* Louis D. Rubin Jr. and Robert D. Jacobs, eds. (Baltimore: Johns Hopkins Press, 1953), p. 97.

that "Faulkner has created Yoknapatawpha County from
the cloth of Lafayette County": "the materials of Lafayette
County and Oxford are so much a part of Faulkner's fiction
that a knowledge of this environment does lead to some
knowledge and understanding of Faulkner's works."[5]

The idea that Faulkner, while "meticulously delineating the
topography," is concerned also with "the permanent and unchanging aspects of human nature" is developed by Olga
Vickery:

This vision of man as related to both the particular and the
universal, to time and eternity, underlies Faulkner's examination
of perception, truth, and reality. Every man is fixed at birth by
the specific coordinates of time and space, through which he comes
to share in the history of his people and the geography of his
land. . . . But beneath such surface changes the land nevertheless
preserves its own identity, maintaining its own rhythms through
the seasonal cycle of life and death, growth and decay. Similarly,
human nature provides the unchanging constant in the evolution
and dissolution of social and economic forms. In one sense, then,
time and place merely provide the setting for the drama of man-
kind; but at the same time, those individuals who contribute
profoundly to the panorama of history find their hearts—the permanent and unchanging aspect of human nature—continually
revivified by the primordial land with which they are intimately
related as a result of deep and abiding connections with a specific
place.[6]

The reader's knowledge of this specific place, Yoknapatawpha
County, is gained by sympathetic imagination, working with
Faulkner's own writings but aided by information and experi-
ence. Yoknapatawpha County existed originally in Faulkner's

[5] *Old Times in the Faulkner Country,* in collaboration with Floyd
Watkins (Chapel Hill: University of North Carolina Press, 1961),
pp. 65, 69. A book of photographs by Martin Dain, *Faulkner's County:
Yoknapatawpha* (New York: Random House, 1964), shows both
county and people as they may be observed at the present time.

[6] *The Novels of William Faulkner* (Baton Rouge: Lousiana State
University Press, 1964), pp. 240–241.

mind and cannot be fully understood in terms of factual information about Oxford and Lafayette County. On the other hand, Yoknapatawpha County does correspond roughly with the salient features of Lafayette County, and the history of Jefferson and its inhabitants and of Oxford follow much the same pattern. Although, in Vahanian's forceful metaphor, Faulkner uses "outrageous regionalism" to express "the region . . . of the human heart,"[7] he uses familiar realism to depict the region of man's outward life. The cumulative impression built up of a complete, concrete world lends conviction to the often partial or distorted world as seen by the characters. The Square and the courthouse in Oxford and the kinds of settlements and countryside in Lafayette County seem familiar to the reader. But he may look in vain for a hamlet that fits in every detail the descriptions of Frenchman's Bend. Acquaintance with Oxford and Lafayette County is extremely helpful if one does not try to identify the creations of William Faulkner's imagination with what man has built or God has created in Mississippi.

Ward Miner's *The World of William Faulkner* is well known and easily available.[8] Miner's facts about Oxford and Lafayette County and his parallels between facts and details in Faulkner's stories are useful, though not invariably accurate. Since this study is concerned with creations of the imagination, the factual parallels will be dealt with chiefly when they throw light on the creative process and when the experience of the reader as observer is pertinent. The most helpful and authentic account of parallels between fact and fiction, Calvin S. Brown's "Faulkner's Geography and Topography," is invaluable to

[7] Vahanian, p. 97.

[8] (Durham: Duke University Press, 1952.) Page references are to the Grove Press edition. All population figures given in this chapter are taken from the United States Census Reports given in the Appendix to Miner's book. Because this chapter is concerned with the country of Faulkner's imagination, supplementary details, confirming or contrasting with the fictitious version, will be cited in notes except in discussion of major changes. What slight inconvenience this procedure may cause in correlation of fact and fiction is compensated for by the more coherent view of the fiction.

the on-the-spot seeker of Faulkner's specific settings.[9] Brown's
initial generalization about the "sense . . . in which it can be
maintained and proved that Jefferson is Oxford and Yoknapatawpha County is Lafayette County" is the indispensable
basis of any attempt to correlate real and fictitious places:

Faulkner habitually imagines his characters moving about the
square and streets of Oxford and the roads, hills, and swamps of
Lafayette County. Since he often describes his settings in detail, it
follows that anyone who knows the town and county well will
frequently recognize these settings, especially if he has known the
territory long enough to recall many features and landmarks now
either obliterated or altered beyond recognition.

Those like Calvin Brown who have known town and county
long enough and know the fiction of Faulkner well are not
numerous. Only the reader who, like Brown, is thoroughly
familiar with Yoknapatawpha can realize the extent to which
Faulkner's Yoknapatawpha County is both a country of the
imagination and a living reality.

Pertinent to the question of the workings of Faulkner's imagination are some of Ward Miner's interpretations of Faulkner's deviations, in Yoknapatawpha County, from basic statistical facts about Oxford and Lafayette County. The map
of Yoknapatawpha County in *Absalom, Absalom!* gives the
area as 2,400 square miles; Lafayette County has only 679
square miles. But distances between Jefferson and other places
in the mythical county, such as Sutpen's Hundred, are too
short to be consistent with the larger area and are close to
actual distances in Lafayette County.

But, oddly enough, Faulkner greatly decreased the population; as late as the 1930s (the map refers to *Sanctuary* and

[9] *PMLA,* LXXVII (December, 1962), 652–659. The article not only
covers salient features as they appear in various novels but traces the
wanderings of Joe Christmas in *Light in August* and the return of
Mink Snopes to Jefferson in *The Mansion.* John Faulkner in *My Brother
Bill* (New York: Trident Press, 1963) gives many examples of specific
places which have parallels in Yoknapatawpha County but is less
directly concerned with places than are Cullen or Brown.

Light in August) the total population of Yoknapatawpha County was 15,611, a figure between the population of Lafayette County in 1850 and 1860 as given in Miner: 14,069 and 16,125. Yoknapatawpha County, therefore, is much more rural and sparsely settled than modern Lafayette County. More curiously still, Faulkner's proportion of Negroes— 9,313 Negroes and 6,298 whites—is larger than at the time of the highest percentage of Negroes in Lafayette County, 47.5%, in 1880. (Unlike the Mississippi Delta, Lafayette County has always had more whites than Negroes.)

In discussing these statistics (pp. 86–88), Ward Miner presents some reasonable explanations. The larger county gave Faulkner more scope to include whatever he wished, but his sense of distance was still conditioned by Lafayette County distances. The greater proportion of Negroes suggests that the white people's psychological awareness of the Negroes may well be greater than the actual numbers of Negroes would indicate. One may well add certain conjectures about the sparser population. It explains the importance of the individual in the rural areas and acquaintanceship between characters who do not live in close proximity. It emphasizes the loneliness of life in the country and the clannish isolation of some families and groups. Lillian Smith emphasizes the effect of "distance and darkness . . . in the making of the rural mind of the South":

Distance was not a word but a force pushing a man hard against his memories and fears, isolating him from a world to which he never felt securely tied. When the sun set, the night began. There were no lights; only a kerosene lamp or a pine knot burning. . . . Country folks have lived in a blackout since time began.[10]

The sparse population makes more plausible a cast of characters relatively small for the time and area covered. The Oxford *Eagle* reflects the function of Oxford-Jefferson as the center of county life and the clearing house for county

[10] *Killers of the Dream* (Garden City, N.Y.: Doubleday Anchor Books, 1963), p. 139.

news. In the 1930s, for example, a decade prominent in
Faulkner's fiction, news from more than twenty communities,
as well as from Oxford, was reported, with all of the usual
trivia of who had been where and visited whom. Many of
the communities do not appear on most maps. The same
family names appear repeatedly. In the natural course of
events, these families would do business in Oxford-Jefferson
and would become known at least to merchants and government officials. Anyone who read the *Eagle* weekly would be
able to identify many families in the area without personal
acquaintance with them. John Maclachlan sounds as if he
had been reading the *Eagle* when he commented on Jefferson:

Jefferson is a hub of the universe. It is a small town, a village,
but it is more. Center and turning point of its surrounding countryside it is, like any point in an infinity of time and space, a place of
departure equidistant from all others. Moreover it is a community
of no secrets. Each knows all that is true, and much that is not,
about each. Not a man's life alone is known, but the life of the
father and grandfather as well, and that of the son. Something
done or said on an occasion fifty years ago may well come into the
talk of explaining what happened, what was done and said, last
Saturday night.[11]

In his deviations from statistical truth, Faulkner, according
to Miner, "is trying to record the real history of a particular
region of this country, . . . to make the reality of the Yoknapatawpha Saga a more real reality than the actuality of Lafayette County" (pp. 110–111). In arriving at and presenting
essential truth, some distortion may be necessary: "that imaginative distortion," described by Lewis Mumford, "which
takes place when a deep emotion or a strong feeling plays upon
some actuality, like a blow-torch on metal, and enables the
mind to twist the thing before it into a new shape."[12] But

[11] "No Faulkner in Metropolis," in *Southern Renascence,* p. 107.
[12] Lewis Mumford, *The Golden Day* (Boston: Beacon Paperbacks,
1957), p. 85.

although the fury with which Faulkner's vision of truth sometimes filled him might demand even the expressionistic technique discussed by Wright Morris in "The Violent Land,"[13] the land itself and the human communities upon it remained for Faulkner the province he chose to be all his knowledge, a microcosm in which human truth was revealed by creative imagination transforming objective reality.

II. *Yoknapatawpha Panorama*

Yoknapatawpha County is somewhat Homeric and Biblical in its boundaries: the rivers that flow near its northern and southern boundaries suggest both the River Oceanus that encircled the human activities depicted on the shield of Achilles and the rivers of the Garden of Eden. With no equally convenient and identifiable boundaries to the east and west, Faulkner refrained from inventing any and made the most of the Tallahatchie and the Yoknapatawpha (now simplified to *Yocona*) Rivers so providentially furnished by the Creator of Lafayette County that they neatly frame its mythical counterpart.

Certain facts about Lafayette County may explain why Yoknapatawpha County fades out east and west. Until recent times, travel by vehicles was chiefly north and south, a point Faulkner stressed in his article "Mississippi."[14] The sparseness of the actual population—22,798 in Lafayette County in 1950— and the nature of the land have resulted in the virtual absence of towns or even tiny settlements along the east and west boundaries of Lafayette County. To simplify his problem

[13] Wright Morris, "The Violent Land: Some Observations on the Faulkner Country," *Magazine of Art*, XLV (March, 1952), 99–104.
[14] *Holiday*, XV (April, 1954), 35. Reprinted in James B. Meriwether, ed., *William Faulkner: Essays, Speeches, and Public Letters* (New York: Random House, 1965), p. 9.

of covering his fictitious county, Faulkner merely took advantage of an actual peculiarity of Lafayette County.

When facts were less suitable to his purpose, however, Faulkner ignored them. The two rivers are not so close to the limits of Lafayette County as they are in Yoknapatawpha County, particularly in the southeast; there a good-sized chunk of Lafayette County, with several towns, lies south of the Yocona River.

In *As I Lay Dying,* the Yoknapatawpha River, in its most impressive flood stage, is both a geographical fact and a natural force against which man must struggle. Darl Bundren's description (pp. 134–135) stresses the "ceaseless and myriad" murmur, the "yellow surface dimpled monstrously into fading swirls," the foam and flotsam, and the "trees, canes, vines" surrounded by water, in "a scene of immense yet circumscribed desolation filled with the voice of the waste and mournful water." In their normal state the Yocona and Tallahatchie Rivers are characteristic of the area, flowing in the center of broad bottom land; a bridge over such a river is often merely a central span in a long viaduct over the land, not a dramatic leap from river bluffs to river bluffs. The rivers themselves, the Yocona for example, are turbid brown or yellow and slow-moving in the flat land, as the Indian name *Yoknapatawpha* signifies (*Faulkner in the University,* p. 74). The Tallahatchie as Isaac McCaslin saw it in "The Bear" was bordered by "an open ridge," approached through a tunnel of cane, and was a "thick yellow river, reflectionless in the gray and streaming light" (*Go Down, Moses,* p. 239). In his last novel, *The Reivers,* Faulkner filled in some details about the Tallahatchie, the story of the settlement of Wyatt (*Wyott* in the novel) and river traffic in the 1830s, and the Iron Bridge across the Tallahatchie near Wyatt, the first and, for some time, the only iron bridge in the county, in fact and fiction.

Between the two rivers, slightly to the north of the center of the area, lies Jefferson. The panorama that Gavin Stevens, in *The Town,* saw from a ridge near Seminary (College) Hill not only provides the basic hub and wheel pattern for the geography of Yoknapatawpha but suggests, in its perspective,

Faulkner himself, brooding over the microcosm that is his
world and his creation:

There is a ridge; you drive on beyond Seminary Hill and in time
you come upon it: a mild unhurried farm road presently mount-
ing to cross the ridge and on to join the main highway leading
from Jefferson to the world. And now, looking back and down,
you see all Yoknapatawpha in the dying last of the day beneath
you. There are stars now, just pricking out as you watch them
among the others already coldly and softly burning; the end of
the day is one vast green soundless murmur up the northwest
toward the zenith. . . .
    Then, as though at signal, the fireflies—lightning bugs of the
Mississippi child's vernacular—myriad and frenetic, . . . pulsing
. . . . And you stand suzerain and solitary above the whole sum of
your life beneath that incessant ephemeral spangling. First is Jefferson, the center, radiating weakly its puny glow into space;
beyond it, enclosing it, spreads the County, tied by the diverging
roads to that center as is the rim to the hub by its spokes, yourself
detached as God Himself for this moment above the cradle of
your nativity and of the men and women who made you, the
record and chronicle of your native land proffered for your perusal in ring by concentric ring like the ripples on living water
above the dreamless slumber of your past; you to preside un-
anguished and immune above this miniature of man's passions
and hopes and disasters—ambition and fear and lust and courage
and abnegation and pity and honor and sin and pride—all bound,
precarious and ramshackle, held together by the web, the iron-
thin warp and woof of his rapacity but withal dedicated to his
dreams [pp. 315–316].

Such passages as this may give a valid basis for identifying
Gavin Stevens with Faulkner, since both are fully familiar
with their culture, in the typically Southern fashion, and
identify themselves with it. But that similarity is limited to
their feeling for the land and the people and does not extend
to their interpretations of their society.
    Gavin continues, working from northwest to northeast to
southeast, to enumerate the spokes of the wheel:

They are all here, supine beneath you, stratified and superposed,
osseous and durable with the frail dust and the phantoms—the
rich alluvial river-bottom land of old Issetibbeha, the wild Chickasaw king . . . the same fat black rich plantation earth still syn-
onymous of the proud fading white plantation names . . . . Then
the roadless, almost pathless perpendicular hill-country of McCallum and Gowrie and Frazier and Muir . . . then and last on to
where Frenchman's Bend lay beyond the southeastern horizon,
cradle of Varners and ant-heap for the northeast crawl of Snopes
[pp. 316–317].

That "northeast crawl," of course, took the Snopeses to Jefferson, the hub.

III. *Jefferson*

The wheel image, with Jefferson the hub, is not merely the
fancy of an imaginative author. The Oxford-Lafayette County
Chamber of Commerce gives this factual statement linked
with Faulkner's image, though not necessarily indebted to it:

Oxford sits squarely on the dividing ridge between the watersheds
of the Tallahatchie and Yocona Rivers. The elevation of its business section is right at 500 feet above sea level.
   Because of its geographical location in the northern third of
the state and because of its radiating state highways, it has been
suggested that Oxford be called "The Hub City of North Mississippi."[15]

The image of the wheel and the hub readily lends itself to
symbolism, such as the wheel of life. The movement of the
characters toward Jefferson shows Jefferson's centripetal power

---

[15] The Oxford-Lafayette Chamber of Commerce (Oxford, Mississippi,
September, 1962), p. 1. A mimeographed brochure and guide prepared
for newsmen.

and reinforces the unifying function of the image: all roads lead to Jefferson, all characters have social, commercial, and political ties with Jefferson. But each point on a spoke is itself a hub. The little Grier boy sees his hamlet as the center of outward, centrifugal motion:

It was like the wheel . . . hubbed at that little place that don't even show on a map, that not two hundred people out of all the earth know is named Frenchman's Bend . . . and spoking out in all the directions and touching them all, never a one too big for it to touch, never a one too little to be remembered . . . ["Shall Not Perish," *Collected Stories,* p. 114].

Ties of common humanity radiate from each point in Lafayette County into the outer world.

As Gavin's description indicates, the wheel of which Jefferson is the hub is broken or unfinished, the spokes not radiating around a full circle; this actual feature of the county suggests symbolically the imperfection of human life. The map in *Absalom, Absalom!* represents the highway engineer's dream of roads straight as a plumbline; maps of Lafayette County show no straight roads and no roads running due north, east, south, and west. Both the basic similarity and the deviations between the real and the fictional county are apparent in the map which superimposes the real pattern on Faulkner's map. On modern highway maps, only six of the seven roads out of Oxford appear in reassuring red or black: there is no first- or second-class road northwest of Oxford beyond College Hill. To travel the red-dirt roads in the northwest sector one would need some such strong motive as going on a hunting trip or being a Faulkner fan. The fact that Gavin's—or Faulkner's —wheel has its source in reality does not lessen its symbolic significance: again the Creator of Lafayette County provided a suitable natural setting, but this time the purposes of man wrought in that setting an appropriate design.

The most obvious and significant deviation from the geography of Lafayette County is the consistent relocation of Oxford and the university forty miles away, outside the county.

It is futile to speculate about the purely imaginary site. Details about "Oxford" and the university in fiction, however, are realistic except for geographical location.[16]

But it is most useful to speculate about Faulkner's reasons for such high-handed chess-playing with "Ole Miss"—a much longer move than a "knight's gambit." The University of Mississippi is literally and figuratively not a part of Oxford; it has its own postoffice, of which William Faulkner was undoubtedly the least efficient postmaster, and it is outside the corporate limits of Oxford. The railroad runs between the campus and the town, through Hilgard Cut. But there is only one telegraph office for Oxford and the university and only one railroad depot, a fact of less consequence now, passenger service through Oxford having been discontinued in 1941.[17] This literal separation of university and town gave Faulkner some reason for increasing the distance between them. The mental distance that separates town and gown is a better reason. Faulkner deliberately removed whatever intellectual influence and cultural activities the university community provides for the town. There is only one state university: Faulkner wanted a town that was typical and therefore he had to remove what is unique.[18]

More significant than the removal of university influence is removal of the non-typical element of the population;

---

[16] There are indications that Faulkner, at least sometimes, put "Oxford" north or northwest of Jefferson. Young Bayard passed the gates of Sartoris going east when driving from near Jefferson to "Oxford" and the university (*Sartoris*, p. 147). Horace Benbow's trip to "Oxford" required changing trains at Holly Springs, which would be consistent with a northeast or northwest location (*Sanctuary*, p. 173); the reference to Sardis Reservoir in "Two Soldiers," "that Government reservoy up at Oxford," specifies northwest (*Collected Stories*, p. 81). Details about the university in *Sanctuary* and *Sartoris* are realistic, and in *Sartoris* "Oxford" has streets and a Square "identical with those in Jefferson" (p. 147). The relation between "Oxford" and Taylor, however, is precisely that between the real Oxford and Taylor (*Sanctuary*, p. 35). Calvin Brown confirms these observations (p. 657).

[17] Brown, p. 652. In *Knight's Gambit* Charles Mallison gets off the train in Jefferson in 1942 (p. 239).

[18] This conjecture is confirmed by Calvin Brown, p. 657.

Jefferson is more representative of the South and of small towns everywhere than Oxford is. Gavin Stevens, a Harvard graduate with a Phi Beta Kappa key, stands out more in Jefferson than he would in the university community. John Faulkner clearly does not include the university when he says about Phil Stone, a real-life parallel, in some respects, to Gavin: "Phil was a Yale graduate, the only 'up East' man in our community."[19] Gavin remains in Jefferson because of family ties and personal interests, much as Faulkner and Phil Stone did. Louis Rubin's comments on the "young Southerner of good family" who returns from college "to assume his role in community life" would apply to Gavin: "He was not . . . an intellectual at all, for the very term presupposes a primary allegiance to ideas, to the life of the mind, as against everyday preoccupation in a world of things."[20] In Oxford Gavin could find a number of intellectually congenial souls and might be able to live the life of the mind, instead of depending on his family and a few close friends like the shrewd but unlettered Ratliff. One Gavin Stevens in Jefferson does not break the pattern: he has to conform to it. But a whole coterie of Gavins would destroy the typical character of the community. Unlike Oxford, with its fairly permanent faculty and staff and its transient population of students, Jefferson is like Rubin's typical Southern community, "self-sufficient, an entity in itself, with a mostly homogeneous population, relatively orderly and fixed in its daily patterns."[21]

Faulkner did not, of course, ignore the role of the university in the lives of people in small towns throughout the state. Individuals from Jefferson go to the university, and the distance between Jefferson and "Oxford" is used to good purpose, especially in *The Town*: Linda Snopes, in her brief stay at the university, escaped from the contagion of Snopesism and the provincialism of Jefferson. When Faulkner in *Sartoris*

[19] *My Brother Bill*, p. 130.
[20] *The Faraway Country: Writers of the Modern South* (Seattle: University of Washington Press, 1963), p. 5.
[21] *Ibid.*

(1929) moved the university away from Jefferson (p. 147),
he could scarcely have anticipated what uses he would make
of the geographical "fact."

Removing the university did not remove the socially elite
element of Jefferson. Jefferson, like the actual Oxford, is the
center of the social life of the county, dominated by a few
leading families and those gentle folks acceptable to them.

The mansions of some families are notable features of
Jefferson and the vicinity, and represent significant facts of
social history and social life. Although the Sartoris plantation
is four miles from town,[22] the Sartoris family play a part in
both the business and social life of the town, Colonel Bayard
being president of one of the banks. On one of the Colonel's
trips home from his office, he viewed the Sartoris estate
(*Sartoris*, pp. 6–7). The house described was built to replace
the house burned by the Yankees (*The Unvanquished*).
Sartoris plantation was four miles north of Jefferson, west of
the railroad built after the war by Colonel John Sartoris. The
road was bordered by gums and locusts, with fields beyond
and "patches of woodland newly green and splashed with
dogwood and judas trees." The house, in "a valley of good
broad fields," stood among locusts and oaks and was approached through "iron gates" and "a curving drive." It
represents the visible survival of a vanished life: "The white
simplicity of it dreamed unbroken among ancient sunshot
trees." Wistaria and rose vines grew at one end of the colonnaded veranda. Indoors, the "seldom violated stateliness" of
the parlor confirms the significance of "dreamed unbroken":
the days of hospitable elegance belong to the past, when
Colonel John Sartoris was alive (*Sartoris*, pp. 6–7, 59–60).
Other characteristic features of the Sartoris plantation were
the cotton gin and the mill where Negroes made sorghum,
the motive power for its long arm being furnished by a mule.
Plantation house, outbuildings, mules, and Negroes present a

[22] Cedar Hill, an ante-bellum house (1852) which was not burned
during the Civil War, stands on the approximate site of Sartoris and
was formerly accessible by a road which crossed the railroad. It is now
owned by James Faulkner, nephew of William Faulkner.

scene typical of the fertile and fairly level parts of Yokna-patawpha County.

In Jefferson, the Benbow house represents the houses of the well-to-do which do not fit the conventional idea of ante-bellum splendor. At the top of a semi-circular drive "in an unbroken arc of cedars," set out by the architect who built the Victorian house in "funereal light Tudor," the "brick doll's house" had more than the usual "bridal wreath and crape myrtle bushes as old as time and huge as age would make them": "in one fence corner was an astonishing clump of stunted banana palms and in the other a lantana with its clotted wounds, which Francis Benbow had brought home from Barbados in a top-hat box in '71" (*Sartoris,* pp. 169–170). Faulkner's usual fidelity to the flora and fauna of the region is illustrated here and in the reference to the mocking birds, catbirds, and thrushes which sang in the "resinous, exhilarating gloom" under the cedars.[23]

The Benbow house, like Sartoris, had ceased to be a scene of social gatherings and normal family life, and was a well-preserved survival.

Much more pretentious to begin with and more significant in Jefferson history is the Compson house, on the Compson Mile which Jason Lycurgus Compson got from Ikkemotubbe for a race horse. After the Civil War the Domain was mortgaged and sold in fragments, until Jason III sold the pasture to a golf club to pay for Caddy's wedding and Quentin's year at Harvard. Although Oxford has no golf course near the location Faulkner assigned to the Compson estate, a "branch" still flows southeast of the Square, within the limits of the "Mile." The Compson Domain, as it appears in *The Sound and the Fury* and in Faulkner's Appendix, consists of "the house and the kitchengarden and the collapsing stables and one servant's cabin" (p. 8). The "square,

[23] The prevalence of cedars, wild or planted, is one of the most distinctive characteristics of this region and, it seems, of the South. One of the rules of Ben Robertson's Grandfather Bowen, who liked to plant cedars in South Carolina, was "Never cut a cedar." *Red Hills and Cotton* (New York: Knopf, 1942), p. 61.

paintless house with its rotting portico" (p. 313) had long
ceased to be the scene of any social life when Benjy, who
loved fire, burned himself up with the house in 1933 (*The
Mansion,* p. 322). After World War II, the carriage house
was converted into a house for Orestes Snopes (*The Mansion,*
p. 328), and finally "the old square mile was even intact again
in row after row of small crowded jerrybuilt individually-
owned demiurban bungalows" (*The Sound and the Fury,*
Appendix, p. 9). In 1945, "Jason's old lost patrimony was
already being chopped up into a subdivision of standardised
Veterans' Housing matchboxes" and was officially entitled
Eula Acres (*The Mansion,* p. 332).[24] The account in *The
Mansion,* incorporated into fiction, is more significant than the
earlier statement in the Appendix, in *The Sound and the Fury.*
The stages through which the Compson place passed from
the days of its reputed glory to the days of its decrepitude,
when it is a setting in the fiction, reflect changes in the history
and physical appearance of Jefferson.

   The decline of the old families gradually changed the face
of the town. The rise of new families transformed or lifted
its face. Close to the street, on the site of an old colonnaded
house which had burned, a hill-man from Frenchman's Bend
"built the handsomest house in Frenchman's Bend on the
most beautiful lot in Jefferson," "chopped out the jungle and
whitewashed the remaining trees and ran his barn- and
hog- and chicken-lot fences between their ghostly trunks"
(*Sartoris,* pp. 24, 26). After the hill-man left, it was the home
of the Mitchells, with a pool and a tennis court, where Miss
Jenny Du Pre and Narcissa Benbow attended sophisticated
card parties with the town's faster set (*Sartoris,* pp. 28–30).

   The hill-man left because the house he built became "the
mausoleum of the social aspirations of his women." Flem
Snopes was perhaps more fortunate in achieving his dream

   [24] The reference to the proposed highway which would run the
length of the subdivision (*The Mansion,* p. 333) is realistic in relation
to the location of the Compson Domain. The parallel to Eula Acres,
Avent Acres, adjoins the cemetery in Oxford, northeast of the Square,
not southeast as in the fictitious location.

of splendor after his women were gone—Eula dead, a suicide, and Linda escaped to New York. Flem's "mansion" was the old De Spain house, but unlike the hill-man, Flem tried to imitate the traditional mansions, as Ratliff ironically indicates:

(it was going to have colyums across the front now, I mean the extry big ones so even a feller that never seen colyums before wouldn't have no doubt a-tall what they was, like in the photographs where the Confedrit sweetheart in a hoop skirt and a magnolia is saying good-bye to her Confedrit beau jest before he rides off to finish tending to General Grant) [*The Town,* p. 352].

But after Linda's return and Mink's release, the Mansion became Flem's mausoleum.

The significance of "colyums" as a cultural status symbol is well brought out by Ulrich Phillips, in *Life and Labor in the Old South*: the fashion began in Virginia, largely through the influence of Thomas Jefferson, and "spread until few dwellings were thought to be full-style without pillars and pediment or entablature. Columns plain or fluted, round or square, every formal house must have . . . ; wood, painted white, was the chief recourse. The columns must rise to the height of the eaves, and the more massive the better."[25]

Ratliff's reference to the magnolia is intended to suggest the "moonlight and magnolia" tradition for which the "colyums" are the background. The symbolism of magnolias and cedars, of honeysuckle and wistaria in Faulkner is based upon distinctive features of the Southern scene which, to Southerners, become symbols. Ben Robertson dwells at some length upon this Southern trait, citing the cape jasmine as the symbol of frail perfection destroyed by a touch, a breath, and concludes:

[25] *Life and Labor in the Old South* (Boston: Little, Brown, 1963), p. 331. An ante-bellum house which closely resembled the description of Flem's mansion, the Turner-Faison-Howry house, formerly stood on North Lamar near the Square. Typical Southern colonial in architecture, it had some distinctive features, including colored Venetian glass panes beside the door to the upper balcony (Oxford *Eagle,* December 10, 1936). The house has been moved outside of town to make way for a motel. Now called Cedar Oaks, it has served since 1964 as headquarters for the annual Pilgrimage.

"We have tried for a hundred years with cape jasmines to
smother death."[26] But the huge magnolia trees and the cedars
are in fact dominant details which realism as well as symbolism requires.

The old mansions preserved but sleeping, the old mansions
with their faces lifted, the old mansions decayed or destroyed,
the sometimes tasteless new mansions—all are or have been
centers and symbols of social life, all reflect the vicissitudes
of Jefferson, all that still stand contribute to the typical quality
of Jefferson and to distinctive local variations. But since 1900,
in none of the old family mansions have life and hospitality
flourished. On the narrow, hilly, shady streets of Oxford can
be found their counterparts, but not their originals. Calvin
Brown's statement that "the houses in which Faulkner's
characters live are never specifically identifiable" confirms the
impressions of a newcomer to Oxford, and his explanation
that it is simpler to invent a house than to put imaginary
people into an actual house seems eminently reasonable.[27]

The impression the reader receives that Jefferson has few
impressive ante-bellum mansions is true of Oxford, in which
there are fourteen ante-bellum houses. Faulkner's own home,
Rowan Oak, built in 1848, and another very similar to it
represent typical architecture. Not visible from any street,
Rowan Oak is one of the few houses that retain spacious
grounds; another is Ammadelle, on North Lamar, "apparently
the only brick ante-bellum house in town now standing";
it was in fact finished after the Civil War. It was designed by
Calvert Vaux, of the New York firm of Olmsted and Vaux.[28]

26 *Red Hills and Cotton,* pp. 63–64.
27 Pp. 658, 659.
28 Miner, p. 43. Miner cites drawings signed "C. Vaux, architect,
N.Y., 1859." Local tradition sometimes ascribes the plans to Upjohn.
The account of historic houses and buildings given by Miner seems
quite complete, but only the impressions of the reader-observer are relevant here. The Olmsted referred to is Frederick Law Olmsted, author
of *The Cotton Kingdom* (1861) and architect-in-chief of Central Park
in New York. Probably the most palatial house in Oxford was the
twenty-room home of Jacob Thompson, United States Congressman and
Secretary of the Interior under President Buchanan. The one house
burned by General Smith when he burned the Square, it was not re-

The map of Oxford, with its very small blocks near the Square, suggests how the spacious old estates were cut up, and also indicates, in the numerous streetless areas, the hills and ravines which break up the town.[29] One of the few descriptions of the ravines which are a dominant feature of Oxford is the account of the Big Ditch "which was a town landmark. The tops of tall trees which grew in it just showed above the rim; a regiment could hide and deploy in it" (*Light in August*, p. 403).

The two Negro sections to which Faulkner refers, Freedman Town and Negro Hollow, have their counterparts in most Southern towns, with unpaved streets and houses ranging in Oxford from flimsy, dilapidated cabins to substantial, well-kept small houses.[30]

The most obvious parallels between Oxford and Jefferson appear on the map or strike the casual observer: the conver-

---

placed by a house of equal size and splendor: tales are told of the dining room which seated a hundred guests.

[29] The newer parts of Oxford, in addition to commonplace subdivisions much like Eula Acres as described by Faulkner, are distinguished by attractive use of hillside locations, new winding streets of comfortable width graced by mimosa trees, and well-kept lawns. Faulkner's failure to feature among his characteristic flora the strikingly beautiful mimosa trees, with their delicate pink blossoms, is apparently the result of the relatively recent popularity of the mimosa in that part of Mississippi. Ben Robertson refers repeatedly to mimosas as traditional favorites in South Carolina (pp. 61, 94, 95).

[30] The segregation of Negro residences in towns, except survivals of servant quarters adjoining white houses, results in extremes of Negro social and economic levels visible in close proximity. In *The Negro in Mississippi 1865–1890* (New York: Harper Torchbooks, 1965), Vernon L. Wharton refers to the "immediate tendency" toward residential and business segregation in Mississippi towns, caused by both the poverty of the Negroes and the "increasing desire of the whites to avoid Negro neighbors" (pp. 129–130). But the segregation process, he adds, "was slow and incomplete" in Jackson and other towns. As W. E. B. Du Bois observes, "the best of the whites and the best of the Negroes almost never live in anything like close proximity" (*The Souls of Black Folk* [Greenwich, Conn.: Fawcett Publications, Premier Americana, 1960], p. 125). Hortense Powdermaker comments on the same characteristic of incongruity and proximity as typical of the Negro section of "Cottonville" and as owing to lumping together all the Negroes (*After Freedom: A Cultural Study in the Deep South* [New York: Viking, 1939], pp. 11–12). Freedman Town was razed in 1974 for urban renewal.

gence of county roads in the center of the town, the Square
and the courthouse in its center, and the mingling of country-
and towns-people in the activity in the Square. In these respects, Jefferson is like most county seats in Mississippi: the
hub and spoke pattern is as characteristic of counties in
Mississippi as is the gridiron pattern of states such as Illinois
where only the larger cities appear as hubs. The layout with
the Square in the center of town is typical:

. . . a Square, the courthouse in its grove the center; quadrangular
around it, the stores, two-storey, the offices of the lawyers and doctors and dentists, the lodge-rooms and auditoriums, above them;
school and church and tavern and bank and jail each in its ordered
place; the four broad diverging avenues straight as plumb-lines in
the four directions, becoming the network of roads and by-roads
until the whole county would be covered with it [*Requiem for a
Nun*, p. 39].[31]

In Jefferson, however, some features are peculiar to Jefferson-
Oxford, most notably the Confederate monument in the
Square, said to be unique in facing south. According to one
story, the unusual position was due to the desire of Faulkner's
grandmother to enjoy the sight of the monument when she
looked toward the courthouse from her house on South

---

[31] A minor difference between Jefferson and Oxford is that in Jefferson the courthouse is on the spot where the two main streets would
intersect. In Oxford, the courthouse breaks the north-south street,
Lamar, but the two east-west streets, forming the north and south sides
of the Square, pass unbroken in front of and behind the courthouse.
The main road to the east joins Lamar several blocks south of the
courthouse but continues west from the northwest corner of the Square.
John Faulkner's initial description of the Square in Oxford, in *My
Brother Bill*, brings out its associations for Oxford residents, especially
for the Faulkner boys. His reminiscence, as he sat in front of the
funeral home waiting for the body of William Faulkner to be brought
there, and the news accounts of the funeral procession of Oxford's
most famous son proceeding around the Square, with its closed stores,
on the way to St. Peter's Cemetery, merge in the reader's mind with
the multitude of memories of fictitious events in the Square. In "The
Ways that Faulkner Walked: A Pilgrimage," *Arizona Quarterly*, XXI
(Summer, 1965), 133–145, H. Edward Richardson describes the route
from Faulkner's house to and around the Square.

Lamar.[32] The museum is distinctive in a small town ("Shall Not Perish," *Collected Stories,* pp. 110–111; *Requiem for a Nun,* p. 253). The federal courthouse, used for scenes in "The Fire and the Hearth" (*Go Down, Moses,* pp. 63–71), is neither unique nor typical; it is the headquarters of the North Mississippi Federal District Court. Other towns have much the same assortment of buildings, some still with the character- istic metal awnings extending over the sidewalks and with second-storey galleries, reached by outside stairways. Other towns have a water tower and cotton gins near the Square. Other towns have loungers in the shade.[33] Although the reader of Faulkner feels at home in the Square in Oxford and with pleasure recognizes specific details, the Square in Jefferson is more typical than distinctive, save in the lack of ante-bellum buildings and in the soldier who turns his back to the foe.

The Square is the center of trade, the daily destination of many of the townspeople, and the weekly mecca of fortunate country folk whose lives provide such heady pleasures as a trip to town on Saturday. The trip might be strictly business:

The wagons and pick-ups of the hill farmers and the five- and ten-ton trucks of the bottomland planters and operators had al- ready backed up to the loading platforms of the seed stores and the fertilizer warehouses, and tractors and spanned and tripled mules would be moving across the dark shearing of the land's winter sleep: plow and middlebuster, harrow and drag and disc ... ["Knight's Gambit," p. 239].

But the throngs and noise, after the silence and space and loneliness of life in the hills or even in the rich bottomland, would make the Square exert a magnetic attraction for the countryman and fascinate, though with less unalloyed bliss, the town dweller. Charles Mallison had a bird's-eye view of the Square from his Uncle Gavin's office the Saturday after

[32] Murry C. Falkner, *The Falkners of Mississippi* (Baton Rouge: Louisiana State University Press, 1967), p. 30.

[33] Hortense Powdermaker's account of "Cottonville," a town essen- tially like Oxford, could almost be a description of Oxford (pp. 11–12).

the Square had almost been the scene of a lynching by a white mob:

. . . he was still standing . . . alone at the window looking down into the Square thronged and jammed as he couldn't remember it before—the bright sunny almost hot air heavy with the smell of blooming locust from the courthouse yard, the sidewalks dense and massed and slow with people black and white . . . and above all the motion and the noise, the radios and the automobiles—the juke boxes in the drugstore and the poolhall and the cafe and the bellowing amplifiers on the outside walls not only of the record-and-sheetmusic store but the army-and-navy supply store and both feed stores and . . . somebody standing on a bench in the court-house yard making a speech into another with a muzzle like a siege gun bolted to the top of an automobile . . . explicitly speaking he couldn't see the Square at all: only the dense impenetrable mass of tops and hoods moving in a double line at a snail's crawl around the Square in an invisible aura of carbon monoxide and blatting horns and a light intermittent clashing of bumpers . . . [*Intruder in the Dust*, pp. 236–238].

What Jefferson means to the poor people in the hills is best seen in *As I Lay Dying*, where the various Bundrens have personal reasons for wanting to go to Jefferson but have to wait until Addie has died before they can make the family pilgrimage, fulfilling their promise to bury Addie in Jefferson and gratifying their own desires. What opportunity Jefferson offers to those with ambition is seen in the career of Flem Snopes; in *The Town*, Flem began by running a back-alley restaurant and living in a tent, became superintendent of the power plant and lived in a rented house in a back street, bought the house after becoming vice president of the bank, and ended, in *The Mansion*, as president of the bank and owner of the De Spain mansion with the "colyums." The Square represents both the opportunities and the limitations in business and pleasure in Jefferson.

As the Square is the center of Jefferson, the courthouse is the center of the Square, the scene of legal activity from the marriage of Flem Snopes and Eula Varner in *The Hamlet* to the trials of Mink Snopes, Lee Goodwin, and Nancy Mannigoe for murder in *The Mansion, Sanctuary,* and *Requiem for a Nun.* From the beginning the courthouse was the nucleus of the town, the symbol of civilized society—church, courthouse, school, in that order, with the courthouse the "catalyst," without which there was no town (*Requiem for a Nun,* pp. 28, 213).

But above all the courthouse; the center, the focus, the hub; sitting looming in the center of the county's circumference like a single cloud in its ring of horizon, laying its vast shadow to the uttermost rim of horizon; musing, brooding, symbolic and ponderable, tall as cloud, solid as rock, dominating all: protector of the weak, judicate and curb of the passions and lusts, repository and guardian of the aspirations and the hopes . . . [*Requiem for a Nun,* p. 40].

When the Square was burned in 1864, the courthouse "simply survived":

harder than axes, tougher than fire, more fixed than dynamite; encircled by the tumbled and blackened ruins of lesser walls, it still stood, even the topless smoke-stained columns, gutted of course and roofless, but immune, . . . so that all they had to do . . . was put in new floors for the two storeys and a new roof, and this time with a cupola with a four-faced clock and a bell to strike the hours and ring alarms . . . [*Requiem for a Nun,* p. 46].[34]

The courthouse still survives, nesting place of pigeons and sparrows, "centennial and serene above the change":

The electricity and gasoline, the neon and the crowded cacophonous air; even Negroes passing beneath the balconies and into the chancery clerk's office to cast ballots . . . ; its fate is to stand in the hinterland of America: its doom is its longevity; like a man,

[34] The courthouse in Oxford before the Civil War was a brick building, almost square, with four chimneys, two porticoes, each with four columns, and a clockless cupola. See Appendix A for an account of the history of the courthouse; see illustration.

its simple age is its own reproach, and after the hundred years, will become unbearable [*Requiem for a Nun*, p. 47].

Gone are "the last of the forest trees," the iron hitching chains looped between the wooden posts around the yard and the watering trough; gone are store fronts of bricks made from native clay. Glass fronts, fluorescent lights, tractors, trucks, and autos prevail, and a French point-seventy-five field piece and an anti-tank howitzer flank the Confederate monument (*Requiem for a Nun*, pp. 243–244).

A necessary adjunct to the courthouse, the jail, older than the courthouse, was left "in the tideless backwater of an alley on a side-street" a block north of the courthouse, gradually transformed but its function and significance unchanged as it harbored Mink Snopes, Lee Goodwin, Nancy Mannigoe, Lucas Beauchamp, and Joe Christmas:

. . . not only was the courthouse finished, but the jail too: not a new jail of course but the old one veneered over with brick, into two storeys, with white trim and iron-barred windows: only its face lifted, because behind the veneer were still the old ineradicable bones, the old ineradicable remembering: the old logs immured intact and lightless between the tiered symmetric bricks and the white washed plaster, immune now even to having to look, see, watch that new time . . . [*Requiem for a Nun*, pp. 222, 224].[35]

When the Square was burned, the jail escaped. It stood diagonally across from the hotel, the Holston House,[36] and housed

---

[35] Accounts of the jail vary. Miner says it was built shortly before the courthouse (p. 30). Harrison says the same contractors built both and adds the corroborative detail of the combined cost (see Appendix A). At the time the new jail was being opened, an article in the Oxford *Eagle* (February 21, 1963) stated that the jail was built in the 1870s. Harrison's more detailed account is closer to Faulkner's fictitious version, which is symbolically significant.

[36] The Colonial Hotel stands where, in Jefferson, Faulkner illogically retained the Holston House, which should have burned when the rest of the buildings on the Square did. The Butler Hotel, which originally stood on that site, did burn. Down the same street in Oxford, just west of the Square, still stands an old hotel which Grant is said

a shifting population of Negroes who worked out their fines during the day, of thieves and moonshiners awaiting trial, of accused murderers awaiting trial or convicted ones awaiting execution. In *The Mansion,* Mink Snopes peered from the jail, "his dirty hands gripping the grimed interstices of the barred windows" (p. 3), vainly watching for Flem to come and rescue him. This jail now belongs wholly to fiction and memory: a white concrete jail replaced it in 1962–1963.

Except for the Square, the railroad depot, down the hill to the west of the Square, at train time was the one reliable source of excitement; even the Square was deserted at night except for patrons of the picture show arriving or going home. With the coming of paved roads and automobiles and airplanes, the depot lost its significance, but it figures repeatedly in the fiction dealing with the period from 1908 through the thirties, with more departures than homecomings.[37] The airport has replaced the depot in the lives of Jefferson travellers. The Sartoris family epitomizes the social history of the town as reflected in transportation: Colonel John Sartoris built the railroad, Young Bayard came home by train from World War I, Old Bayard lost his life in an automobile driven by Young Bayard, Young Bayard died in an airplane crash.

And Young Bayard was laid to rest, if rest he could, in the cemetery northwest of the Square (*Sartoris,* p. 373). This is the last inevitable feature of a Southern town, the cemetery, populated in Jefferson by Compsons and Sartorises who even in death cannot escape the encroaching Snopeses: "whiter than white itself in the warm October sun against the bright yellow and red and dark red hickories and sumacs and gums and oaks like splashes of fire itself among the dark green cedars" (*The*

---

to have used as his headquarters during his occupation of Oxford. Faulkner may have had in mind this hotel as the old Holston House and the Colonial Hotel as its modern transformation.

[37] Watching the trains come in was a favorite amusement in any small town before the motor age. John Faulkner described the rivalry of the hackmen at the depot and the swarm of boys collecting Sunday papers there after Sunday School (pp. 60–61). Now piles of pulp wood beside the station indicate one of the present uses of the natural resources of the area.

Town, p. 354), the marble medallion face of Eula Varner Snopes,[38] above Flem Snopes's ironic tribute to a virtuous wife—who had had a lover for eighteen years—gazes perhaps at the figure of Colonel John Sartoris:

· He stood on a stone pedestal, in his frock coat and bareheaded, one leg slightly advanced and one hand resting lightly on the stone pylon beside him. His head was lifted a little in that gesture of haughty pride which repeated itself generation after generation with a fateful fidelity, his back to the world and his carven eyes gazing out across the valley where his railroad ran, and the blue changeless hills beyond, and beyond that, the ramparts of infinity itself. The pedestal and the effigy were mottled with seasons of rain and sun and with drippings from the cedar branches, and the bold carving of the letters was bleared with mold, yet still decipherable:

COLONEL JOHN SARTORIS, C. S. A.

1823   1876

Soldier, Statesman, Citizen of the World

For man's enlightenment he lived
By man's ingratitude he died

Pause here, son of sorrow; remember death
[*Sartoris,* p. 375].

Faulkner provided the marble colonel with a gratifying view by moving the cemetery from its location in Oxford, northeast of the Square and east of the highway to Memphis, to the vantage point northwest of the Square from which the railroad

---

[38] The description of Eula's monument fits that of Faulkner's grandmother, on which the inscription, from Proverbs 31:11, 28, includes part of that on Eula's: "Her children rise and call her blessed." Flem may have intended "A virtuous wife is a crown to her husband" to recall to observers the rest of the verse, Proverbs 12:4—"but she that maketh ashamed is as rottenness in his bones." In Eula's monument, fiction imitates fact. On the tombstone of Dean Faulkner, who was killed in an airplane accident in 1935, fact imitates fiction: the inscription, "I bare him on eagles' wings and brought him unto Me" is that on John Sartoris's tomb in *Sartoris* (1929) (p. 374).

could be seen.[39] Except for the inscription and minor details in the description of the monument, the effigy of Colonel John Sartoris and its relation to the railroad fit the effigy of Colonel William Falkner in Ripley.

The many references in the Yoknapatawpha novels to the cemetery reflect a characteristic of the South which is better represented by Aunt Jenny in *Sartoris* (pp. 373–376) than in the morbid Compson obsession with death and cemeteries, in *The Sound and the Fury*. But the idiot Benjy, in his weekly visit to the cemetery, was following precedent which, as Ben Robertson shows, could be sane and wholesome:

We like to visit cemeteries. We do not feel we are strangers among tombs. . . . Graveyards in the South are like the Southern hills: there is the same looming eternity about them, and we understand eternity in our lonely country. It gives you a proper perspective to spend an hour among tombs.[40]

The visitor to Oxford, as he follows Benjy's route to the cemetery, knows that along this route passed the funeral procession that carried William Faulkner to his grave beneath the oak trees. Fame had not changed his love of simple things and sense of closeness to the earth; the remark he made to J. W. Harmon in 1928 or 1929 might well have been true when he died: he said "he had rather be hauled to the cemetery by a wagon and mules—a team—than to be taken in a Cadillac limousine."[41] No vain-glorious effigy of William Faulkner

[39] Calvin Brown notes (p. 658) discrepancies in Faulkner's references to the cemetery. It should also be noted that Faulkner's description of the approach to the cemetery, which would accurately describe the Oxford cemetery, immediately precedes his description of Colonel Sartoris's monument in the fictitious location.

[40] Robertson, p. 94. Like the Bundrens, the Robertsons refused to let "hell nor high water" keep them from funerals. Thomas D. Clark refers to the "sprawling graveyards" found "among the pine hills of the rural South" and comments: "Death has ever been a subject of primary interest in the region" (*Pills, Petticoats and Plows: The Southern Country Store* [Indianapolis and New York: Bobbs-Merrill, 1944], p. 261).

[41] *William Faulkner of Oxford*, James W. Webb and A. Wigfall Green, eds. (Baton Rouge: Louisiana State University Press, 1965), p. 94.

points at the town which he immortalized in his creations,
as Colonel Falkner's effigy points with pride at the railroad.
A simple, classic monument shows where Oxford's greatest
citizen, unlike the Sartoris men, lies "dead in the ground
without strutting and swaggering" (*Sartoris,* p. 374).

IV. *The Northwest Sector*

The railroad and the highway to Memphis, which runs parallel
to the railroad on the east, lead to the outside world of trade
and cities: for Oxford or Jefferson, Memphis is the big city, to
which cotton is sent, in which the well-to-do can shop and, in
Faulkner's day of state prohibition, could replenish their
liquor supply, and in which any male who can raise the price
can indulge the lusts of the flesh. In building the Sartoris
legend, using parallels from his own family history, Faulkner
deviated from the facts concerning the railroad and had it put
through after the Civil War, simply transferring to Jefferson
the facts about the railroad through Ripley, as he transported
the effigy of Colonel Falkner to the Jefferson cemetery. The
only railroad in Oxford was built in 1857, the Mississippi
Central, now the Illinois Central; it is clearly shown on a
Civil War map which also clearly shows the absence of any
railroad in Ripley. In Yoknapatawpha, after the Civil War a
branch line from Jefferson was built into the main line from
Memphis to the East coast; in fact and fiction, there are
junctions in Holly Springs and Grand Junction. The story of
the building of the railroad in *Sartoris* resembles that of
the railroad in Ripley built by Faulkner's great-grandfather,
Colonel William Falkner, after the Civil War. The legend
of Colonel Falkner and his railroad endured to such a degree
that the Oxford *Eagle* for August 18, 1926—before the name
of *Faulkner* had gained new luster—reprinted a quotation
from the *Southern Sentinel,* recalling the first train to Chicago

passing through on the Colonel's railroad: "At last this dream has become realized and great through trains pass daily within sight of the artistic marble likeness of Col. Falkner in the Ripley cemetery where rests [sic] his bonès and by the place that was his home for many years." Because in this one part of the fiction Faulkner fused Oxford and Ripley, the geography of Yoknapatawpha County may by logical extension include the little crossroads hamlet of Falkner on the railroad north of Ripley, its tiny disused station with broken windows a melancholy reminder of the Colonel's dream of greatness. In his article, "Mississippi," Faulkner refers to Sartoris's railroad with no mention of his deviation from geographical and chronological fact.

In *The Unvanquished,* the location of the railroad described is in Alabama; there was not yet a railroad in Jefferson. The boy Bayard had seen a railroad and locomotive when he visited the Dennisons at Christmas:

It was the straightest thing I ever saw, running straight and empty and quiet through a long empty gash cut through the trees, and the ground, too, and full of sunlight like water in a river, only straighter than any river, with the crossties cut off even and smooth and neat, and the light shining on the rails like on two spider threads, running straight on to where you couldn't even see that far . . . like they were getting up speed to jump clean off the world.

. . . and then we heard it; it whistled and then it got louder and louder fast . . . . It came roaring up and went past; the river they had cut through the trees was all full of smoke and noise and sparks and jumping brass, and then empty again . . . [pp. 99–100].

Imaginative truth provides a glimpse of a significant aspect of Southern experience, even though Faulkner, for understandable reasons, located that experience outside of Yoknapatawpha County. The fifteen-year interval between the time when Oxford got its railroad and when Jefferson did may serve, like the larger and more sparsely populated fictitious county, to increase the effect of loneliness and isolation in the earlier history of Yoknapatawpha County and to emphasize

the changes brought about after the war by trains and roads
and automobiles and airplanes.

Only one area west of the railroad in Yoknapatawpha
County is dealt with by Faulkner, the region northwest of
Jefferson near the Tallahatchie River. That section of Lafayette County consists of river bottom and swamp, of eroded
hills beginning to be covered with pines, with red dirt roads
that descend into mud holes and peter out into trails or that
cut through the red hills and lead to the shore of Sardis Reservoir. Here the old ferry landings on the river are replaced
by boat ramps on the reservoir which has been created by the
Sardis Dam to the west. Faulkner's fiction gives little idea of
this feature of the present landscape. Erosion is more visible
in the northwest sector than in other parts of the county
where reforestation and other measures to control erosion have
been more extensively practiced. In the 1830s the Natchez area
resembled Lafayette County of the 1930s: "By degrees acre
after acre of what was a few years previous beautiful undu-
lating ground . . . presents a wild scene of frightful precipices
and yawning chasms."[42] Faulkner's frequent references to erosion scarcely prepare one for the reality of "Mississippi canyons."

In this northwest part of the county, Faulkner locates two
major stories of the past. Twelve miles from Jefferson, in a
hundred square miles of wilderness and swamp, Thomas Sutpen in the 1830s hewed out his estate, built, according to his
Grand Design, in imitation of Tidewater plantations.[43] For

---

[42] Phillips, *Life and Labor in the Old South,* p. 8. Phillips is quoting
from an account of the Natchez area in 1835. The Oxford *Eagle* for
April 18, 1930, stated that 40,000 acres in Lafayette County were worth-
less because of erosion. On February 2, 1933, the *Eagle* quoted the
Assistant State Forester as saying that four to six generations of
Lafayette County farmers had "worn out" 170,000 acres, that 194,000
acres were never cultivated because they were unsuitable, and that only
56,000 acres were in cultivation, with fewer farms than twenty years
earlier. By 1937, according to the *Eagle* for May 13, only 50,000 acres
were in cultivation, as compared with 100,000 in 1917. Statistics support an observer's impressions and testify to what Du Bois called "the
hard ruthless rape of the land" (*The Souls of Black Folk,* p. 97).

[43] The one hundred square miles from which Sutpen's Hundred got

three years he lived there in isolation, "in the Spartan shell of
the largest edifice in the county, not excepting the courthouse
itself, . . . without any feminized softness of window-pane or
door or mattress" (*Absalom, Absalom!,* pp. 39–40). Here he
hunted game with slaves, who "could creep up to a bedded
buck and cut its throat before it could move" (p. 40). Sutpen's
Hundred was eventually feminized by Sutpen's frivolous wife,
but after her death during the war it lapsed into "scaling desolation . . . marooned and forgotten in a backwater of catastrophe" (p. 132).

Years later Quentin Compson remembered Sutpen's Hundred as he saw it when quail-hunting with his father:

. . . he looked up the slope before them where the wet yellow
sedge died upward into the rain like melting gold and saw the
grove, the clump of cedars on the crest of the hill dissolving into
the rain as if the trees had been drawn in ink on a wet blotter—
the cedars beyond which, beyond the ruined fields beyond which,
would be the oak grove and the gray huge rotting deserted house
half a mile away [p. 187].

And he remembered his earlier venture with some other boys:

. . . *coming up from the rear, into the old street of the slave
quarters—a jungle of sumach and persimmon and briers and
honeysuckle, and the rotting piles of what had once been log
walls and stone chimneys and shingle roofs among the under-*

---

its name exceeds by 2,400 acres the holdings of A. H. Pegues in the
Oxford area; his career bears a superficial resemblance to Sutpen's before the Civil War. One wonders whether Sutpen—or Faulkner—had
in mind the famous Virginia plantation of Berkeley Hundred, without
knowing the meaning of "Hundred": Clifford Dowdey says that the
Hundreds were so called "either because one hundred settlers was the
ideal figure for a plantation or because of the hundred-acre basic grant
for a share of stock" (*The Great Plantation: A Profile of Berkeley
Hundred and Plantation Virginia from Jamestown to Appomattox*
[New York: Bonanza Books, 1957], p. 28). The scale of Faulkner's
map in *Absalom, Absalom!,* in which the Tallahatchie River is only
sixteen miles due north of Jefferson, scarcely allows room for an estate
of one hundred square miles twelve miles from Jefferson, south of the
river.

growth . . .[p. 214]. . . . *the rotting shell of the house with its sagging portico and scaling walls, its sagging blinds and plank-shuttered windows, set in the middle of the domain which had reverted to the state and been bought and sold and bought and sold again and again and again* [p. 213].

In imagination, Quentin saw it collapse in flames. If there was a plantation like Sutpen's in the northwest sector, it is now at the bottom of Sardis Lake. But for the reader, it still stands, in all its vicissitudes, as part of Faulkner's haunted landscapes.

Farther north, in the river bottom and completely outside the range of the settled population and cultivation, lay De Spain's hunting and fishing camp, where Wash Jones killed Sutpen with a scythe (*Absalom, Absalom!*, pp. 285–289). Five miles down the river from the camp is the Indian Mound referred to in "A Bear Hunt." De Spain's camp and the surrounding area are the scenes of "The Bear."

When Ike McCaslin returned from the camp every year as a boy, the transition from the Big Bottom to the precariously cultivated land was abrupt: "the wagon winding on among the tremendous gums and cypresses and oaks where no axe save that of the hunter had ever sounded, between the impenetrable walls of cane and brier" would emerge suddenly and "skeleton cotton- and corn-fields would flow away on either hand"; "house, barn, fences" would show "where the hand of man had clawed for an instant" ("The Old People," *Go Down, Moses,* pp. 176–177).

The only dwellers in the Big Bottom or along its edge were "the swamp dwellers, the gaunt men who ran traplines and lived on quinine and coons and river water, the farmers of little corn- and cotton-patches along the Bottom's edge" ("The Bear," p. 248).

At the time of Ike's youth, the northwest triangle of Yoknapatawpha County also included lumbering camps, with a log-line and log-train which joined the railroad to Memphis at Hoke's, a sawmill. By 1885 a planing mill at Hoke's marked the end of the wilderness.

Although the river bottoms in Lafayette County were full
of virgin timber when Faulkner's father was a young man,
Faulkner's own hunting took place first near Batesville, at
the edge of the Delta. The scene and many of the incidents
of "The Bear" are based upon Faulkner's own experiences
but are located in Yoknapatawpha County where the Big
Woods really did exist at the time the story took place. The
same succession of changes that finally made it necessary for
Ike to go two hundred miles to hunt, in "Delta Autumn,"
took place in Lafayette County, and both William Faulkner
and Uncle Ike hunted in the triangle between the Yazoo and
the Mississippi Rivers.[44] The recreation which Faulkner finally
enjoyed where the Big Woods used to be was boating on
Sardis Reservoir. What big trees remain there are now surrounded by water, and the Indian Mound is almost an island,
as no doubt it was during floods in ancient days.

v. *The Northeast Sector*

East of the railroad and the highway to Memphis there is less
swamp than to the west, and the Tallahatchie River narrows.
The country is still wild, with pine hills which, in Lafayette
County, are now being reforested where they had been cut
over. The Holly Springs National Forest covers very nearly
the northeast quarter of Layafette County, preserving or re-
storing the area so that, for scenic purposes, it presents a pleas-
ant wildness. In both Lafayette and Yoknapatawpha Counties
a good road traverses the area, with many dirt roads in various states of passableness. The most striking feature of any of
the roads out of Oxford except those to the northwest is the
kudzu vine, planted to check erosion, which in summer covers

[44] John Faulkner, pp. 91–92; Cullen, pp. 12–13, 25–30; Webb and
Green, pp. 152, 154–161.

road embankments with mantles of green and envelops trees
and bushes until the roadside looks like an endless topiary
garden. Even in its leafless state, when it looks like gray veils,
there is something fantastic and extravagant about it that fits
"the violent land." Since both the Holly Springs National
Forest and kudzu are more recent in Lafayette County, "the
reforestation capitol of the world," than the action in most
of the Yoknapatawpha fiction, Faulkner's omission of these
distinctive features is consistent with his general policy of
using accurate and typical details.

Nearest to Jefferson to the northeast is the county subdivision called Beat Four which figures prominently in *Intruder
in the Dust*. Charles Mallison describes it objectively in
"Monk" (*Knight's Gambit*):

. . . the pine hill country in the eastern part of our county: a
country which twenty-five years ago . . . was without roads almost and where even the sheriff of the county did not go—a
country impenetrable and almost uncultivated and populated by
a clannish people who owed allegiance to no one and no thing
and whom outsiders never saw until a few years back when good
roads and automobiles penetrated the green fastnesses where the
denizens with their corrupt Scotch-Irish names intermarried and
made whiskey and shot at all strangers from behind log barns
and snake fences [pp. 40–41].

A more detailed and inclusive account, much less objective, is
given in *Intruder in the Dust,* when Charles drove with
Gavin Stevens to the country churchyard in Beat Four where,
the night before, he and Miss Habersham had dug up a grave.
The passage complements Gavin's bird's-eye view, from northwest of Jefferson, by giving color and specific details whereas
Gavin gave basic pattern:

. . . now he could see the white bursts of dogwood in the hedge-
rows marking the old section-line surveys or standing like nuns in
the cloistral patches and bands of greening woods and the pink
and white of peach and pear and the pinkwhite of the first apple
trees in the orchards . . . and always beyond and around them

the enduring land—the fields geometric with furrows where the
corn had been planted when the first doves began to call in late
March and April, and cotton when the first whippoorwills cried
at night around the beginning of May a week ago: but empty,
vacant of any movement and any life—the farmhouses from which
no smoke rose . . . the paintless Negro cabins where on Monday
morning in the dust of the grassless treeless yards halfnaked children should have been crawling and scrabbling after broken cul-
tivator wheels and wornout automobile tires and empty snuff-
bottles and tin cans and in the back yards smoke-blackened iron
pots should have been bubbling over wood fires beside the sagging
fences of vegetable patches and chickenruns which by nightfall
would be gaudy with drying overalls and aprons and towels and
unionsuits . . . but most of all the empty fields themselves in each
of which . . . there should have been fixed in monotonous repetition the land's living symbol—a formal group of ritual almost
mystic significance identical and monotonous as milestones tying
the county-seat to the county's ultimate rim as milestones would:
the beast the plow and the man integrated in one foundationed
into the frozen wave of their furrow tremendous with effort yet
at the same time vacant of progress, ponderable immovable and
immobile like groups of wrestling statuary set against the land's
immensity . . . [pp. 146–147].[45]

When the car had climbed the crest, there was another pano-
ramic view of Yoknapatawpha County and a vision of the
continent beyond, from a point northeast of Jefferson, with
"the long wall of the levee and the great River itself" to the

[45] The details of clothes drying on the fences and of treeless, grassless
yards are characteristic of cabins in Lafayette County. Yards with the
dust swept "into an intricate series of whorls" (*Intruder in the Dust*,
p. 8) are not so noticeable to the passer-by. Ben Robertson's explanation of sanded yards, surrounded by flowers—"The white of the sand,
shaded by the thick trees, formed an oasis" (p. 60)—seems inapplicable
to cabins which usually lack both shade and color. Andrew Lytle, in
the thoughts of Lucius Cree, explains this regional peculiarity as evidence of instinctive living "in and by the dirt," the yards "swept bare,
to bring the dirt right up to the door sill" (*The Velvet Horn* [New
York: McDowell, Obolensky, 1957], p. 290). But cotton might be
planted "up close to the door," Robert Canzoneri of Mississippi recalls,
when the cabin was in a field of cotton (*"I Do So Politely": A Voice
from the South* [Boston: Houghton Mifflin, 1965], p. 17).

southwest, and ahead of him to the northeast "the long reach of rich bottom land marked off into the big holdings, the plantations (one of which was Edmonds' where the present Edmonds and Lucas both had been born, stemming from the same grandfather)" and "the dense line of river jungle" (pp. 151–152). Charles's feeling for his native land, which suffuses the long passage quoted above, resembles that of his Uncle Gavin and of Faulkner and shows a similar awareness of the world beyond. The two visions from the heights, Gavin's and Charles's, orient the reader geographically and emotionally in Yoknapatawpha County. Faulkner's frequent use of limited point of view and the consequent scarcity of description from the author's point of view make such passages doubly useful and important.

Although Charles does not mention the McCallums, their farm lies somewhere between Charles's vantage point and the Edmonds plantation. In *Sartoris* and "The Tall Men" the McCallum farm seems more in the hills than the river bottom, although the "tall men" grow cotton and raise cattle. When Bayard reached the McCallums' after his grandfather had died in Bayard's car, the isolation and the closeness to the woods are stressed, with reference to Bayard's past hunting expeditions with the men. In "The Tall Men," over twenty years later, the draft investigator saw chiefly the "stout paintless gate" and picket fence, the walk between two rows of cedars, and "the rambling and likewise paintless sprawl of the two-storey house," its lower storey of logs.[46]

Beyond McCallums', nearer the Tallahatchie, the old McCaslin plantation, run by Roth Edmonds at the time of "The Fire and the Hearth," is the closest approximation of the old order of paternalistic plantation surviving in Faulkner's stories. The few large plantations in the county are in the river bot-

---

[46] *Collected Stories,* p. 46. Faulkner's farm is about the same distance from Oxford, in the same direction, as the McCallums' from Jefferson. On Faulkner's farm the unpainted house with its metal roof and the piece of bottom land with a creek are typical. John Faulkner's account of the people in the area (Chapter 17) fits Charles Mallison's account of Beat Four, in the corresponding location in Yoknapatawpha County.

toms. During the Civil War, Uncle Buck and Uncle Buddy lived in a two-room log house and housed their slaves in the "big colonial house," built by their father, "one of the finest houses in the country" (*The Unvanquished,* p. 52). A different version of the house and its history is given in "The Fire and the Hearth": on an oak and cedar knoll, two log wings, with an open hallway between, were built by Carothers McCaslin; the open hallway "Cass Edmonds had enclosed and super-posed with a second storey of white clapboards and faced with a portico" (pp. 44–45).[47] The plantation has two thousand acres, with a drive almost a mile long leading up to the house (*Intruder in the Dust,* p. 7).

The Edmonds plantation is typical, a self-sufficient, some-what feudal organization, with its own commissary, no doubt its own cotton gin, as on the Sartoris plantation, and quarters for Negro employees and tenants employed at the sawmill (*Go Down, Moses,* pp. 96, 137). The cabin of Lucas Beauchamp is not completely typical, having been built for him and standing by itself on its own ten acres; but typical enough are the "savage gash" of a road and the paintless house and fence, the grassless, neatly swept yard.

Such plantations, four miles in this instance from both the sawmill and the crossroads store, made master and slaves or landlord and tenant depend upon each other in their isolation. Not only has this area failed to grow more thickly populated, but Lucas comes on ruins of a mansion when searching for buried treasure (*Go Down, Moses,* pp. 91–92).[48]

The far northeast end of the county, apparently beyond the river bottom and off the edge of Faulkner's map, peters out in barren pine hills with "poor soil" and "little tilted and barren patches of gaunt corn and cotton" and narrow, winding, rutted, and dusty roads; Fentry's "two-room log house with

[47] From the settling of Virginia, this was a standard pattern for a homestead house; such a house was often later covered with weatherboards and plastered (Phillips, pp. 329–330). The influence of this basic plan of a central hallway is still apparent on every scale, from the dog-trot cabins to the porticoed mansions.
[48] The ruined mansions might represent the ravages of either war or peace. See Appendix B.

an open hall" rounds out the typical scenes by adding the poverty-stricken but independent farms in the barren hills.[49]

vi. *The Southeast Sector: Frenchman's Bend*

No better than Fentry's farm are those in the poorer places near Frenchman's Bend, in the southeast sector. The farms of the Bundrens and the Griers, with their incompetent occupants, might be comparable, but we are given no objective descriptions of them by which to judge. Frenchman's Bend is a rural settlement, the only one in the county with which Faulkner deals in detail. Between the rivers in Lafayette County there are seven towns with a population of less than 250 and one between 250 and 1,000. Faulkner's reasons for decreasing the population are now apparent: he wished to concentrate on one hamlet and to feel free to combine details from several communities without encouraging identification of Frenchman's Bend with any one of them. The decreased population might also be a kind of extrapolation of what could be observed over an adult's life-time: the decline of towns like Tula, across the river south of the Frenchman's Bend area, where the fairly substantial two-storey houses, unusual in this locality, recall the days when the town had eight stores and was a thriving center, with a normal school; modern transportation brings it too close to Oxford to compete with the county seat, and it is somnolent, if not dead. Lafayette Springs, seventeen miles east of Oxford, now almost invisible, was on a post road and had daily stage-coach service from Oxford; its hotel, almost as old as the county, accommodated guests who sought the benefits of the twenty springs.[50] The

[49] "Tomorrow," *Knight's Gambit,* p. 90. The distance, thirty miles from Frenchman's Bend and northeast of Jefferson, would put this area outside of the county except in terms of the 2400 square miles which Faulkner rarely remembers.

[50] The Oxford *Eagle*: December 13, 1928; April 3, 1930; April 10, 1930. John Faulkner tells of a family trip by carriage and buggy to Lafayette Springs (p. 70).

dying communities and the prevalence of ruins convey a sense of declining population that would powerfully affect one who could remember the more vigorous past.

Frenchman's Bend is southeast of Jefferson, near the north bank of the Yoknapatawpha River. According to Faulkner's maps, it is twelve miles from Jefferson, the same distance as Sutpen's Hundred on the map in *Absalom, Absalom!* The distance varies in the stories from twelve to twenty-two miles.[51] The original grant of river-bottom land to the Frenchman, Grenier, straddled two counties (*The Hamlet*, p. 3). Here also Faulkner did not imaginatively assimilate the size he designated for Yoknapatawpha County; the longer distances, however, increase the isolation of the country people and their difficulty in getting to town. An imaginatively satisfying reason for accepting the twelve-mile figure, which fits the geography of Lafayette County, is that it places Frenchman's Bend and Sutpen's Hundred equi-distant, southeast and northwest, from Jefferson.

Both Sutpen's Hundred and the Old Frenchman's Place represent the ruins of grand designs, the decayed grandeur that is more melancholy than dilapidation of more modest structures. Sutpen was determined to establish "a place on an even more ambitious and grandiose scale than Grenier's":

(his [Grenier's] plantation: his manor, his kitchens and stables and kennels and slave quarters and gardens and promenades and fields which a hundred years later will have vanished, . . . leaving nothing but the name of his plantation and his own corrupted legend like a thin layer of native ephemeral yet inevictable dust on a section of country surrounding a little lost paintless crossroads store) [*Requiem for a Nun*, pp. 37, 33].

Although the legend haunts *The Hamlet*, which ends with Henry Armstid frantically digging for treasure on the Old

---

[51] Twelve miles agrees with the map of Lafayette County and twenty miles puts Frenchman's Bend out of the county. Calvin Brown notes the essential similarity, even to "Yellowleaf" for Whiteleaf Creek, between the road from Jefferson to Frenchman's Bend and "Old 6" from Oxford (p. 653, n.).

Frenchman's Place, the ruins themselves are seen more clearly in *Sanctuary*, as they appear first to Horace Benbow and then to Temple Drake, a suitably ominous setting for a nightmarish episode:

The gaunt ruin of the house rose against the sky, above the massed and matted cedars, lightless, desolate, and profound. The road was an eroded scar too deep to be a road and too straight to be a ditch, gutted by winter freshets and choked with fern and rotted leaves and branches [p. 18].

The house came into sight, above the cedar grove beyond whose black interstices an apple orchard flaunted in the sunny afternoon. It was set in a ruined lawn, surrounded by abandoned grounds and fallen outbuildings. But nowhere was any sign of husbandry —plow or tool; in no direction was a planted field in sight—only a gaunt weather-stained ruin in a sombre grove through which the breeze drew with a sad, murmurous sound [p. 40].

With Popeye, Tommy, Lee Goodwin, and the old blind man secreting themselves in the Old Frenchman's Place, as earlier Clytie and Jim Bond and Henry Sutpen had hidden away in the Sutpen ruins, early grandeur is succeeded by later horror. Such ruins do exist in Lafayette County, although they are seldom visible to the casual visitor and may be unknown even to long-time residents.[52] Others must have been submerged by Sardis Dam or burned, but it is unlikely that many have been torn down, the Southerners' treatment of their "towers and hall" being like Edward's in the ballad: "let thame stand tul they doun fa."

Frenchman's Bend, unlike Sutpen's Hundred, was inhabited by white farmers who never owned slaves; at first, Will Varner's cook was the one Negro in the district (*The Hamlet*, p. 10). Most of the farmers lived in unpainted one- or two-room cabins; they planted cotton in the bottom land and corn at the foot of the hills, living almost as meagerly as sharecroppers.

[52] Two actual ruins, both southwest of Oxford, provide factual parallels, on a less magnificent scale, to the Sutpen and Grenier mansions. See Appendix B.

Although the whole county is cotton country, with the cotton gin as characteristic of the area as the grain elevators are of the Midwest, most of the cotton is grown in patches, large fields being chiefly in the bottom lands.[53]

Will Varner, the leading citizen of Frenchman's Bend, owned the only house with more than one storey (*The Hamlet,* p. 10), the store, the cotton gin, and the combined grist mill and blacksmith shop (p. 5). His store, the gathering place for the men in the vicinity, was at the crossroads from which, according to Faulkner's map, a road led northeast to the farms of the Tulls, the Griers, the Bookwrights, and the Quicks and to Mr. Whitfield's church; a road to the south crossed the Yoknapatawpha River to the Bundren farm. Gavin Stevens saw Frenchman's Bend as he approached it to attend a coroner's inquest:

Then, across the long flat where the highway began to parallel the river bottom, Stevens saw the store. By ordinary it would have been deserted, but now he could already see clotted about it the topless and battered cars, the saddled horses and mules and the wagons, the riders and drivers of which he knew by name [*Knight's Gambit,* p. 67].

Yocona is the hamlet still extant which is closest to the location given Frenchman's Bend.[54] A two-storey house, a two-storey building which resembled Mrs. Littlejohn's hotel, and a blacksmith shop were noticeable a few years ago. Two other towns offer enough parallels in details though not in location to suggest that Frenchman's Bend is a composite of several

[53] The huge level cotton fields typical of good plantation country are found in the Delta area west of Lafayette County and in the area to the northeast, near Ripley, where the Falkner family lived before and for a time after the Civil War.

[54] Calvin Brown identifies Frenchman's Bend with Cornish, on the basis of the location of Cornish on an old map, at the junction of "Old 6" with the road south to Tula. There are Varners living on "Old 6" at present. In Webb and Green, Emily Stone tells about hearing a story about an idiot and a cow, like that of Ike in *The Hamlet,* in that area of the county. Faulkner had already written one version of the story before she heard about it (p. 99).

places. Taylor, used with its own name and location in *Sanctuary,* on the railroad southwest of "Oxford," has several stores more like Varner's, with its gallery, than most of the filling-station-stores along the highways. A disused store in Taylor belonged to the Tatum family, whose history as related by a local resident remarkably resembles that of Will Varner. "Varner's Grocery" is actually in this area but resembles the fictitious store only in name. Toccopola, just outside Lafayette County to the east, not only has an overall resemblance to Frenchman's Bend but has graves in the cemetery with the name of the family which residents of Oxford cite as the originals of the Snopeses. Since Faulkner included only one "hamlet" in his county, he combined details from several hamlets to make a typical community in which characters could not be easily identified with real people.

Few details are given about the farms near Frenchman's Bend. Apparently they ranged from the comparative prosperity and comfort of the Varners' and Houstons' down through the easy-going poverty of the Bundrens' and Griers' to the destitution of the Armstids' (*The Hamlet,* pp. 215, 355). The tenant farms on the little back roads in the hills presented pictures of incredible poverty. Ratliff turned into Mink Snopes's rutted lane:

. . . at the end of it a broken-backed cabin of the same two rooms which were scattered without number through these remote hill sections . . . . It was built on a hill; below it was a foul muck-trodden lot and a barn leaning away downhill as though a human breath might flatten it [*The Hamlet,* p. 73].

Even on the main highways one sees many such cabins; one would swear no human being could live in them, except that the inhabitants are frequently visible at any hour of the day on the front gallery or there are such other signs of life as clothes drying or wash-machines on the gallery or television aerials on the roof.[55] Such cabins, inhabited by Negroes or

[55] Except for such modern details, the cabins still resemble those described by Du Bois (pp. 101–103) and described and pictured by James

poor whites, are the most common man-made features of the landscape in all parts of Yoknapatawpha or Lafayette County, even as the natural landscape is dominated by pine hills and cotton fields, by the miniature canyons of erosion or the enshrouding kudzu vines. But as W. J. Cash observes, "the countryside, with its wide dispersion of population and its fields and woods and long blue reaches" tends "to soften even the horrible into the merely picturesque."[56]

Only one other town remains on—or rather off—Faulkner's map. Twenty miles south of Jefferson, on the railroad, lies Mottstown or Mottson, county seat of Okatoba County, a kind of peripheral parallel to Memphis on the north as a scene of action outside Yoknapatawpha County. Since these two places tie Yoknapatawpha County into the non-fictitious South, identification of Mottstown is useful. Water Valley, county seat of Yalobusha County, fits the details given for the location of Mottstown, in a valley ("That Will Be Fine," *Collected Stories,* p. 273). It is near the Otuckalofa River, which sounds much like "Okatoba."

Although Faulkner makes little use of the southwest sector, except for Taylor, the highways to both Water Valley and Batesville add typical scenes suggesting that Faulkner omitted this sector because he wished to concentrate on fewer localities, not because the southwest area lacked suitable material. The fact that both of the actual ruins described (Appendix B) are in this sector may or may not be significant: similar ruins

Agee and Walker Evans, in *Let Us Now Praise Famous Men* (Boston: Houghton Mifflin, 1960). Their account of white tenant families and their housing is very similar to Charles S. Johnson's account of six hundred Negro families in Macon County, Georgia, in the 1930s (*Shadow of the Plantation* [Chicago: The University of Chicago Press, Phoenix Edition, 1966]).

[56] *The Mind of the South* (New York: Vintage Books, 1960), pp. 206–207. Cash points out that the miserable hovels provided for millworkers in towns were, by the standards of tenants or croppers, "entirely acceptable," being painted and tight against the rain, "both rarities in the rural South" (p. 212). The lack of industries in Oxford, other than two small factories, explains the absence of such millworkers' housing as Cash describes and as may be seen, for example, in Starkville, Mississippi.

in other areas may exist or may have existed in Faulkner's youth. The existence of these ruins at present and the innumerable visible parallels to Faulkner's cabins and country stores and hamlets and to the geography and topography of Jefferson and Yoknapatawpha County establish the factual basis for Faulkner's settings.

VII. *Yoknapatawpha Peripatetics and Periphery*

The completeness with which Yoknapatawpha County is depicted is due largely to the frequency with which the characters travel, usually slowly, about the countryside. By this device and by having most of his characters visit Jefferson, the center of trade and of government, Faulkner knits together his widely scattered characters in fascinating patterns. But he uses different reasons for travel to make plausible the frequent or exceptional journeys. The Yoknapatawpha fiction shows the history of transportation in the county, and therefore the pattern of roads graphically represents one of the most vital concerns, in fact or fiction, of the inhabitants.[57]

Two characters in a number of novels and stories travel for business or professional reasons and observe and interpret a great deal of the action. Ratliff, the sewing machine agent, is the modern equivalent of the peddler who furnished the chief contact between backwoods dwellers and civilization and who

---

[57] In the Oxford *Eagle* since 1900 a constant theme is the need first for roads, then for hard-surfaced roads, then for paving, and finally for an airport. As late as 1928, there was no all-weather road out of Oxford (Oxford *Eagle,* August 30, 1928). By this time, however, the railroad was reducing passenger service. The 1930s were the heyday both of local interest in aviation and of highway construction. The change from horsetrading and blacksmith shops and livery stables to auto agencies and garages and auto graveyards in the economy of Oxford-Jefferson lends itself easily to symbolic details. Clark, in *Pills, Petticoats, and Plows,* stresses the social and economic effects of these changes.

knew every inhabitant in a large and thinly settled area. His business trips, most prominent in *The Hamlet,* mark the stages in transportation and consumer goods, from wagon to truck and from sewing machines to radios to television (*The Mansion,* p. 321). Gavin Stevens as a lawyer knows people throughout the county and in *Knight's Gambit* takes a number of professional trips in rural areas.

Ratliff even took a peddler's holiday, with no hope of selling a sewing machine, when in "A Bear Hunt" he joined a group of hunters, the chief characters who travel for pleasure. The older generations of hunters, most notably Ike McCaslin, hunted in the Big Woods. The Indians belonged, of course, to the Big Woods but played no part in other scenes in Yoknapatawpha after the establishment of Jefferson. Young Bayard and Charles Mallison hunted in the McCallum-McCaslin region. Young Bayard's frantic driving on the country roads around Jefferson, his expeditions with his drinking pals, and his flight to and from the McCallums' afford some of the best descriptions of the countryside. Without such characters and their activities, important areas in the county would be omitted.

There are such habitual or occasional travelers and repeated journeys. But a significant number of novels deals with journeys for special purposes or occasions. Thus the travel pattern of action serves also to unify Yoknapatawpha and to acquaint the reader with the county. The journey of the Bundrens from Frenchman's Bend to Jefferson by way of Mottson is dealt with so subjectively that it does not serve so much to depict the countryside as to present the inhabitants. In *Light in August,* Lena Grove's journey in search of her lover, Joe Christmas's travels and flight, and the Hineses' trip from Mottson to Jefferson are prominent narrative elements. In *Intruder in the Dust,* Charles Mallison's memories of Edmonds's plantation and his practically unremitting and frantic expeditions to Beat Four and within Jefferson give the reader a lively sense of the locality. *The Mansion* gives evidence that this is one of Faulkner's favorite and most successful devices: Mink's trips to Jefferson and to Memphis to buy ammunition and a gun, in 1908 and 1946, are among the most vivid passages

because of Mink's original naïve ignorance and child-like interest in what he sees and because after his thirty-eight years
in prison he confronts the modern world like a Rip Van
Winkle. *The Mansion* includes the state penitentiary at Parchman as a scene of action. *Requiem for a Nun* both relates the
history of Jackson and has a scene in the governor's mansion.
Thus prominent on the periphery of the county, within the
state, are places which are reminders of man's sin and guilt,
of justice and punishment. In *The Mansion* Mink's second
journey and Montgomery Ward Snopes's account of an earlier
trip to Memphis, repeating some of the scenes from the Memphis portion of *Sanctuary,* extend the range of the fiction outside the county into non-fictitious geography. And finally *The
Reivers* returns to some of those Memphis scenes and a
younger Miss Reba, fills in the old route from Jefferson-
Oxford to Memphis, and to the peripheral geography adds
Parsham Junction, Tennessee, clearly recognizable as Grand
Junction. In the Linscomb—actually the Ames—plantation,
near Grand Junction, Faulkner introduces his most luxurious
modern plantation.[58]

Named or identifiable places on the periphery of Yoknapatawpha County and the many details drawn from Oxford
lend Faulkner's narratives the advantages of reality without
sacrificing the freedom of imagination he gains by establishing a mythical geography within the county. The imperfect
wheel of roads in Lafayette County gives him his basic pattern, typical in general of Southern counties but distinctive in
its imperfection. But identification of specific buildings in
Oxford, except a few on the Square, seems largely conjectural.
Identification of places outside Oxford would be possible to
no casual observer and, apparently, not even to residents of
Oxford. Many of the farms or plantations he describes are

---

[58] Cleanth Brooks quotes a letter identifying not only the setting but
specific persons and incidents referred to: *William Faulkner: The
Yoknapatawpha Country* (New Haven: Yale University Press, 1963),
p. 446. In *The Falkners of Mississippi,* Murry Falkner tells about a trip
to Memphis, in his grandfather's 1909 Buick touring car, which included episodes like some of those in *The Reivers* (pp. 70–77).

on back roads that could not be discovered without a geological survey map, unless one is a native like Faulkner. But he is so faithful to the kinds of terrain and to typical details of various kinds of dwellings and settlements that even the casual observer can easily fuse Lafayette and Yoknapatawpha Counties without being distracted by whatever liberties Faulkner may have taken in using specific places as the originals of his settings.[59]

Whatever changes have been wrought since the white man came to Mississippi, Lafayette County is remarkably unmarred by industrial civilization: time seems to have stood still, unless one is unduly conscious of the television aerials on the cabin roofs and the washing machines on the porches and the cars in the yards.

Extensive passages quoted from Faulkner both convey the information about Yoknapatawpha County and suggest the emotional coloring which illuminates Faulkner's vision and transforms Lafayette County into Yoknapatawpha. If, with this survey of the county in mind, the reader can pick up any part of the Yoknapatawpha chronicles and find himself immediately at home and enjoy some sense of the larger scene, this chapter will have accomplished its purpose, that of orienting the reader and providing imaginatively some of the pleasure derived from familiar scenes. But, as Calvin Brown concludes: "the aesthetic qualities which make *Absalom* and *Light in August* and *The Sound and the Fury* important are rooted in the universality of these novels rather than in their localization."

[59] Calvin Brown says that one scene in *Sartoris,* Hub's place, is such a "complex" of careful details that he would immediately recognize it if he happened to know the place (p. 658).

3

CASTE AND CLASS SOCIETY IN YOKNAPATAWPHA COUNTY

1. The South as a Conditioning Factor in Faulkner's Realism

LAFAYETTE County, with its history and its people, provided William Faulkner, out of his own experience and tradition, with the material for the creation of Yoknapatawpha. In dealing with the society, Faulkner exercised the same power of selection and emphasis as he did in creating his fictitious county from what reality offered: his inclusion of only one hamlet, his transplanting of the university, and his virtual omission of one of the four sectors is paralleled by his incomplete coverage of the society and its history. The reader must neither expect certain patterns to emerge nor complain about omissions and focus: he must see first what is included and what is omitted in the world of Yoknapatawpha before judging its meaning. Examination of the "factual" aspect of Faulkner's Yoknapatawpha is only a preliminary, but an essential, step toward the consideration of the meaning revealed by the narrative action and the literary art. The statement of Charles Mallison, as narrator in "Monk," would apply to Faulkner: "it is only in literature that the paradoxical and even mutually negativing anecdotes in the history of a human heart can be juxtaposed and annealed by art into verisimilitude and credibility" (*Knight's Gambit*, p. 39). The verisimilitude and credibility of the Yoknapatawpha fiction are intensified by the cumulative effect: thus a survey of the society depicted—its distinctive characteristics, its history, its classes and castes, its institutions, its patterns of action—is a first step designed to explain essential features of the subject matter but by no means intended to imply that subject matter and art can be divorced. Faulkner's repetition of factual details throughout the Yoknapatawpha fiction and his use in *Requiem for a Nun* of historical prologues to the acts of the drama suggest that an overall survey is not contrary to his intentions as an artist and that he hoped that the ideal reader would ultimately arrive at a synthesis, a vision of the whole affording a God-like view of the artist's creation.

As a Southerner, Faulkner was using "the quickest tool to hand," the part of the South he knew best, to explore the truths of the human heart revealed in "man in conflict with himself, with his fellow man, or with his time and place" (*Faulkner in the University*, pp. 3, 19). In so doing, though he had no Balzacian intent, he did in fact, as Arlin Turner observes, draw "a wonderfully rich and complete society" and virtually exhausted "the list of elements habitually considered Southern."[1] The contrasts apparent in the countryside and towns, with the extremes symbolized in the mansions and the cabins, have their root in Southern culture. Mississippi, the state in the Deep South most resistant to change, most fully exemplifies the paradoxes in the Southern heritage discussed by Howard Odum: the abundance of natural resources and

[1] Arlin Turner, "William Faulkner, Southern Novelist," *Mississippi Quarterly*, XIV (Summer, 1961), 129.

"the greater cultural tradition . . . of exploitation of the land and its resources"; the mansions from which "came low attainment" and "the dark places" from which "came flashing gleams of noble personality."[2] The paradoxes of the South, preserved in their most extreme form in Mississippi, represent a basic tendency to hold contradictory attitudes or beliefs and to resist the self-examination which might reveal the contradictions. The region which most prides itself on rugged individualism exerts such pressures toward conformity that dissidence is crushed and the holders of unpopular opinions are persecuted. The region in which the old-time religion flourishes treats human beings with incredible inhumanity. Pride in hospitality is matched with hostility and violence toward strangers; white people's pride in the family is matched with their destruction of family unity and stability among Negroes. Pride in the founders of their society is accompanied by betrayal of the *noblesse oblige* which represented the best of the aristocratic code and by blindness to the fact that those founders were not only the adaptable, mobile, forward-looking individuals from the older regions, exactly the opposite of their ancestor-worshiping descendants, but also rapacious, ruthless opportunists. The state which resisted the federal government in 1962 eagerly accepts the greatest proportionate amount of federal aid of any state, and is trying, as James Silver says, to attain "mutually exclusive" ends: "to freeze the social status quo while revolutionizing the economic order."[3] Understanding of these basic characteristics facilitates understanding of specific social phenomena.

Any tendency by the reader to discount the more distressing and alarming aspects of the South as Faulkner reveals it is likely to be counteracted by events in both South and North since 1954: the South is no longer a spectacle, better than *Ben Hur* as the Sutpen story was to Shreve, but part of the whole "American dilemma," part of the nightmare that threat-

[2] Howard W. Odum, *The Way of the South* (New York: Macmillan, 1947), pp. 81, 94.
[3] James W. Silver, *Mississippi: The Closed Society* (New York: Harcourt, Brace & World, 1964), pp. 75, 77.

ens the American dream. Faulkner retained "artistic devotion to a locale," as Warren Beck observes, but "transcended provincialism" in "the excruciation of a Hamlet, forced to chide his own mother, on the grounds of his realistic discernment of fact and the demands of his indomitable idealism."[4] But the reality of Faulkner's South should not cause the regional aspects of his art and the national implications of the sociological facts to obscure the larger, the universal truths conveyed by the new myth of the South revealed in Yoknapatawpha County. The nature of the society, however, must be understood before the characters and events can be interpreted, the artistic achievement appreciated, and the myth and its meaning deciphered.

Although the reality of Faulkner's South is not diminished by the larger truths or by his technical virtuosity, the nature of his realism becomes apparent only when the whole body of the Yoknapatawpha fiction is considered. In discussing the French writers who are called "anti-realists" or "new novelists" because they seek "a re-apprehension of the real," Peter Brooks defiines *realism* in terms especially applicable to Faulkner:

"Realism" is a question of interest, of a writer's desire to explore and describe the concrete phenomena among which man lives, at the same time that the writer records a man's moral or psychological history. Although he is no more "unselective" than any well-aimed camera, the realist refuses to abstract or internalize what, in its externality, seems to him as irrefutable as Dr. Johnson's stone, and therefore important to man. There would seem to be a sense in which one could say that if the novel exists as a genre, it is because it permits a reconstruction of this phenomenological world . . . .[5]

[4] Warren Beck, "Faulkner and the South," *Antioch Review,* I (Spring, 1941), 84.
[5] "The Laboratory of the Novel," *Daedalus,* XCII (Spring, 1963), 265–266. The relevance of this article to Faulkner becomes explicit in Brooks's discussion of Faulkner's influence on Claude Simon. "Antirealistic" elements in Faulkner's *As I Lay Dying* and *The Sound and the Fury* are noted by David Littlejohn in "The Anti-Realists" in the same issue of *Daedalus,* p. 259.

The camera analogy suggested by Peter Brooks may help
further to define the nature of Faulkner's realism. Photographic realism which reports objective reality with a minimum
of selection and a lack of "effective" camera angles is like the
literary naturalism which is closer to sociology than to art.
Photographic art which imaginatively selects significant aspects of human life and the "phenomenological world," with
focus and lighting designed to convey the artist's perceptions
or those of his characters, is like the realism Brooks describes,
which seeks "re-apprehension of the real." Photographic effects which depend upon illusion, whether false moonlight and
bogus magnolias or Gothic horror, are like Hollywood romanticism, in which the everyday world is lost in fantasy or
nightmare. Faulkner could and did on occasion use naturalism
or romanticism to reveal the world as seen by his characters,
but the total effect on the reader of the Yoknapatawpha fiction
resembles, on a much larger scale, that of *The Sound and the
Fury*: the final restoration in Section IV ("April 6, 1928") of
the familiar real world after seeing it through the distorted
or perverted vision of various characters.[6]

The essential faithfulness of Faulkner's fictional world to
reality even while it is a world of the imagination is recognized by critics and can be verified by observation and experience. Faulkner's characters belong so completely to their world
and in general are so fully limited to it or emotionally bound
by it that the natural surroundings and the man-made environment are essential parts of the human experience. The
love of the land and of familiar scenes which animates the

---

[6] The concept of *realism*, as determined by René Wellek in *Concepts
of Criticism* (New Haven: Yale University Press, 1963), embraces both
Faulkner's subject matter and the range of his techniques: realism as
"the objective representation of contemporary social reality" admits
taboo subjects, excludes the fantastic, the symbolic, and the extraordinary, and implies "a lesson of human pity, of social reformism and
criticism, and often of rejection and revulsion against society" (pp.
240–241, 242). The ultimate consequence of "the main technical demand of realist theory"—"impersonality, the complete absence of the
author from his work"—is "an inward turn toward a subjective, symbolic art which is at the other pole of realism" and is most clearly
represented in the stream-of-consciousness method (pp. 247, 251).

geography of Yoknapatawpha lends the same concreteness to the characters and their everyday life and to the dramatic episodes.

Although in *Faulkner at West Point* Faulkner disclaimed any primary intention "to be drawing a picture of a region" and said that "the sociological qualities" in his writing were "coincidental to the story," he also said that if an author "feels that social evil enough, it will be there" in his stories "dealing with men and women in the human dilemma," and that it is part of the writer's dilemma not to be able to keep out the awareness of the evil (pp. 50, 51, 85). Although individual works in which the author does not speak in his own voice or through characters may lack explicit statement of moral judgments, Faulkner's intensely moral view of life becomes clear when his entire work is surveyed. By asking what social evils Faulkner felt so keenly about that he could not exclude them, one gains knowledge about the author and his fictional world. David Daiches, asking what kinds of work sociological criticism may prove helpful in, notes that in both nineteenth- and twentieth-century novels "society is *there,* to be taken account of and accepted as a basic fact about human life," regardless of the author's attitude toward it, and that sociological questions may profitably be asked even about Faulkner, "though in his own way he operates as a poet." Similarly, David Daiches says, understanding of the author is aided by social history which explains the quality to be found in his work.[7] Since Faulkner wrote about his own environment and largely about his own times, some knowledge of the social background serves to throw light on both the work and the author.

Robert Canzoneri, a native Mississippian and at times a resident of Oxford, confirms the validity of Faulkner's picture of Mississippi but views it in a proper perspective:

. . . Faulkner's account of Mississippi is so accurate and so nearly complete that the temptation is to say to those curious about the

---

[7] David Daiches, *Critical Approaches to Literature* (Englewood Cliffs, N.J.: Prentice-Hall, 1956), pp. 371, 347.

state, simply, "Read Faulkner." But his is not a literal picture; that is, the literal element is often true to its specific locale and conditions, all right, but the deep sources of motive are true far beyond the characters . . . so that they illuminate both Mississippi and the age-old world.[8]

Robert Penn Warren, in his seminal article on Malcolm Cowley's editing of *The Portable Faulkner*, said that "no land in all fiction is more painstakingly analyzed from the sociological standpoint." After listing some of the social classes and types included, Warren continues:

Nature and sociology, geography and human geography, are scrupulously though effortlessly presented in Faulkner's work, and their significance for his work is very great; but the significance is of a conditioning order. They are, as it were, aspects of man's "doom" . . . but his manhood in the face of that doom is what is important.[9]

This chapter will deal in part with the social classes to which Warren refers; the next one will deal with institutional aspects of society and patterns of social action: the family and womanhood, the churches, the courts, lawlessness and violence. But in both chapters it must be kept in mind that "the significance is of a conditioning order."

A survey of Yoknapatawpha society is necessarily limited to what Faulkner selected from the entire time-span covered, from the coming of the white man to the present. The central facts of slavery and a caste society are basic to themes and narrative in Faulkner's depiction of the human world of Yoknapatawpha County. Of the three kinds of contact between the white people and Negroes indicated by Gunnar Myrdal—the casual, the economic, and the criminal[10]—this

[8] Robert Canzoneri, *"I Do So Politely": A Voice from the South* (Boston: Houghton Mifflin, 1965), p. 91.

[9] Robert Penn Warren, "William Faulkner," *William Faulkner: Three Decades of Criticism,* Frederick J. Hoffman and Olga W. Vickery, eds. (East Lansing: Michigan State University Press, 1960), p. 110.

[10] *An American Dilemma* (New York: Harper & Row, 1962), p. 650. Myrdal's monumental study is indispensable in all aspects of the caste

chapter will focus on the casual: the nature of a caste society invests these contacts with tremendous significance, quite literally sometimes that of life and death. Therefore the ordinary aspects of life must be examined before dealing with the major episodes in the whole social structure and the beliefs on which that structure is based. Historical background relevant to Faulkner's fiction will be considered in relation to the settling of the country and the development of the caste-class system and as a body of fact and legend conditioning modern characters.

ii. *The Dispossession of the Indians*

Although in Act II of *Requiem for a Nun* Faulkner traces the evolution of Yoknapatawpha County and Mississippi from the dawn of terrestrial time, his treatment of human

---

society and race problem in the South. Relevant to social classes and castes are Part VII, "Social Inequality," and Part VIII, "Social Stratification." Sociological studies of single communities, history and social history, and personal experience of Southerners will be used as sources to explain or confirm Faulkner's fiction, which will generally provide the organizational pattern. Many points which may be unfamiliar to readers outside of the South are common knowledge in the South or represent attitudes and experiences common to Southerners who, like Faulkner, subject their culture to critical scrutiny in the light of American ideals. In a review of the paperback edition of *An American Dilemma,* James Silver, writing from experience and a personal point of view close to Faulkner's, said that he found there "the most satisfactory explanation for everything that has happened in Mississippi" in his thirty years' residence in Oxford and that "what Myrdal wrote more than 20 years ago is as up to date as the latest newscast from the Magnolia State," because Myrdal's work is "a genuine classic" and "because Mississippi has been the most rural, backward, poor, Negroid, and enamored of the fiercest resistance to change of all the Southern states." He states "without reservation": "the first requisite to an understanding of insurrection, murder, bombings, legal double-talk, super- and pseudo-patriotism, and an 87.2 per cent vote for Goldwater is a thoughtful perusal of *An American Dilemma*" (*Book Week,* Paperback Issue [January 10, 1965], p. 3).

history is less comprehensive. He begins, not with prehistoric man, but with the Indians at the time the first white men came to Mississippi. As natural processes during geologic time had carved out the county and foreordained the rich black alluvial soil and the red earth of the pine-covered hills that would erode when stripped of their forests, so the human factors in operation at the beginning of the white man's occupation of the county determined the nature of the society which developed. The white society of the Yoknapatawpha fiction has been dominated from its beginnings by the presence of a subject race and a caste system and by natural and historic factors which determined its specific social structure and patterns. When the Yoknapatawpha works are arranged in chronological order of events, they present a logical continuity, with an inexorable chain of cause and effect, from the coming of the white man until the time when Faulkner wrote *The Reivers*. To show the forging of that chain by man's greed and inhumanity, an account of the social world of Yoknapatawpha must begin with the arrival of the first settlers.[11]

Although none of the novels deals directly with the Indian period and the first settlers, short stories, numerous scattered allusions, and the historical preludes in *Requiem for a Nun* give the essential details and emphasize their significance. Faulkner's own statement of why he included the Indians and Negroes and of what they mean in the Southern tradition has greater significance in relation to the Indians, whom he might have omitted, since they disappeared before the Civil War, than to the Negroes:

They represent the dispossessed, the people who racially or ethnically have received injustice from the hands of people who were more fortunate than they, and my use of them in my work is from pity, that I believe that people should not be treated unjustly

[11] In an unpublished thesis, "A Comparison of Yoknapatawpha and Lafayette Counties" (Harvard, 1958), Frederick S. Kullman covers the period from the settling of the counties to 1904, the beginning of the "new age."

. . . just because they happen to be red in color or black in color
[*Faulkner at Nagano,* pp. 86–87].

The dispossession of the Indians began when, after a period
of white infiltration, they sold land to white men. Faulkner
gives some account of the historical facts in *Faulkner in the
University*: the land records, which are only a hundred and
fifty years old, go back to Indian patents; the Indians disappeared as a separate race, being compelled to leave or remain
outside the culture or mix with Negroes and descend into
Negro status (pp. 9, 43).[12]
But before the Indians were dispossessed, they were ruined
by the corrupt ways they learned from the "superior" white
race. Faulkner shows how the Indian leaders abandoned their
own values and way of life for the white man's materialism
and how they prepared the way for violation of their own
rights by violating the rights of others. The names of Faulkner's Indian characters and their family relationships vary
from one story to another. The most detailed and latest account is that in *Requiem for a Nun,* in which Issetibbeha
was the Chickasaw chief who befriended the first white
settlers. He was succeeded by his nephew, Ikkemotubbe, who
swapped a square mile of what was later the heart of Jefferson
to the first Compson for a race horse. He thus set a precedent
of arbitrary and irresponsible action by an Indian leader. Regardless of which name is given to which Indian, the childish
vanity, the ruthlessness, and the abuse of power of the Indians
are apparent: Issetibbeha's gilt bed and girandoles from Paris

[12] Myrdal notes that equality of social status favored intermingling of
Indians and Negroes, though the Negroes were sometimes the slaves
of the Indians, and that there is more Indian blood in American
Negroes than was formerly realized (p. 124). John Cooper Hathorn
deals with land sales and migration of Indians from Mississippi in a
thesis, "A Period Study of Lafayette County from 1836 to 1860 with
Emphasis on Population Groups" (University of Mississippi, 1938). He
gives the real names of the Indians who sold land to the settlers. By
1839 most of the Indians had left the county (p. 6). Hortense Powdermaker notes that the lower-status Indians mingled freely with the
Negroes until the departure of the Indians (*After Freedom: A Cultural
Study in the Deep South* [New York: Viking, 1939], p. 6).

gracing the squalid ruins of a house made from the saloon of a steamboat; Ikkemotubbe's poisoning of his uncle and his uncle's son to become Doom—the Man ("A Justice"). The Indians kept slaves for which they had no need and even raised slaves like cattle to sell to white men, a practice which they perhaps learned from the white men.[13] Even the thrill of the hunt became inhuman, when Indians coursed Negroes with dogs to entertain guests[14] and hunted down a slave to be a human sacrifice to the dead chief. To such tales as these in "Red Leaves" and "A Justice," Faulkner adds that of a historical Choctaw chief (*Requiem for a Nun,* p. 237), who derived his name, LeFlore, from that of a Canadian voyageur. He became a wealthy planter and furnished his mansion with importations from France. A notable exception to the rule among Indians in Mississippi or elsewhere, LeFlore could adopt white man's ways and succeed on white man's terms. According to the legend, Faulkner said, LeFlore was loyal to the Union and, rather than accept an oath to the Confederacy, died in a burning barn, set afire by Confederate troops. The loyalty to the Union was fact, but the manner of his death was legend.[15]

[13] Myrdal comments that some Indian tribes "were active in the internal Negro slave trade" (p. 124). In *Black Reconstruction in America, 1860–1880* (Cleveland and New York: The World Publishing Company, Meridian Books, 1962), W. E. B. Du Bois discusses the practice of breeding slaves in the border states for sale in the Deep South (pp. 41–44). In *The Peculiar Institution: Slavery in the Ante-Bellum South* (New York: Vintage Books, 1964), Kenneth Stampp discusses slave breeding and cites an example in Mississippi of an unsuccessful farmer who "succeeded very well in raising young negroes" (pp. 245–251).

[14] In this amusement, as well as in slave breeding, the Indians imitated or had a parallel in the whites, among whose "best anecdotes of the good old days" were those of chasing fugitive Negroes with "nigger dogs," according to J. W. Schulte Nordholt, in *The People that Walk in Darkness* (New York: Ballantine Books, 1960), pp. 87–88. Stampp states: "The tracking of runaways with dogs . . . was a common practice in all slave states, defended and justified in the courts. Groups of slaveholders sometimes rode through the swamps with their dogs and made the search for fugitives comparable to fox hunting" (p. 189). The pursuit of the French architect in *Absalom, Absalom!* and of Tomey's Turl in "Was" are serious and comic versions of the practice.

[15] *Faulkner in the University,* p. 44. According to the historical

Parallel images of complete corruption and degeneration of the Indians appear twice, involving different characters: the Parisian shoes with red heels which were a motive for murder in "Red Leaves" and the "crusted slippers" which a slave child carried when Mohataha, having ratified the dispossession of her people, set out toward the West without a backward glance.[16] Neither Moketubbe nor Mohataha could wear the shoes they treasured, nor could they step into the shoes and power of the white men.

Sam Fathers, son of an Indian chief and a Negro slave ("A Justice"), atoned for his Indian father's violation of human rights by preserving the code of the wilderness and transmitting its values to Ike McCaslin ("The Bear"). Except for the hunting camp and the hunting parties, society had no place for Sam Fathers. From Sam, Ike learned that God gave the earth to man to hold "mutual and intact in the communal

account by Mrs. N. D. Deupree, "Greenwood LeFlore" (*Publications of the Mississippi Historical Society,* VII [Oxford, 1903], 141–151), the death of LeFlore occurred unsensationally after the end of the Civil War; his life, however, was far more spectacular than any of Faulkner's tales about Indians in Yoknapatawpha County. LeFlore's journey to Washington to interview President Jackson, for redress against a dishonest Indian agent, slightly suggests the mission of Francis Weddel to Washington in Faulkner's "Lo."

[16] *Requiem for a Nun,* p. 217. The Oxford *Eagle* for December 10, 1936, the centennial issue, describes the historical event upon which the story of Mohataha is based: "On June 12, 1836, the Chickasaw Indian woman, Ho-kah, No. 372, affixed her signature, a cross mark, to a deed" selling land to John J. Craig, John Chisholm, and John D. Martin and "Oxford came into being." Faulkner referred to the dispossessed Indians as either Chickasaw or Choctaw, sometimes using both terms for one Indian. This inconsistency Faulkner explained in a letter to Malcolm Cowley, published in *The Faulkner-Cowley File: Letters and Memories, 1944–1962* (New York: Viking, 1966): "The line dividing the Chickasaw and Choctaw nations passed near my home; I merely moved a tribe slightly at need, since they were slightly different people in behavior." The shift in the later Indian stories from Choctaw is also explained: "The Indians actually were Chickasaws, or they may so be from now on" (pp. 25, 26). Elmo Howell noted the inconsistency and the shift to Chickasaw as the Yoknapatawpha chronicles developed. As Howell observes, the details of the burial of Sam Fathers, in "The Bear," are based on Choctaw customs ("William Faulkner and the Chickasaw Funeral," *American Literature,* XXXVI [January, 1965], 523–524).

anonymity of brotherhood," in pity and humility ("The Bear," *Go Down, Moses*, p. 257).

The implicit and explicit concept of man's relationships to the land throughout Faulkner's work approximates Ike's idea. This was the first curse on the land: the Indians' irresponsibility in bartering their domain for false values and glittering vanities. But the white men who persuaded them to do so were the more guilty as they knew better than the Indians the worthlessness of what they gave the Indians and the worth of what they gained in return and would quickly ruin. Because the white men could get large tracts of land so cheap, the second curse, still potent, was visited upon the South: slavery. Faulkner's account of the dispossession of the Indians conforms in essential circumstances to historical fact.

III. *The Establishment of Jefferson and the Plantation System*

The migration of the Chickasaws to Indian Territory, represented by Faulkner as the procession of Mohataha, took place in the early 1830s. The Chickasaw Agency trading post in what became Jefferson was established before 1800; the first settlers who helped to establish the town and the county plantations began to arrive about 1815.[17] The foundation of the social structure and the establishment of a social tradition had their inception with the arrival of the three "coeval pioneers and settlers" of Yoknapatawpha County, who represented both town and country occupations (*Requiem for a Nun*, p. 7).[18]

[17] Mississippi became a state in 1817. By the Treaty of Pontotoc, 1832, Lafayette was one of the ten counties of the Chickasaw Cession, the last of the Indian lands opened to settlement. Lafayette County was created in 1836.

[18] In his "Period Study of Lafayette County," John Hathorn classifies the original settlers in Lafayette County as (1) younger sons of slaveholding families in the older Southern states, (2) unfortunates, used to good society and trying to recoup their fortunes, (3) adven-

Dr. Habersham and his small son came from Carolina. The son's emigration to Oklahoma with his wife, an Indian chief's daughter, prevented the Habershams from maintaining leadership in the community. Dr. Habersham was succeeded by Dr. Peabody, who enjoyed some of the prestige of his predecessor (*Requiem for a Nun*, p. 15).[19] Alec Holston, "half groom and half bodyguard" to Dr. Habersham, became the first tavern keeper in the embryonic town which preserved his name in the leading hotel, the Holston House. The third of this group, Louis Grenier, a French Huguenot younger son, brought the first slaves into the county and "was granted the first big land patent."[20] He lived too far from Jefferson and died too soon to become a social force in the community. He left "nothing but the name of his plantation and his own fading corrupted legend" in Frenchman's Bend and the Old Frenchman's Place (*Requiem for a Nun*, p. 33). The story of

---

turers, promoters, and wanderers, (4) poor whites. They came from Virginia, the Carolinas, Georgia, Alabama, Kentucky, and Tennessee, with the influx between 1835 and 1840. Many of them traveled by the Natchez Trace, which, as a federal highway, was much traveled from 1800 to 1830. Faulkner may have known, when he chose *Habersham* for the name of one of his first settlers in Jefferson, that in 1801 Joseph Habersham suggested that United States troops build the road (Lena Mitchell Jamison, "The Natchez Trace: A Federal Highway of the Old Southwest," *Journal of Mississippi History*, I [1939], 82–99). John L. Swaney, one of the first actual mail messengers on the Trace, traveled with a leather mail pouch and a tin horn, like Faulkner's Thomas Jefferson Pettigrew (*Requiem for a Nun*, p. 10).

[19] The three first settlers in Oxford bought land from Ho-kah in 1836, but before that date Dr. Isom came to the site of Oxford and Dr. Robert Carter came to Wyatt, from which he moved to Oxford (Oxford *Eagle*, December 12, 1935).

[20] *Requiem for a Nun*, p. 7. According to *The Reivers* (p. 8), Grenier came in 1790, a date which allows a more probable length of time for the establishment and decline of his plantation. Faulkner twice introduces the Huguenot strain in the South. Among the Huguenots who provided a distinct cultural strain for a time in South Carolina, a leading family was the Manigaults, referred to by Ulrich Phillips in *Life and Labor in the Old South* (Boston: Little, Brown, 1963), pp. 47–48, 255. Faulkner uses *Manigault* as the source of Nancy's name, Mannigoe, and refers to "the old Charleston family name" (*Requiem for a Nun*, pp. 50, 118). L. Q. C. Lamar, Oxford's most distinguished citizen before William Faulkner, was of Huguenot descent.

his last descendant, the degenerate Lonnie Grinnup, is told in "Hand upon the Waters," in *Knight's Gambit.*

The plantation system which Grenier introduced, late in the history of the South when slavery elsewhere was a dying institution, was the foundation of a social order based on a feudal control of labor. The formula for fortune was cheap land and large, slave-operated cotton plantations: as Ulrich Phillips said, "A cotton crop in western prospect became a golden fleece."[21] Faulkner's Jason Compson and the other plantation owners who sought the golden fleece brought a varied tradition and heritage, but they all owned slaves and helped to build a plantation system that endured after the Old Frenchman's Place was a ruin. Jason Lycurgus Compson, the founder of the family in Jefferson, was the descendant of a Jacobite printer from Glasgow who founded a family doomed to support lost causes and to lose their gambles. Jason Lycurgus, the one successful exception, "was a bold ruthless man who came into Mississippi as a free forester to grasp where and when he could and wanted to, and established what should have been a princely line" (*Faulkner in the University*, p. 3). The dates given in the Appendix to *The Sound and the Fury* are a little earlier than those in *Requiem for a Nun*, but the former are the more definite and occur in the more complete account: Jason Lycurgus came in 1811 and by 1812 owned a square mile of land in the growing community of Jefferson (*The Sound and the Fury*, p. 6). Jason sold part of Compson's Mile to the town for the site of the courthouse (*Requiem for a Nun*, p. 197).[22] The Compson estate before

---

[21] Phillips, p. 100. The introduction of slavery into new territory in the South was part of "continued vigorous growth" of the system which prevailed, according to Stampp, through the 1850s, with demand for slaves exceeding the supply. He denies that slavery in the South, Old or New, was on "the verge of collapse" in 1860 (p. 388). Clement Eaton, in *The Growth of Southern Civilization* (New York: Harper Torchbooks, 1963), subscribes to "the Ramsdell thesis of the natural limits of slavery expansion," determined by the lack of rich soil in the new Territories to the west and north (p. 70).

[22] In the settlement on the site of Oxford, Craig, Chisholm, and Martin, the historical "coeval pioneers," bought land from Ho-kah and donated fifty acres to the board of police for the county seat (*Oxford Eagle,* December 10, 1936).

the Civil War was a park with extensive quarters and gardens and a "columned porticoed house" (*The Sound and the Fury,* p. 6). The Compsons had not been landed gentry nor, as Jacobites, were they a common Southern type. W. J. Cash's statement that "actual Cavaliers or even near-Cavaliers were rare among Southern settlers" is confirmed by numerous other authorities who stress the point to disprove the romantic legend of descent from Cavaliers, familiar in the myth of the South.[23] Jason Lycurgus seems less like the Cavalier of tradition than like the men Cash describes as making up a great part of the planter class: "men distinguished by something of the same hard and coarse stamp as the horse-trader."[24] The Compsons were not preserving a tradition: they were establishing one.

This is even more true of Thomas Sutpen, a poor white who had conceived a Grand Design involving both a magnificent plantation copied after the Tidewater pattern and a dynasty to perpetuate the Sutpen name and fame. He arrived in Jefferson in 1833, bought "a hundred square miles of some of the best virgin bottom land in the country," and paid for it in Spanish gold coins (*Absalom, Absalom!,* pp. 31, 34).[25] The ruthlessness with which he ruled his slaves and even the French architect was as much part of the legend as the magnificence of the estate. Sutpen most completely represents the

· [23] W. J. Cash, *The Mind of the South* (New York: Vintage Books, 1960), p. 3. *The Mind of the South* is an excellent work, of moderate length, to provide background in Southern social history and culture pertinent to Faulkner's fiction. Published in 1941, it shows so much parallelism to the social facts reflected in Faulkner's fiction and to their implications that Cash and Faulkner seem to have been exploring simultaneously the same historical aspects of the South; they arrived at very similar conclusions. For further information on the Cavalier tradition, see Appendix C.

[24] *Ibid.,* p. 20.

[25] The size of Sutpen's holdings, 64,000 acres, may have a parallel in those of Colonel Barr, whose former slave became "Mammie Callie" to the Faulkner boys. Colonel Barr owned most of the land from Oxford to Burgess, about twelve miles; the north and south dimensions are not given (John Faulkner, *My Brother Bill* [New York: Trident Press, 1963], p. 48). See Appendix D for further information about Mississippi plantations.

patriarchal isolation of the plantation owner who was, as Cash says, "if not strictly alone, then accompanied only by his slaves and members of his own family, to all of whom his individual will would stand as imperial law."[26] "He was amoral, he was ruthless, completely self-centered," but his main motive was "to take revenge for all the redneck people against the aristocrat who told him to go around to the back door" (*Faulkner in the University,* pp. 80, 97).

But the self-styled aristocrats did not welcome Sutpen as one of their group. John Sartoris from Carolina was a kind of foil to Sutpen and, less obviously, to the Compsons, whose early history in Jefferson is not presented in the novels and stories.[27] Sartoris was the genuine but rare pioneer aristocrat from an older part of the country. He came with slaves and money and established a plantation which was never a show-place like that of Grenier or Sutpen. In his concern for the welfare of the community, as well as for his own aggrandizement, John Sartoris provides a contrast to the completely self-centered attitudes of the Compsons and Sutpen. The Sartoris treatment of their inferiors usually showed that they were "quality" and not upstarts. John Sartoris seems to represent the few members of the established aristocracy of Carolina or Virginia who migrated to the wilderness.[28]

---

[26] Cash, p. 33.

[27] *Sartoris* and *Sutpen* are among the few less usual names Faulkner uses which are not still common in Lafayette County. In *William Faulkner: The Yoknapatawpha Country* (New Haven: Yale University Press, 1963), Cleanth Brooks refers to a letter from Miss Brenda Sartoris whose father attended high school at Sardis near Oxford (p. 383). If Faulkner browsed through old copies of the Oxford *Eagle,* he could have noted there an item about the marriage of U. S. Grant's daughter, Nellie, to Algernon Sartoris, in 1874. If he did, and used the name deliberately, he must have enjoyed his little ironic joke in taking as the name for his most admirable, though not ideal, character, the one who resembled his great-grandfather, a name associated with the general who occupied Oxford and brought defeat to the South. It is more likely that this is a rare instance of unconscious irony.

[28] Cash, pp. 3, 4. In background and in migration to Mississippi there is no parallel, as there is in some later events, between John Sartoris and Colonel W. C. Falkner, Faulkner's great-grandfather. The latter entered Mississippi as a destitute orphan boy seeking an uncle in

Not the Sartorises but the McCaslins illustrate the typical ruling class before the Civil War, in either Carolina or Mississippi, as described by Cash: "the strong, the pushing, the ambitious . . . . The frontier was their predestined inheritance." The specific case used by Cash to illustrate the point bears considerable resemblance to Carothers McCaslin,[29] who established the most lasting family and plantation, with the most obvious mixture of races. Except for the degree to which Grenier and Sutpen tried to ignore the frontier and build in a style and on a scale suited only to more civilized surroundings, Faulkner's account of the McCaslins applies to these other families:

They were the aristocracy of provincial Mississippi at that time. It was still frontier. In Natchez they had the fine Empire furniture, . . . they spent their money on *objets d'art* from Europe, furnishings and fine clothes. In the country, these people, they were aristocracy, but they were still frontier, they were still the tall man with the long rifle, in a way. That even their splendor was a little on the slovenly side, that they went through the motions of living like dukes and princes but their life wasn't too different from the man who lived in a mud-floored hovel [*Faulkner in the University,* pp. 37-38].

The McCaslins provide the chief account of Yoknapatawpha plantation life before the war. Although "Was" is a comic

---

Ripley. Except for the help of his uncle, who provided a home and an opportunity to read law, W. C. Falkner was a self-made man, with literary tastes and ambitions lacking in all of the Sartorises. In a recent study, *The Falkner Feuds* (Chapel Hill: The Colonial Press, 1964), Thomas Felix Hickerson gives some of the facts about Colonel Falkner's life which had been obscured by legend. A much more complete and reliable source of biographical information about Colonel Falkner is an unpublished Ph.D. thesis by Donald P. Duclos: "Son of Sorrow" (University of Michigan, 1962). For further information about Colonel Falkner see Appendix E.

[29] Cash, pp. 14–15. The scene of Cash's example is Carolina. Carothers McCaslin began with slaves, only three brought from Carolina so far as the ledger entries indicate ("The Bear," *Go Down, Moses,* p. 266). He might be a second or third generation of a slaveholding family, beginning again in a new territory.

version of the pursuit of a runaway slave, it has serious implications, not only that of the reduction of a human being to
animal status. In running away, Tomey's Turl was violating
the rule that a slave was to be in his cabin after "horn blow,"
and he was legally a runaway in Mississippi if found without
a pass more than eight miles from home. (It took Buck and
Cass from breakfast to dinner, on horseback, to reach Beauchamps'.) The reluctance of the owners to allow the marriage
between Tomey's Turl and Tennie was more typical than
was the ultimate capitulation to the claims of romance.[30] Miss
Sophonsiba represents a typical heroine "who persists in trying to force the chivalric image on the life about her," especially on Buck who recoils from her "favor," a red ribbon
(p. 15).[31] Buck and Buddy pursued enlightened policies
toward their slaves, in addition to allowing Turl and Tennie
to marry. They not only winked at the nocturnal escapades
of their slaves, so long as they were in quarters in the morning,
but also manumitted some of their slaves after their father's
death (Roskus and Fibby did not accept freedom, and Thu-
cydus stayed and worked it out and set up as a blacksmith
with his earnings) ("The Bear," *Go Down, Moses*, pp. 266–
267). Private manumission was not only uncommon but became illegal in the lower South unless the freed persons left
the South.[32] The McCaslin departures from prevailing customs serve to reveal the customs.

Ike McCaslin, viewing his heritage, saw the cost at which

[30] Stampp describes measures taken to insure that slaves remained
in their cabins at night (p. 149), and gives the distance prescribed in
the Mississippi laws concerning fugitive slaves (p. 213). Slave marriages
were not recognized by law, and "most owners refused to allow slaves
to marry away from home," but sometimes a sale was made to unite
slaves belonging to different owners (Stampp, p. 341).

[31] William R. Taylor, *Cavalier and Yankee: The Old South and the
American National Character* (Garden City, N.Y.: Doubleday Anchor Books, 1963), p. 181.

[32] Stampp, pp. 94–97, 233, 234; Eaton, p. 91. According to Stampp,
instances of rejection of offers of freedom have been exaggerated (p.
93). Nat Turner's insurrection, 1831, caused the position of free
Negroes to deteriorate. In 1860 there were only 773 free Negroes in
Mississippi (Eaton, pp. 91, 92).

the land had been tamed and the wilful pride of those who bought it from the Indians:

. . . had bought with white man's money from the wild men whose grandfathers without guns hunted it, and tamed and ordered or believed he had tamed and ordered it for the reason that the human beings he held in bondage and in the power of life and death had removed the forest from it and in their sweat scratched the surface of it . . . in order to grow something out of it which had not been there before and which could be translated back into the money he who believed he had bought it had had to pay to get it and hold it and a reasonable profit too: and for which reason old Carothers McCaslin, knowing better, could raise his children, his descendants and heirs, to believe the land was his to hold and bequeath since the strong and ruthless man has a cynical foreknowledge of his own vanity and pride and strength and a contempt for all his get . . . ["The Bear," *Go Down, Moses*, pp. 254–255].

Before the Civil War the pattern had been set: an agrarian society dependent on slave labor had been established; the town would recognize the big plantation owners as social leaders, and town society would adopt the same basic concepts, derived from the assumption that the white man takes what he wants from the red man and derives a profit from it by the labors of the black man. The ruling class was much like that described by Cash, merely "a close clique of property," representing chiefly "the natural flower of the back-country grown prosperous" by industry and luck and unscrupulous opportunism.[33] James Silver notes the striking parallels between Mississippi in 1850 and 1950: by the middle 1850s Mississippi had swung from the frontier spirit of the West to

[33] Cash, pp. 21, 19. Faulkner does not deal with yeoman farmers and poor whites before the war, although yeoman farmers constituted the largest single group in the South; in Mississippi about half of the families owned slaves, a relatively high proportion (Stampp, pp. 29, 30). Later arrivals among upper-class white settlers and the yeoman farmers and the poor whites will be dealt with as they appear in Yoknapatawpha. The trader Ratcliffe, ancestor of Ratliff, does play a part in the story of the courthouse (*Requiem for a Nun*, Prologue, Act One).

the orthodoxy it has maintained most of the time since; it
had become, in James Silver's terms, a closed society.

IV. *The Civil War and Its Aftermath*

Although the Civil War affected the course of social history
and checked the progress of some of the leading families, it is
dealt with directly in only a small part of the Yoknapatawpha
fiction. The tradition fostered by obsessive memories of heroic
exploits and past grandeur did as much in Yoknapatawpha
to determine the destinies of families and individuals as did
the effects of the war. Faulkner dealt with the Civil War
chiefly in *The Unvanquished,* in which limitation of point of
view plus restriction to Yoknapatawpha County and areas
covered in refugee flights excluded major military engage-
ments. Far from glorifying the war, Faulkner tended to show
the futility of deeds of daring inspired by trivial or selfish
motives.

Episodes in the history of the town which are common
memories have their parallels in the history of Oxford and
the vicinity: the mustering of troops; Van Dorn's raid on
Grant's military stores; the burning of the Square. Faulkner's
use of these incidents illustrates his mingling of history and
fiction. In 1861, John Sartoris, in the first Confederate uniform
seen in town, stood on the south balcony of the courthouse
during the enrollment of troops (*Requiem for a Nun,* p. 45).
In Yoknapatawpha, the burning of the Square is not prominent in local memory and the destruction of the courthouse
is less complete than it appears in a contemporary photograph
(*Requiem for a Nun,* p. 46). Van Dorn's raid is correctly
located in Holly Springs in *Sartoris* (p. 226), but in *Light in
August* it is transplanted to Jefferson as the event which attracted Hightower to the town where he wasted his life in
obsessive romanticizing of his grandfather's trivial and ignoble

part in the raid.[34] The basically realistic references to General Forrest throughout *The Unvanquished* are echoed, then over-shadowed in the story of the jailer's daughter who scratched her name on a pane of glass through which she saw for a moment the lieutenant who later came back and married her.[35] The proportions given to private life and public events here are significant.

The leaders of the second group of settlers played parts in the war. John Sartoris was elected colonel in 1861, fought at First Manassas, was not re-elected in 1862, returned to Mississippi and organized a cavalry troop under Forrest.[36] Sutpen,

[34] The date given for the burning of the Square in *Requiem for a Nun* (p. 46), 1863, is incorrect in reference to Oxford: General A. J. Smith burned the Square in Oxford in August, 1864. Only the foundation of the courthouse was actually used in the rebuilding. These and other inaccuracies in Faulkner's historical references are tedious to recount and irrelevant to the fiction; the essential point is that Faulkner felt free to change details but that "historic" facts relating to Jefferson usually have a historic basis. Faulkner relocated the Van Dorn raid in Jefferson to preserve the unity of setting by having the action of *Light in August* centered there and also to make use of the raid as an image from history in the story of Hightower.

[35] *Requiem for a Nun*, pp. 232–233, 235–237, 253–257. The same story, with a different name for the girl, is told in *Intruder in the Dust*, with the burning of the Square given three lines and the story of the girl given half a page (pp. 50–51). Faulkner's statement about the glass perhaps being preserved in a museum (*Requiem for a Nun*, p. 253) is based on fact. In the Mary Buie Museum in Oxford is a piece of glass with "Jane T. Cook" scratched on it and the following information about it. As Confederate troops retreated past her house on South Lamar in 1863, Jane Cook scratched her name on the window and then went into the street and "cursed the men Out" for running away. General Forrest's son, a Captain in the troop, so admired her that he returned and married her. Faulkner omits the more lurid facts about Forrest, though he does bring in his past as a slave-trader ("The Bear," *Go Down, Moses*, p. 264). E. O. Hawkins gives an account of Faulkner's uses of this story and the historical details: "Jane Cook and Cecilia Farmer," *Mississippi Quarterly*, XVII (Fall, 1965), 248–251. Nordholt, in *The People that Walk in Darkness*, sums up Forrest: "after growing rich on his trade in human beings, he . . . was allowed to move in the best circles. He was promoted to general during the war and became notorious for the slaughter of Negro prisoners at Fort Pillow. After the war he quickly became the leader of the Ku Klux Klan" (p. 71).

[36] The election of officers by popular vote continued in the Confed-

who desired to be heroic, lacked the character to live up to his dreams (*Faulkner in the University,* p. 204). His chief distinctions, a citation for valor by Lee and his election as colonel, supplanting Sartoris, are given in parentheses (*Absalom, Absalom!,* pp. 68, 189). His duty to his cause and to his men he subordinated to his own vainglory in having marble tombstones sent by blockade runner from Italy and transported by the regiment for almost two years until they reached Mississippi (*Absalom, Absalom!,* pp. 188-190). General Compson was more modest but somewhat more successful: "Brigadier General Jason Lycurgus Compson II who failed at Shiloh in '62 and failed again though not so badly at Resaca in '64, who put the first mortgage on the still intact square mile to a New England carpetbagger in '66" (*The Sound and the Fury,* p. 7). For forty years more he kept selling fragments of the estate until he died at the camp on the Tallahatchie "where he spent most of the end of his days." This expository account in the Appendix of *The Sound and the Fury* exposes the exaggerated idea the Compsons had of their "glorious" past. Of the other leading families, Theophilus McCaslin, Ike's father, was in Colonel Sartoris's horse troop under Forrest ("The Bear," *Go Down, Moses,* p. 234); Amodeus, his twin, fought in Virginia (*The Unvanquished,* p. 57).

The one example of dissent from Confederate principles was Mr. Coldfield, a conscientious objector with a background of fidelity to the Union instead of to an agrarian tradition

---

erate Army until 1862. Failure to be re-elected was likely to indicate the aversion of "men who would not submit to discipline" to an efficient officer and their preference for a "good fellow," as Mary Chesnut explained in *A Diary from Dixie* (Boston: Houghton, Mifflin, 1961), pp. 132, 249-250, 245. The election of Sutpen in Sartoris's place is not wholly explained by Mrs. Chesnut's comments: although Colonel Falkner was a "martinet," according to William Faulkner (*Faulkner at West Point,* p. 108), Sutpen was scarcely "a good fellow." The "facts" given about Colonel Sartoris are essentially true of Colonel Falkner, except that the colonel of the partisan rangers who " 'rode with Forrest' was not the Mississippian W. C. Falkner, but the Kentuckian W. W. Faulkner," according to Duclos, who says that Falkner resigned from Confederate service in October, 1863, and was inactive thereafter (p. 178). Hickerson repeats this information (*The Falkner Feuds,* p. 27).

involving slavery. As Faulkner said, Coldfield lacked "enough courage to do anything about it except to hide his head in the sand" (*Faulkner in the University*, p. 274): he nailed himself into his attic and died there (*Absalom, Absalom!*, pp. 82–84).[37]

Of the four leading families which were represented in the Confederate Army, none declined primarily because of loss of life or property. *The Unvanquished,* the only novel which deals chiefly with the war period, shows the hazards and privations of civilians rather than warfare, except for Colonel John's capture of some Union men and escape from others, in "Retreat." Lack of food, loss of stock, the burning of the house, and a refugee flight to Hawkshurst Granny Millard endured, with the two boys, Ringo and Bayard.[38] Like many wives and mothers referred to by Clement Eaton,[39] not only did Granny keep the plantation going in her son-in-law's absence and keep all of the slaves but Loosh and his wife from running away to the Yankees, but she supplied the destitute in the area with the mules and horses they desperately needed, until her Robin Hood frauds practiced on the Union officers led to her involvement with Ab Snopes and Grumby and to her death. Granny is the heroine of *The Unvanquished*; Colonel John Sartoris is the hero of some of the stories. Judith Sutpen and Clytie struggled also to keep the plantation going, but the Negroes left and Wash Jones was of little use. There is one brief reference to nursing the wounded in Jefferson (*Absalom, Absalom!*, p. 125); the removal of the

[37] There seems to be no historical parallel for the story of Mr. Coldfield, but his name may be adapted, perhaps to suggest sterility, from that of "Colonel" J. R. Cofield, the Oxford photographer who took many pictures of William Faulkner (e.g., see frontispiece).

[38] Faulkner's fidelity to history, in addition to his carelessness with dates, is apparent in *The Unvanquished*. The reading of the cookbook and even the discussion of cocoanut cake as a Christmas luxury (*The Unvanquished,* p. 21) are paralleled by Mary Chesnut's account of reading a dessert recipe as a substitute for eating when food was scarce during the war (*A Diary from Dixie,* p. 516) and by Thomas Clark's account of cocoanut cake as a seasonal delicacy (*Pills, Petticoats, and Plows* [Indianapolis and New York: Bobbs-Merrill, 1944], p. 134).

[39] Clement Eaton, *A History of the Southern Confederacy* (New York: Collier Books, 1961), p. 206.

university from Jefferson also removed the stories of the use
of the university as a hospital which are featured in accounts
of Oxford during the war. By having his characters leave
railroadless Jefferson, Faulkner was able to include a description of rails tied "around a tree like you knot a green
cornstalk around a wagon stake,"[40] and an account of a locomotive chase in which a Confederate "iron knight" defied
and escaped from a Yankee locomotive (*The Unvanquished,*
pp. 79–80).[41]

The railroad motif prepares for the activities of Colonel John
Sartoris after the war. Both the strength and the weakness of
leaders of the South were apparent in the achievement of
Colonel John Sartoris after the war and in his downfall. He
rebuilt Sartoris, built the railroad with Redmond, and successfully ran for the legislature. He represents the aristocrats who
succeeded, according to Cash, because of the "latent energy"
which enabled them to hold "fast to the better part of their
heritage" and "ride triumphantly through by sheer force."[42]
But because of his "violent and ruthless dictatorialness and
will to dominate" he antagonized Redmond; after the final
triumph of Sartoris as a political rival, Redmond shot and
killed John Sartoris ("An Odor of Verbena," p. 258).[43] The

[40] *The Unvanquished,* p. 100. Bayard would not know that these
were called "Sherman's hairpins" (Katherine Du Pre Lumpkin, *The
Making of a Southerner* [New York: Knopf, 1947], p. 72).

[41] This is one of the few episodes with a historical parallel which
Faulkner significantly alters. It is a kind of reversal of the famous
Andrews raid. Andrews stole a Confederate train but ran out of fuel
and was overtaken and captured by the Confederates. Andrews and six
of his men were hanged. Faulkner gives the Confederates a bloodless
triumph in a kind of epic race between "iron horses." In the chapter
"The Great Locomotive Chase," in *The Civil War,* Harry Hansen
gives a detailed account of the Andrews raid. Elmo Howell deals with
Faulkner's use of the episode: "William Faulkner and the Andrews
Raid in Georgia, 1862," *Georgia Historical Quarterly,* XLIX (1965),
187–192.

[42] Cash, p. 157.

[43] The legend of Colonel Falkner parallels this part of the story of
John Sartoris. Faulkner's own version of the story in *Faulkner at West
Point* (pp. 108–109) is incorrect only in the point noted above (footnote 36) concerning Forrest. For further details about Colonel Falkner,
see Appendix E.

bravest deed of a Sartoris is not part of the legend of Colonel Falkner or of the Sartoris legend in Jefferson: told in "An Odor of Verbena," in *The Unvanquished,* it was a departure from the traditional code of honor and hence would not become one of the cherished and repeated anecdotes. The Colonel's son, Bayard (the "Colonel" Bayard of *Sartoris*), refused to follow the code of revenge by continuing the violence and bloodshed. Instead, he confronted Redmond, unarmed, and risked his life rather than take another's as "honor" required. The swashbuckling exploits of the legend suited the popular taste better than this act which, had it established in Jefferson a pattern of physical and moral courage, based on individual conscience, would have caused Faulkner's fiction to deviate from fidelity to social truth.

The decline of General Compson, already mentioned, was due to lack of character (*Faulkner in the University,* p. 204), specifically to an immaturity which made him retreat to a life of idleness, with hunting his major interest, instead of trying to save his property which, being in the heart of Jefferson, had not been destroyed and had considerable value. Sutpen's failure to rebuild after the war was due to the subordination of every thing and every one to producing the son without whom his Grand Design would perish. His principle, announced to nightriders in March, 1866, that the South would be restored if every man saw to the restoration of his own land, was sound and courageous (*Absalom, Absalom!,* p. 161). Sutpen's "little country store" not only shows energy and initiative and willingness to humble himself but is also a characteristic feature of the post-war South. Thomas Clark says: "Crossroads stores popped up like mushrooms" because "Confederate veterans everywhere turned to storekeeping as a side line to operating disorganized plantations."[44] The relationship between Sutpen and Wash, which proved to be Sutpen's doom, is, up to a point, a perfect example of the way in which, Cash says, the Southerner "found in the prescriptions of his captains great expansion for his ego." Wash, the one example in nineteenth-

---

[44] Clark, *Pills, Petticoats, and Plows,* pp. 21, 23.

century Yoknapatawpha of Cash's poor white who escaped both toil and actual want, throws light on Sutpen's difference from other master-class captains: because Sutpen did *not* know "how to handle the commoner, . . . to manipulate him without arousing his jealous independence," Wash killed him.[45] Even Wash would not submit to having his granddaughter, mother of Sutpen's daughter, treated worse than an animal.

The sole example of the rehabilitation of a plantation as a major enterprise, unaccompanied by railroads or banks or commercial ventures, is found in the story of the McCaslins. Before the war, the humane and eccentric Uncle Buck and Uncle Buddy had established a relationship with their slaves and the poor whites which gave them the control of "white trash" votes in the army and insured a stable supply of labor: they persuaded the whites to pool their land with that of the Negroes and promised them "nobody knew exactly what, except that their women and children did have shoes . . . and a lot of them even went to school" ("Retreat," *The Unvanquished,* p. 35). This method may not have been unique, but it was certainly highly exceptional. Faulkner does not specify it as a reason why McCaslin Edmonds was able to maintain the plantation as a going concern which represented the "mazed and intricate entirety" of the plantation system, to keep it "not only still intact but enlarged, increased" during "the debacle and chaos . . . where hardly one in ten survived" ("The Bear," *Go Down, Moses,* p. 298). Ike's failure, when he reached his majority, to conceive of and carry out any such scheme for the benefit of the workers, instead of repudiating his inheritance, becomes the more obvious when the story of his father and uncle is recalled.

The effect of the war on those at the other end of the scale, the Negroes, is presented incidentally but significantly: the conventional faithful slaves who identified their interests with those of their masters and mistresses are represented by all of the Sartoris servants except Loosh, but most notably by Ringo, Bayard's companion. The same age as Bayard but smarter,

---

[45] Cash, pp. 115, 114.

Ringo called Rosa Millard "Granny," helped Bayard shoot at the Union soldiers coming, they thought, to free the slaves, cooperated with Granny in her schemes for getting horses and mules from the Union forces, and accompanied Bayard in seeking out and killing Grumby, in vengeance for Granny's death. The companionship and equality between Ringo and Bayard lasted until after the war, when Bayard could be educated and Ringo could not. Atlhough the other slaves were loyal to Granny and accepted her authority, Loosh showed the Union soldiers where the silver was buried and claimed his freedom, choosing the danger of misery and starvation in order to belong to himself and God rather than to John Sartoris who buried him "in the black dark" ("Retreat," *The Unvanquished,* p. 85).[46]

One of the most moving episodes in *The Unvanquished* is that of the Negro fugitives moving in a cloud of dust toward General Sherman and his forces, to cross Jordan into the Promised Land. J. W. Schulte Nordholt quoted John Eaton's memoirs: "There was no plan in this exodus, no Moses to lead it."[47] These wanderers in the wilderness are described with

[46] Loosh was informed of news of armies and possible emancipation (*The Unvanquished,* pp. 5–6) by means of the Negroes' "grapevine telegraph" described by Vernon L. Wharton in *The Negro in Mississippi: 1865–1890* (New York: Harper Torchbooks, 1965), p. 20. The Sartoris slaves illustrate both the legendary faithful Negroes who aided the family by burying silver and hiding livestock and those who cooperated with the Federal troops (Wharton, pp. 20, 21). Faulkner did not use the most striking instance of disloyalty to masters, an uprising in Lafayette County in 1863 in which "the Negroes drove off their overseers, divided among themselves the mules and other property of their masters" (Wharton, p. 17).

[47] P. 153. The enormous numbers Faulkner describes—"the dust didn't even settle for two days"—may not be wildly exaggerated. According to John Eaton's account of the fugitives he supervised, near Grand Junction, Tennessee, in 1862: "The arrival among us of these hordes was like the oncoming of cities." Another witness said it was "like thrusting a walking stick into an ant-hill" (quoted in Wharton, pp. 28, 26). To Malcolm Cowley's statement of why he chose "Raid" for inclusion in *The Portable Faulkner*—"if the book didn't have those black people tramping the roads to Jordan, it wouldn't be the book I want it to be"—Faulkner replied: "GOOD!!! Would have done so myself to begin with" (pp. 56–57).

sympathy by Bayard and Drusilla. Isaac McCaslin is less sympathetic toward the free Negro who married Fonsiba and who sat reading in the midst of the desolation that to him was the new Canaan of freedom ("The Bear," *Go Down, Moses,* pp. 278–279). With his grant of land, inherited from his father for the latter's United States military service, his hopes and ambitions, and his desire for education, Fonsiba's husband adds another type of free Negro which is historically accurate: W. E. B. Du Bois describes the type, to whom freedom "was the fulfillment of prophecy and legend. It was the Golden Dawn."[48] Du Bois states the substance of their dreams: little farms and education.

Not only what Faulkner included but what he omitted in the account of Yoknapatawpha after the war is significant: by not presenting the most admirable leaders in the actual history of Oxford or dwelling upon the carnage and suffering during the war and Reconstruction, he avoided glorification of the South and sympathetic pleading for it.

Reconstruction was mild in Yoknapatawpha County as it was in Lafayette County. It is dealt with in the fiction chiefly in summaries: that of Ike speaking to McCaslin Edmonds ("The Bear," *Go Down, Moses,* pp. 290–292), and Faulkner's own summaries in *Requiem for a Nun;* the first (p. 233) is merely a brief preliminary to the story of the return of the young man to marry the jailer's daughter, and the second (pp. 242–243) is a parenthetical reference to the illiterate Negro marshall "Mulberry," who sold illicit whiskey. He figures in Ike's account under the name of "Sickymo," hiding his stock in trade under a sycamore instead of a mulberry tree. References to carpetbaggers and KKK activities are brief and general. There is no reference to the tale that from seventeen to thirty Negroes were drowned by the Klan in the Yocona River.[49] The only specific episode of the Recon-

---

[48] Du Bois, *Black Reconstruction in America,* pp. 122–123.
[49] Kullman, p. 71; Wharton, p. 220. In "William Faulkner, the Man and his Work" (reprinted in the *Mississippi Quarterly,* XVII [Summer, 1964]), Phil Stone no doubt reflects the local tradition behind Faulkner's account of Reconstruction in his explanation that "the usual

struction period is that in "Skirmish at Sartoris," in which, on his wedding day, Colonel Sartoris shot two carpetbaggers and took control of the voting to prevent an illiterate Negro coachman, Cassius Benbow, from being elected marshal. This episode, especially as related by old Falls in *Sartoris* (pp. 235–236), well illustrates the attitudes of the masses toward those who had been their leaders during the war, as described by Cash: their "deep affection" and "profound trust," their memories of their former commanders as "bold, dashing, splendid," "fit to cope with the problem in hand," are reflected in all of the reminiscences of Falls.[50] He remembered everything but what they were fighting for (*Sartoris*, p. 227). Sartoris also organized nightriders and it was he who visited Sutpen ("An Odor of Verbena," p. 256). In relating this episode, Bayard is sympathetic to Sutpen. In Joanna Burden's story of the "carpetbaggers" whom the Colonel shot, her grandfather and brother, we find that they were Northern abolitionists, a one-armed old man and a boy, and that the graves were concealed by Joanna's father so that they would not be violated (*Light in August*, pp. 217–218). But Joanna recognized the love of the land and the tradition behind Colonel Sartoris's action (p. 223). This episode exemplifies methods used even by moderates during Reconstruction to control voting by violence. In discussing "Skirmish at Sartoris" as representing Faulkner's limited treatment of Reconstruction, James B. Meriwether points out that "Faulkner has obviously taken some pains to prevent his story from pointing out a simple moral": though the Burdens were wrong in attempting "by force and bribery to elect an incompetent

---

troubles of the Reconstruction period" were less exaggerated in Lafayette County because the whites outnumbered the Negroes and soon "white supremacy reasserted itself" (p. 159). Wharton regards the report cited of KKK activity as one of the unreliable "boastful tales of mass slaughter" which nevertheless indicate how unsafe life was for Negroes in 1869–1870. Faulkner did not deal directly with the Klan in any period but always spoke of it scornfully as "the dull dreary minority" who provided "nothing dramatic enough" for fiction (*Faulkner in the University*, p. 94).

[50] Cash, p. 113.

candidate," Colonel Sartoris was wrong in killing them and
disenfranchising the Negroes by equally dubious election
procedures. Meriwether notes the irony in the Colonel's question, "Don't you see we are working for peace through law
and order?" Faulkner's neglect of the Reconstruction period
in his fiction, Meriwether concludes, was due not to lack of
interest or "even of strong feelings," but to "a determination
to avoid a subject which has been overworked, overtalked,
overwritten, perhaps, and been used too often as an excuse to
account for ills due to other, less honorable causes."[51]

An omission of considerable significance is that of the cult of
the Confederate hero. Faulkner does describe the unveiling of
the Confederate monument on Confederate Decoration Day,
1900, by Aunt Jenny Depre [sic] (*Requiem for a Nun*, p. 239).
Katharine Lumpkin's account of what Confederate reunions
were like in her childhood in South Carolina and of the way
in which children were taught to love the "Lost Cause" makes
one realize what memorable childhood experiences Faulkner
omitted from his fiction.[52] Specifically, Faulkner was old
enough to have witnessed the dedication of the Confederate
monument on the University campus, May 10, 1906. (The
unveiling took place before Faulkner's family moved to

---

[51] "Faulkner and the South," in *Southern Writers: Appraisals in
Our Time*, R. C. Simonini, ed. (Charlottesville: University of Virginia
Press, 1964), pp. 156, 159. The first account Faulkner wrote (*Sartoris*,
pp. 235–236) is told by old Falls; the date, 1872, is more realistic than
that in "Skirmish at Sartoris," 1865, which is too early: the Reconstruction Act was passed March 2, 1867. In both accounts, Sartoris let
the Burdens shoot first. There seems to be no local parallel to this
episode, which illustrates the use of violence to keep Negroes from
voting. Nordholt gives a much more horrible example which took
place in Mississippi in 1875, of the murder of a Negro senator and
four other Negroes, all shot "all to pieces" (pp. 185–186). Colonel
Sartoris exemplifies the moderates in Mississippi who were willing to
use "violence to drive the Negro from his new privileges, from what
offices he held, and from the polls" (Silver, p. 13). The political careers
of three Mississippi Negroes, Hiram R. Revels, Blanche Kelso Bruce,
and John R. Lynch, however, won them national fame and esteem
(Wharton, pp. 159–163).
[52] Katherine Du Pre Lumpkin, *The Making of a Southerner*, pp.
113–127. Aunt Jenny Sartoris married a Carolina Du Pre.

Oxford.) As one might suppose, the omission was not due to lack of actual patriotic fervor in Mississippi: James Silver refers to Faulkner's Hightower, in *Light in August,* as an example of the contrast between legend and history and of the obsessive sense of the past. He continues:

Even for the average citizen, patriotic societies make up an integral part of his social life. It is in the life of these organizations, in the accounts in the press, and in the common routines of political oratory that the romanticism of the Old South as well as the cult of the Confederacy flourish—always renewed by bitter stories of Reconstruction.[53]

The most notable omission, had Faulkner been seeking the admirable and exceptional in history as a basis for his fiction, was the actual Oxford resident and political leader for whom the central thoroughfare is named: Lucius Quintus Cincinnatus Lamar.[54] Faulkner split his name among Lucius Quintus Carothers McCaslin and Lucius Quintus Carothers Priest and Ruby Lamar. No other reference to Lamar is apparent in Yoknapatawpha. The facts of Lamar's life would have made him ideal for a central figure reflecting both the Southern tradition and a critical examination of and deviation from it:

[53] Silver, p. 5. James Silver lived in Oxford from 1936 to 1964 and was a friend of Faulkner's. Evidence such as this of romantic aspects of history which Faulkner avoided is helpful in counteracting unsound conclusions of some critics, based on incomplete knowledge of the Yoknapatawpha fiction and of Mississippi. A little-known fact about the South, illustrated in Oxford, would offer wonderful opportunity for romanticizing based on fact. Tilting tournaments, modeled after *Ivanhoe,* were popular in the South before and after the Civil War (Nordholt, p. 58). In 1867, one was held in Oxford, with a horse, a saddle, and a silver set among the prizes, the total worth of the prizes being $1,100. The entrance fee for knights was $10.00. Profits were for the benefit of the cemetery. (Oxford *Eagle,* December 10, 1936.) Detailed accounts of such tournaments are given in *The Ring Tournament in the United States* (Richmond: Garrett and Massie, 1936), by Esther J. and Ruth W. Crooks.

[54] John F. Kennedy's study of the life and political significance of Lamar, as one of his ten *Profiles in Courage* (New York: Pocket Books, 1963), is sufficient testimony to the achievements of Lamar and to his exceptional character.

he was a pro-Southern Congressman before the war, devoted
to "the promotion of Southern interests" and "the preservation
of Southern honor." He was the drafter of Mississippi's
ordinance of secession.[55] He discovered the unsoundness of
the slavery system when he saw the consequences of the war.
He supported the post-war amendments to the Constitution
and believed that disenfranchisement of the Negro was impossible: "universal suffrage being given as the condition of
our political life, the Negro once made a citizen can not be
placed under any other condition."[56] In his eulogy on the death
of Charles Sumner, in 1875, he pleaded for reconcilation between North and South: "My countrymen! know one another,
and you will love one another!"[57] He followed his conscience
and his rational convictions rather than popular sentiment,
in voting against the Bland Silver Bill, and wrote to his wife:
"Can it be true that the South will condemn the disinterested
love of those who, perceiving her real interests, offer their
unarmored breasts as barriers against the invasion of error?"
He said on a political tour: "I prize the confidence of the
people of Mississippi, but I never made popularity the standard of my action."[58] Until the time of William Faulkner,
Oxford had no resident of equal fame. Faulkner's omission of
Lamar and of any character who can possibly be identified
with Faulkner himself in achievements can mean only that
Faulkner wished to deal with the typical or the predictable
products of Southern small-town environment, not with the
unparalleled.

[55] Kennedy, *Profiles in Courage,* p. 135.
[56] Quoted in Myrdal, p. 1312.
[57] Kennedy, p. 130.
[58] *Ibid.,* pp. 147, 149.

v.   *The Caste System and Caste Etiquette*

The complexities of the Southern class and caste system, unfamiliar in its ramifications and details to Northerners and
taken for granted by Southerners, must be understood before
considering the modern world of Yoknapatawpha County.
To arrive at that understanding, it is necessary to pass through
what C. Vann Woodward calls "the twilight zone that lies
between living memory and written history" which "is one of
the favorite breeding places of mythology."[59] Louis D. Rubin
and Robert D. Jacobs cite the awe expressed by Ralph Ellison,
the Negro novelist, "at the way that William Faulkner has
gone about exploring each and every facet of the Negro's
role in the South" as it involves both the white man and the
Negro.[60] Because this multi-faceted caste role had its beginning, in its modern aspects, in the twilight zone, some light on
the history of the post-Reconstruction period is necessary. And
because Negroes must play their caste role according to complicated and often unwritten rules, learned by both whites and
Negroes from earliest childhood, it is necessary to indicate the
range of racial etiquette and the stereotypes upon which it is
based. For this reason Faulkner's work must serve to illustrate
points, rather than to provide the structural basis for analysis,
and historical facts omitted by Faulkner cannot be relegated to
footnotes.

The brief period of the Reconstruction ended with the Com-
promise of 1877, when the freed Negroes had had only a few
years to demonstrate their capacities: as C. Vann Woodward

[59] C. Vann Woodward, *The Strange Career of Jim Crow* (New
York: Oxford University Press, Galaxy Books, 1957), p. viii.

[60] Quoted in *South: Modern Southern Literature in its Cultural Setting,* Louis D. Rubin and Robert D. Jacobs, eds. (Garden City, N.Y.:
Doubleday Dolphin Books, 1961), p. 17.

says, the Negro problem again became that of the South, with the North ceasing the attempt "to guarantee the freedman his civil and political equality."[61] Thus the "closed system" of slavery,[62] with its "withering, blasting effects," was gradually replaced by the closed society[63] in the South which James Silver finds in its most complete American form in Mississippi at the present time, a hundred years after the Civil War (*Mississippi: The Closed Society*).

By a series of Supreme Court decisions from 1873 to 1898, including one in 1883 declaring the Bill of Rights of 1875 unconstitutional, the North acquiesced in the South's denial of civil rights to Negroes, ending in 1898 with approval of the Mississippi plan for disenfranchising Negroes by "the use of the riot as a political instrument."[64] The result was the extension of plantation paternalism into a paternalistic, segregated society, dominated by the principle of white supremacy in a caste system. Cash explains that this philosophy served

to strengthen and expand the planter's narrow class pride, to increase his private contempt for the common whites, to ratify his complacency and harden toward arrogance the conviction which was growing up in him, as a natural result of the paternalistic habit, that it was his *right* to instruct and command . . . .[65]

The Southern paradox is apparent in its paternalism: Gunnar Myrdal describes its "romantic and individualistic" quality, its humor and sentimentality[66]; the other side of the coin is its denial to the Negro of human status in order to justify in the name of God, home, and country the ideology of caste.[67]

[61] Woodward, *The Strange Career of Jim Crow*, p. 6.
[62] Charles E. Silberman, *Crisis in Black and White* (New York: Random House, 1964), p. 89.
[63] By a curious coincidence, this "withering" denunciation of slavery as the cause of the ruin of the rich land of the South was uttered by Charles James Faulkner in the Virginia Convention of 1832, in which he urged gradual abolition. (Quoted in Nordholt, pp. 45–46.)
[64] Silver, p. 13. C. Vann Woodward deals with the Supreme Court decisions in *The Strange Career of Jim Crow*, pp. 53–54.
[65] Cash, p. 91.
[66] Myrdal, p. 459.
[67] Howard W. Odum, *The Way of the South*, p. 40.

The creed of white supremacy, of which paternalism is the rationalized justification, is based on a social, not a biological, concept of the Negro, as Myrdal explains.[68] Faulkner explicitly denied the "scientific" view of race with which Southerners attempt to justify white supremacy in terms of inherent racial differences:

There is no such thing as an "Anglo-Saxon" heritage and an African heritage. There is the heritage of man. Nothing is extinct in any race, only dormant. You are brave and tough when you have to be. You are intelligent when the age demands it. There are all things in like degree in all races.[69]

In essence white supremacy means that the lowest white person is superior to the finest Negro; that, as Ralph McGill says, the Negro is excluded from "the Fatherhood of God and the brotherhood of man."[70] The creed of racial orthodoxy outlined by Thomas Pearce Bailey in 1914 is still the creed of race relations in the Deep South:

1. Blood will tell. 2. The white race must dominate. 3. The Teutonic peoples stand for race purity. 4. The Negro is inferior and will remain so. 5. This is a white man's country. 6. There must be no social equality. 7. There must be no political equality. 8. In matters of civil rights and legal adjustment, give the white man, as opposed to the colored man, the benefit of the doubt; and under no circumstances interfere with the prestige of the white race. 9. In the educational policy let the Negro have the crumbs that fall from the white man's table. 10. Let there be such industrial education of the Negro as will fit him to serve the white

[68] Myrdal, p. 136.

[69] Quoted by Russell Warren Howe, "Prejudice, Superstition, and Economics," *Phylon,* XVII (1956), 223.

[70] Ralph McGill, *The South and the Southerner* (Boston: Little, Brown, 1963), p. 232. In the Milwaukee *Journal,* August 4, 1964, Edward Blackwell, a Negro member of the *Journal* staff writing from "Behind the Cotton Curtain," refers to a mural in the Federal Building in Jackson, Mississippi, in which "white people are pictured as doctors, farmers, engineers, Negroes are faceless forms in cotton fields."

man. 11. Only Southerners understand the Negro question. 12.
The status of peasantry is all the Negro may hope for, if the
races live together in peace. 13. Let the South settle the Negro
question. 14. Let the lowest white man count for more than the
highest Negro. 15. The above statements indicate the leadings of
Providence.[71]

Bailey's twelfth item is revealing: as George Washington
Cable put it: "the moment the relation of master and servant
is visibly established between race and race there is the hush
of peace."[72] Faulkner provides the perfect symbolic expression
of the principle in the edict of Colonel Sartoris, as mayor: "no
Negro woman should appear on the streets without an apron"
("A Rose for Emily," *Collected Stories,* pp. 119–120).

The inexorable permanence of Negro caste status, as compared with class status, may most easily be suggested by the
comparison between caste and sex, relevant especially in a
society where women have been dominated by men and
hedged in by restrictions to a degree unusual in modern
American society.[73] Lillian Smith, in *Killers of the Dream,*
has much to say about both Negroes and Southern women;
in a Faulknerian parallel between the exploitation of the land
and the "washed-out women of the rural South whose bodies

---

[71] From *Racial Orthodoxy in the South,* quoted by Bertram Doyle,
The Etiquette of Race Relations in the South (Chicago: The University
of Chicago Press, 1937), p. 141. Myrdal, "The Southern Defense Ideology" (pp. 441–445), deals with the same concepts and explains their
origins and implications. Hortense Powdermaker lists both the items
of the creed and the corollary stereotypes, in *After Freedom: A Cultural Study in the Deep South* (New York: Viking, 1939), pp. 23–24.

[72] G. W. Cable, *The Negro Question: A Selection of Writings on
Civil Rights in the South* (Garden City, N.Y.: Doubleday Anchor
Books, 1958), p. 132. Not only do Cable's writings on the Negro question sound up-to-date, but there are strong parallels between Cable and
Faulkner. By an interesting coincidence, Cable gave his first public
address at the University of Mississippi in 1882 (Jay B. Hubbell, *Southern Life in Fiction,* p. 814). Although, as Hubbell points out, Cable was
a literary pioneer, followed by a number of Southern novelists, including Faulkner, Arlin Turner questions whether Faulkner had read
Cable's fiction ("William Faulkner, Southern Novelist," p. 129).

[73] Myrdal develops the analogy in detail, pp. 667–668, 1075, 1077,
1078.

were often used as ruthlessly as was the land," she compares the segregation of Negroes with that of women.[74]

To keep the Negro in his place, legal and social restrictions had to be supplied to substitute for slave status. Negroes gradually lost their suffrage by requirements for voting which were not applied equally to whites. Beginning in 1881 and continuing through the first two decades of the twentieth century, Jim Crow laws—discriminatory and segregation laws —imposed legal restrictions on Negroes in every phase of public life, and, according to C. Vann Woodward, "there is more Jim Crowism practiced in the South than there are Jim Crow laws on the books."[75]

Basic to the rationalizations by which the Negro was as-signed to a permanent inferior status was the sense of guilt and the fear of retaliation for the miscegenation which mingled white blood with Negro, largely by relations between white men and Negro women. Hence the confusion between civil and social relations: the rational difference between civil relations, matters of impersonal right, and social relations, matters of personal choice, is obscured by irrational, guilty fears. The Jim Crow laws legalized segregation in all in-stitutional aspects of life and those in which the individual Negro confronts white groups. As Lillian Smith states: "segre-gation became the South's highest law."[76]

To provide further controls over Negro conduct, the elabo-rate system of racial etiquette established behavior patterns that neither white nor Negro could safely violate, under pain

---

[74] Lillian Smith, *Killers of the Dream* (Garden City, N.Y.: Double-day Anchor Books, 1963), p. 148. Taylor finds in Beverley Tucker's *George Balcombe* the same bracketing of Negroes with women, there revealed as due to fear of insubordination from the inferior race or sex (p. 153).

[75] *The Strange Career of Jim Crow*, p. 87. Wharton explains that the racial code was intended to apply "to all possible situations and places in which the races might be thrown together" and therefore was a matter of ritual as well as of law (p. 232). The Jim Crow laws put into effect a much more complete system of segregation than existed under slavery, when a Negro servant could accompany white persons in public places.

[76] Smith, p. 180.

of punishment ranging from ostracism of whites to violence against either race. This racial etiquette, covering "all the little things it means to be a Negro in the South," which Carl Rowan set out to discover,[77] is reflected in the everyday contacts between persons of different race, and builds up tensions to the explosion point. Any one of the major episodes of racial violence in Faulkner's stories has a background of minor situations involving racial etiquette and racial stereotypes before the specific occasion for violence occurs. The stereotypes and the etiquette which is based upon them and which, in a vicious circle, fosters them can be summed up briefly: The Negro is an inferior creature, with innate racial virtues and weaknesses, who must never be treated as a dignified, adult human being worthy of respect.[78] The unspoken assumption is that equality between the races in civil relations is tantamount to social equality, and that Negroes seek not merely social equality but interracial sexual relations, intermarriage, and the mongrelization of the white race. (The degrading mongrelization of the Negro race, like the rape of a Negro woman, is regarded as a physical impossibility.)

Myrdal lists the segregation-discrimination measures reflected in the racial etiquette and legislation in order of most to least abhorrent to the whites, which is precisely opposite to the order of desirability in which Negroes would rank them: 1. intermarriage and other sex relations between white women and Negro men; 2. taboos and etiquette in personal contacts; 3. segregation in schools and churches; 4. segregation

---

[77] Carl Rowan, *South of Freedom* (New York: Knopf, 1952), p. 11. Carl Rowan became director of the United States Information Agency. John Howard Griffin's *Black Like Me,* except that the author is a white man who traveled in the South disguised as a Negro, is a comparable view of segregation and racial etiquette from the point of view of an upper-class but lower-caste person (New York: Signet Books, 1962). The most complete treatment of racial etiquette is Bertram Doyle's *The Etiquette of Race Relations in the South.*

[78] "Strategy for Students at Oxford," in dealing with James Meredith or any other Negro student admitted to the University of Mississippi, included isolating the student as an "NAACP leper" and treating him "as if he were a piece of furniture of no value." Quoted in Silver, p. 56.

in social public places; 5. segregation in transportation; 6. discrimination in public services; 7. inequality in politics; 8. inequality in justice; 9. inequality in breadwinning and relief.[79]

With the basic rule for whites of not treating whites and Negroes alike,[80] the Negro is denied titles of respect such as *Mr.* or *Mrs.* but may be called *Doctor* or *Professor,*[81] often in mockery, but he must always use titles of respect for a white person; the Negro cannot enter a white person's house by the front door or eat at a white man's table[82]; a Negro must not keep his hat on before a white person and must stand in a white person's presence. A Negro should accept gratefully the condescending patronage of a white person and not presume to be his equal in a man-to-man relationship which would exist between two white men. Always the white person takes the initiative in such permissible but not customary social gestures as shaking hands. The tremendous significance of a trivial social gesture, inconsequential in most situations, is revealed in James Baldwin's remark about warfare in the heart "so powerful that the interracial handshake or the interracial marriage can be as crucifying as the public hanging or the secret rape."[83] And for a Negro even to look with interest or impudence at a white woman is dangerous to the point of

[79] Myrdal, pp. 587–599. See also Powdermaker, pp. 43–50.

[80] Sarah Patton Boyle, *The Desegregated Heart* (New York: William Morrow, 1962), p. 24.

[81] Silver (p. 147) cites the example of Ross Barnett hunting with a Negro friend whom he calls "Professor" because the Negro trains bird-dogs. Barnett's generosity to individual Negroes is a good example of the self-gratifying paternalism of whites toward "good niggers."

[82] The taboo against eating together has the strongest sexual implications. Specific examples given by Lillian Smith (p. 42), Katherine Lumpkin (p. 206), and Sarah Boyle (p. 25) show the enforcement of the rule in relation to highly educated, refined Negroes. As Sarah Boyle shows, a filthy poor white would be invited to eat at the table with the family, but a Negro college president would be served a dinner on a tray in another room. As Lillian Smith puts it, if a town has only one drinking fountain, "the town's white idiot can drink out of it" but not "the town's black college professor" (p. 80).

[83] James Baldwin, *Notes of a Native Son* (Boston: Beacon Press, 1957), p. 18.

being suicidal. Segregation enforced by separate public facili-
ties for whites and Negroes must be rigidly observed. Unfortunately it is only too familiar a fact that Mississippi, of all
the Southern states, adheres most rigidly to the racial etiquette
and segregation pattern. Specific examples of etiquette observed and etiquette violated will be cited in discussing Faulkner's Negro characters.

This systematic denial to the Negro of maturity and dignity
makes him socially undesirable. The stereotype of the Negro
has prevented the white people from seeing Negroes as they
really are, as individuals, has forced Negroes to act the stereotyped role in order to avoid trouble, and has caused, by environmental influence, the traits which are assumed- to be
innate. Ike McCaslin in his conversation with McCaslin Edmonds distinguishes between the Negroes' own innate virtues
—"Endurance—and pity and tolerance and fidelity and love
of children"—and the "vices aped from white men or that
white men and bondage have taught them: improvidence and
intemperance and evasion—not laziness; evasion" of tasks
forced upon them. McCaslin adds: "Promiscuity, Violence,
Instability and lack of control," and dishonesty ("The Bear,"
Go Down, Moses, pp. 295, 294).[84] To illustrate how the stereotype creates the reality because of white people's expectations:
Negro servants are paid low wages on the expectation that
they will pilfer enough to eke out their earnings; when they
do so, they are treated indulgently, having proved the truth
of the stereotype—not, of course, the inadequacy of the wages.
Abram Kardiner and Lionel Ovesey present evidence of the
falsity of some of the chief traits attributed to the Negro,
according to the stereotype, and the environmental cause of
others. Some characteristics are the result of attempts to bolster

[84] The love of children is stressed by Charles Johnson in *Shadow of
the Plantation* (Chicago: University of Chicago Press, Phoenix Books,
1966), pp. 58–59. The stereotypes about Negroes listed by Myrdal include happy-go-lucky laziness, thriftlessness, amorality, lower intelligence and immaturity, servility, and criminal tendencies. The odor
which is supposed to be a barrier to social integration, Myrdal notes,
has been no hindrance to "the utilization of Negroes in even the most
intimate household work and personal services" (pp. 106–107).

self-esteem in the face of degradation: flashy dress, alcohol, drugs, gambling. Some are the consequence of suppressed aggression against whites: dancing and sports, impulsive crimes against Negroes. Some are induced by the social and economic facts of Negro life: male indolence and lack of responsibility are due to the predominance of women as breadwinners; passivity and ingratiation are the opposites of the self-confidence and autonomy which they are denied.[85] The supposed sexuality of both Negro men and women eases white men's consciences for their offenses against the women and justifies their fears of retaliation from the men. Kardiner and Ovesey, however, find sexual drives in abeyance especially in lower-class Negro males, because of their lack of prestige in their society, and find "none of the expected sexual hedonism" among Negro women.[86]

Cash explains both the stereotype in the white man's mind and the Negro conformity to it as defense mechanisms: the South, in defense against Yankee criticism and its own doubts, projected "its own mawkish tears and its own mawkish laughter over the black man, incarnations of its sentimentalized version of slavery," and the Negro, with his "quick, intuitive understanding of what is required of him" and his mimetic talents, conformed to the stereotype so well that the

---

[85] Abram Kardiner and Lionel Ovesey, *The Mark of Oppression* (Cleveland and New York: World Publishing Company, Meridian Books, 1962). Part Three, "Negro Adaptation: A Psychodynamic Analysis," presents the conclusions based on personality studies. The points cited merely suggest the basic relations which may be observed between stereotypes and traits exhibited. Robert Penn Warren cites Faulkner's Joe Christmas as a Negro "by social definition and not by blood; to state it in another way, Faulkner here undercuts the official history and mythology of a whole society by indicating that the 'nigger' is a creation of the white man" ("Faulkner: The South, the Negro, and Time," in *Faulkner: A Collection of Critical Essays,* p. 259). Charles Nilon makes the same point about Faulkner's characters with mixed blood: "Most of his studies of miscegenation are examinations of the connotative meanings of the word Negro and illustrations of the compulsive force of those meanings in the determination of social attitudes" (*Faulkner and the Negro* [New York: Citadel Press, 1965], p. 73). Those attitudes create Negro identity and personality.

[86] Kardiner and Ovesey, pp. 312, 347.

South accepted it as reality and could believe in it "as honestly as they believed in so many other doubtful things."[87]

The projection which helps to create the stereotype is particularly relevant to characterization of Negroes in literature. Faulkner's Negro characters will be discussed in their social context, but it may be interesting at this point to compare a list of stereotypes of Negro characters in literature with characters in Faulkner which fall into the categories.

The Contented Slave is found in the Sartoris servants during the Civil War, but is contrasted with Loosh, willing to give up security for freedom, and the hordes of Negroes seeking Jordan and the Promised Land (*The Unvanquished*). The Wretched Freeman is illustrated in Fonsiba's husband, but his wretchedness is chiefly in Ike McCaslin's eyes and is a single glimpse ("The Bear"). The Comic Negro is seen in Simon Strother and Uncle Ned McCaslin; Simon, as a character in an early work, *Sartoris,* is closer to the stereotype than Ned, in Faulkner's last work, *The Reivers*; Ned assumes the mask of the comic Negro for practical purposes but is intelligent and assumes a role of importance and dignity, as well as of deliberate humor. The Brute Negro is perfectly and ironically represented in Rider, in "Pantaloon in Black," of which the whole point is Rider's depth of passion for his dead wife. The Local Color Negro is represented by such occasional characters as old Job in *The Sound and the Fury* and Old Het in *The Town,* both of whom show self-knowledge and understanding of white people that remove them from classification as mere stereotypes. The Exotic Primitive is genuinely exemplified in both the Negro to be sacrificed and the Indians in "Red Leaves," where the time of action and the setting lend authenticity. The stereotype which comes closest to reality has the greatest potentiality for dignified literary treatment: the Tragic Mulatto. Faulkner's Joe Christmas (*Light in August*) and Charles Bon and his son (*Absalom, Absalom!*) are among the most notable examples of the type in literature. No ironic inversion is necessary, for the very concept of the type is

[87] Cash, pp. 86–87.

based on the reality of a profound human dilemma raised to a dignified level of treatment.

Sterling Brown, from whose study, cited by Myrdal, the above character types were taken, has evaluated Faulkner's Negro characters in a more recent study, "A Century of Negro Portraiture in American Literature." Although Brown somewhat questions Faulkner's "essential liberalism on race," he confirms the validity of Faulkner's later characterizations of Negroes: after accepting "the myths of *his* own tribal past" in *Soldier's Pay,* "soon he steadily began to see Negroes whole, and with *Go Down, Moses* he defied several of his region's set beliefs concerning the Negro."

There is no questioning . . . that in ploughing deeply into the soil of his single county, Faulkner was wise, prescient, and rewarded. What seems at first glance the familiar stereotyping becomes, on true reading, complex and revelatory, e.g. Dilsey is far more than the old mammy; Joe Christmas more than the tragic mulatto; Nancy Manigault more than the depraved "wench." But Faulkner also presents new people, unnoticed before but here candidly portrayed: the admirable Lucius Beauchamps [sic], Sam Fathers, and the Centaur in Brass. When spouting the Southern liberal's ambivalent credo (cf. Gavin Stevens' long-windedness in *Intruder in the Dust*) Faulkner is unconvincing or wrong, but when he stands back and lets his Negro character speak out and act out, Faulkner is right, and often superb.[88]

The failure of Southerners and many Southern authors to observe differences between stereotypes and realities or to understand the relation between racial etiquette and stereotypes as a circle of cause and effect may be explained in several ways. First of all, both etiquette and natural inclinations prevent most Southerners from ever knowing a cultured

[88] Quoted in Myrdal, p. 1196. "A Century of Negro Portraiture in American Literature," *The Massachusetts Review,* VII (Winter, 1966), 89–90. Charles Nilon reaches the conclusion that perhaps "the most distinctive thing about Faulkner's creation of Negro character is his destruction of the Negro stereotype" (p. 110).

Negro. James Meredith's fellow students at Ole Miss harassed him: they did not try to know him. A few who did were themselves harassed. Nationally known superior Negroes, Carl Rowan testifies, or "any dignified, competent Negro" are regarded as freaks.[89] Even white people who are well disposed toward the Negro find it hard to break out of the patronizing attitude. Faulkner is a rare exception: he recognized not only the Negro's merits but his superiority, in that the Negro surpasses the white man who is subjected to the same limitations and shows qualities of greatness in the calm and wise way in which he has "put up with this situation so long with so little violence."[90] The ability of the white-supremacy advocates to believe that such barriers as have been erected between the races are necessary to prevent white women from marrying Negro men and at the same time to assert that there is an instinctive, God-given antipathy between the races— disproved by their own secret actions and by the evidence of racial mingling that has occurred—illustrates how impervious belief can make them to fact. Negro behavior is naturally dominated by protective secrecy and evasion: the Negro shows the white man a mask. As James Baldwin says, of the Negro face, "the general desire seems to be to make it blank if one cannot make it white."[91] The boast that Southerners know and love their Negroes is an empty one, nourished by the gratifications experienced by whites in their paternalistic, superior, condescending roles. The love is like that for dogs and horses. The claim to understanding is denied by thoughtful Southerners, from the Civil War to the present.[92] On each side of the invisible barrier of caste exists a separate class

[89] Rowan, p. 146. Blackwell, the Milwaukee *Journal* writer, never had a "social conversation with a white Mississippian."

[90] Quoted by Russell Warren Howe, p. 223.

[91] Baldwin, p. 26.

[92] Myrdal says that the Southerner's guilt makes him clothe his "systematic ignorance in stereotypes" (p. 357). Sarah Patton Boyle, Lillian Smith, and Katharine Lumpkin testify to their own ignorance and painful education in racial understanding and human etiquette. In Oxford before 1954, Robert Canzoneri said, "white life went along smoothly in ignorance of the Negro world around it" (p. 27).

society, with those in the inferior caste feeling that they are
unseen and unheard.[93]

VI. *Class and Caste Structure in Twentieth-Century Jefferson*

Yoknapatawpha County was never predominantly plantation
country like the Delta, but the plantation economy and its
patterns of life survived the Civil War even though the
planters as such ceased to be the dominant social class and a
separate aristocracy,[94] and many of the plantations, such as
Sutpen's and Grenier's, ceased to exist. In fact, the legend of
the Old South, the gilding of the past and the "Lost Cause,"
gained strength precisely because it had ceased to be a reality.
W. J. Cash explains the paradox: "while the actuality of
aristocracy was drawing toward the limbo of aborted and unrealized things, the claim of its possession as an achieved and
essentially indefeasible heritage, so far from being abated,
was reasserted with a kind of frenzied intensity."[95] The

[93] In *Dusk of Dawn*, W. E. B. Du Bois develops the analogy of a
"thick sheet of some invisible but horribly tangible plate glass" between
Negroes and whites (Quoted in Myrdal, p. 690). From the other side
of the plate glass Robert Canzoneri reports: "it is impossible to convey
what an essentially alien group is like, a community which has operated—must operate—in secret, so far as 'we' are concerned" (p. 9).

[94] This was true generally after 1870, according to Du Bois, *Black
Reconstruction in America*, p. 54. Phil Stone states that, although there
had been large plantations in the area before the war, "the old manorial
plantation living became largely a thing of the past" after the war (p.
152).

[95] Cash, p. 127. The same point about glamour of the past as a
kind of Golden Age is made by Nordholt (p. 190) and Hubbell (p.
704). Taylor and Gaines trace the development of the tradition in ante-
bellum literature. The question asked by Jack Burden in Robert Penn
Warren's *All the King's Men*, in a similar society with similar traditions, is pertinent: "if it was such a God-damned fine, beautiful time,
why did it turn into this time which is not so damned fine and beautiful if there wasn't something in that time which wasn't fine and
beautiful?" See Appendices C and D.

preservation of ante-bellum attitudes toward the Negro, often
on the part of those whose families had not been slaveholders,
was part of the desire to identify with the aristocracy and
aristocratic paternalism; for this reason the legend was one of
the forces in establishing the caste system in a non-aristocratic
society.

Brief though the history of Jefferson and the period of
prestige of the Compsons and Sartorises had been, pride in
family and contrast between past splendor and present lack
of wealth and power encouraged the nostalgic glorification
of the past which has characterized the South and has been
prominently reflected in literature. The Southern tendency
to rhetoric and reminiscence was stimulated by conditions in
which the present generation lacked opportunity to display the
initiative and adventurousness of their predecessors or faced
insurmountable obstacles. But the narrow geographic range
of activities, with successive generations being born, living, and
dying within the same community and even in the same
family house, cast glamour on those ancestors who, showing
initiative and energy lacking in their descendants, carved out
a whole new civilization in the wilderness. The order they
established, contrasted with the new disorder in which people
did not know their place, took on a nostalgic glow. Consequently resistance to change developed, with pressure toward
conformity and exclusion of criticism from within or without.
What C. Vann Woodward said of the South in 1850 applies
also to the post-war South: "it set about to celebrate, glorify,
and render all but sacrosanct with praise" the very system
responsible for the plight of the South.[96]

Twentieth-century society in Jefferson, therefore, represented
a conservative, stratified class and caste structure strongly
marked by the traditional values of those who clung to the

---

[96] C. Vann Woodward, "The Irony of Southern History," in *Southern Renascence,* Louis D. Rubin and Robert D. Jacobs, eds., p. 73. In
The Growth of Southern Civilization, Eaton notes that the worst
effect of the slave regime was "the suppression of freedom of thought
and expression . . . and the creation of a profoundly conservative attitude toward social reforms" (p. 97).

past because the present had little to offer.[97] The descendants
of plantation aristocracy or of the original settlers of the town
had the strongest motive for this attitude: they could retain
prestige if their society continued to respect families eminent
in the past, regardless of present economic status. Analysis of
Southern aristocracy by sociologists, such as Powdermaker
and Dollard, or by social historians, such as Cash, and the
personal testimony of Southerners of leading families, such as
the Percys, the Pattons, and the Lumpkins, all serve to describe and explain the best families in Jefferson, maintaining
their aristocratic prestige regardless of their lowered economic
status and declining social activity. Social preeminence had
passed to the merchant, the banker, the lawyer in the New
South[98]; in Jefferson the Sartorises and the Stevenses combined aristocracy and social function.

The Compsons best represent what might be called the
aristocratic syndrome: exaggeration of the origins of the family
in claiming high estate, with failure to admit middle-class
status past or present[99]; the emphasis, characteristic of a closed,
rigid class system, on family background instead of merit[100];
emphasis on family rather than on wealth, poverty being a

[97] Hortense Powdermaker's "Cottonville," in *After Freedom,* closely
resembles Oxford-Jefferson, in being a Mississippi county seat between
Memphis and Jackson, the center of county life, and being similar in
layout. It dates back only to the 1850s and has a larger proportion of
Negroes, with a more fully developed Negro class society. In *Deep
South,* by Allison Davis and Burleigh and Mary Gardner, Old City and
Old County offer many parallels with Yoknapatawpha (Chicago: The
University of Chicago Press, Phoenix Books, 1965). James Silver says
in the Foreword: *"Deep South* is a reliable guide to an understanding
of the revolution now taking place in Mississippi."

[98] In *Revolt of the Rednecks: Mississippi Politics, 1876–1925* (Lexington: University of Kentucky Press, 1951), Albert D. Kirwan lists the
merchant, the banker, and the lawyer as having social preeminence (p.
43).

[99] Powdermaker, p. 19. Davis and Gardner describe the upper class
as deriving status from the family past, with the "founder of the
family line" being the "first wealthy planter in the local community."
"The lineage must be a strictly local one" (pp. 75, 85, 191).

[100] Myrdal, p. 674.

badge of superiority.[101] The shallowness of the Compson
pretension to aristocracy is evident in their lack of the principles of *noblesse oblige,* of responsibility beyond the family, to
justify privilege by moral superiority and good works.[102]
The Compsons also illustrate, pathetically or tragically, the
retreat into the past and withdrawal from participation in the
present which occurs when members of a leading family cannot retain or regain eminence by their own merits and can
only cling desperately to their family tree. After Jason Lycurgus I, the lucky gambler, won the domain from the foolish
and irresponsible Ikkemotubbe, the family under General
Compson reverted to the tradition of being on the losing side
and lapsed into apathy. Jason III, trained as a lawyer, a prestige profession, "sat all day long with a decanter of whiskey
and a litter of dogeared Horaces and Livys and Catulluses,
composing . . . caustic and satiric eulogies on both his dead
and his living fellowtownsmen" (*The Sound and the Fury,*
p. 8). Like Cash's "dwindling few who still clung to nostalgia
and barred shutters,"[103] Mrs. Compson was a whining hypo-
chondriac, eaten up with self-pity and jealous pride in her
own family, the Bascombs, of which her brother Maury was a
prize specimen. Lacking paternal guidance and maternal love,
Caddy was driven to rebellion and violation of the taboos that
hedged in pure Southern womanhood, Quentin committed
suicide, and Miss Quentin repeated her mother's rebellion.
Jason IV enacted a travesty of the role of the responsible head
of a family. The essential vulgarity of Jason is most evident
in his harsh and contemptuous manner toward Negroes.
When Faulkner referred to the Compson "degeneracy into

[101] The multiple aspects of the syndrome are covered in Boyle (p. 6),
Cash (pp. 126–129), and John Dollard, *Caste and Class in a Southern
Town* (Garden City, N.Y.: Doubleday Anchor Books, 1957), pp. 79–80.
[102] Such responsibility is illustrated in the assumption, by the father
of Sarah Patton Boyle, of debts which he was not legally required to
pay and by the political career of Leroy Percy and the personal battle
against prejudice of William Percy. Ralph McGill said of the tradition
of *noblesse oblige*: "There had never been much of nobility in it. It
was paternalistic and, with some few exceptions, the Negro was right
to reject it because of its connotations of inferiority" (p. 188).
[103] Cash, p. 211.

semi-madness," he was not speaking of Benjy, the idiot (*Faulkner in the University,* p. 119). That Faulkner regarded Jason and Quentin as more typical than exceptional is apparent in his remark that "there are too many Jasons in the South who can be successful, just as there are too many Quentins in the South who are too sensitive to face its reality" (*Faulkner in the University,* p. 17).

Faulkner's comment on the Compsons' semi-madness is followed by one on the "moral weakness of the Sartorises." This is significant because too often critics of Faulkner have assumed that the Sartorises represent an ideal, an interpretation borne out by neither the fiction nor Faulkner's direct comments. Colonel John Sartoris was, as has been indicated, an attractive and energetic man but no great leader or superman. He was the only Sartoris who exemplified the rarer kind of aristocrats with vision and energy. After Bayard's one act of moral heroism, when he refused to avenge his father's death, he became so rigidly conservative that he won fame in Jefferson as the sponsor of an edict "that no gasoline-propelled vehicle should ever operate on the streets of Jefferson" (*The Town,* p. 11). Modest as his role in Jefferson was in later years, he was the last of the family to attain any degree of eminence. His son John existed "for the simple continuity of the family" (*Faulkner in the University,* p. 251). His twin grandsons met violent deaths, John, killed in air combat in World War I, exhibiting the family trait of "rash recklessness which passes for physical courage" (*Faulkner in the University,* p. 250). The other twin, Bayard, seeking to equal John's daring and having.lost the will to live without his brother, caused his grandfather's death by his reckless driving and lost his own life in an airplane crash. He anticipated the James Dean type of "rebel without cause."[104]

---

[104] Although young Bayard would seem to illustrate Carlos Baker's description of the young rebel in Faulkner, "a compulsively driven, almost obsessive figure" who lacks understanding of the cause of his rebellion and power to articulate, Baker omits Bayard from his discussion of examples ("William Faulkner: The Doomed and the Damned," in *The Young Rebel in American Literature,* Carl Bode, ed. [London: Heinemann, 1959], p. 146).

In the Sartoris family, Aunt Jenny Du Pre, Colonel John's sister, represented the genuine high-minded, courageous, self-disciplined woman of quality, and Narcissa, who married young Bayard, represented the counterfeit image of pure Southern womanhood. "There Was a Queen" resolves any doubts as to Narcissa's character which *Sartoris* and *Sanctuary* may have left in the reader's mind. It is women like Granny Millard and Aunt Jenny who are the unvanquished. And it is Aunt Jenny who pronounces the verdict on the Sartoris men and their bombast and strutting and swaggering; after the famous passage near the end of *Sartoris,* about the Player and the game and "a dying fall of horns along the road to Roncevaux," Aunt Jenny remarked to Narcissa, who intended to call her infant son Benbow, not John, Sartoris: "Do you think . . . that because his name is Benbow, he'll be any less a Sartoris and a scoundrel and a fool?" The trumpet is the echo of the past, the aristocratic dignity that moved, as Cash said, to "the sound of faraway trumpets forever heralding the charge."[105] Aunt Jenny could hear the trumpets without sinking into bemused nostalgia; her exasperation with her menfolk was rooted in her devoted love. The only thing she could not bear was the dishonor brought upon the family by Narcissa ("There Was a Queen"). As the mother of the last Sartoris, Narcissa may be the answer to why the family seems to end with Benbow: in 1942, on his last appearance in Yoknapatawpha, he was a bachelor, commissioned in the air force.[106] Thus ends the old family with the best claim in Jefferson to aristocratic origin.

In his last novel, *The Reivers,* Faulkner introduces a new family, related to the McCaslins and like them from Carolina, who are obviously intended to serve as a kind of implicit comment on the Sartorises. Boss Priest, president of the other bank in Jefferson, reacted to Old Bayard's edict against automobiles by buying one, not because he wanted one but because

[105] Cash, p. 71.
[106] *Knight's Gambit,* pp. 239–240. Benbow Sartoris is mentioned in *The Mansion,* in 1937. *The Reivers,* narrated in 1961, mentions only Colonel John and old Bayard Sartoris.

he "could not permit himself to allow to stand" Colonel Sartoris's "arrogant decree" (*The Reivers,* p. 29). Young Lucius, in 1905 driving the first automobile he had ever ridden in, at the tender age of eleven, is still living in 1961, having seen the motor age transform the land and having been able to adapt with it. The code of the gentleman was taught to Lucius by his father and grandfather and is being transmitted, in solution, as it were, in the tale he tells to his grandson. The Priests thus provide an example of aristocrats who can survive while maintaining the best of the old tradition of gentility.

Members of the older families of the gentry which did not, in Faulkner's narratives, figure prominently in Jefferson before the war play a part in community life in the twentieth century suitable to their social position but display the same lack of aggressive and progressive leadership which characterizes the later generations of the ante-bellum aristocracy. Doc Peabody continued the function of his father, Dr. Habersham's successor, and remained on terms of easy friendship with the Sartorises. Professionally he associated with all classes of society. His son is a surgeon in New York. Horace Benbow, a guest with Doc Peabody at the last Thanksgiving dinner of Old and Young Bayard, was both an old friend and a family relation after Narcissa's marriage to Bayard. The descendant, presumably, of Judge Benbow and himself a lawyer, Horace by profession as well as family belongs to the socially preeminent. Because Horace lacked enough force of character and shrewdness to put into effect, as a leader of the community, his idealism, he is another example of the inability of the well-born to maintain control of society.

Gavin Stevens, another lawyer and descendant of one of the second group of settlers, like Horace is Quixotic, but as a lawyer he is more successful. A leading character in three major novels and in the short stories in *Knight's Gambit,* as well as an incidental character in other stories, Gavin has admirable qualities but is not intended to be an ideal. His evolution from the thoughtful spectator toward the active participant in community affairs remained incomplete. Faulkner admitted Gavin's lack of judgment and of knowledge of people, his reluctance to become personally involved in the world of reality, but thought him capable of learning from experience (*Faulkner in the University,* pp. 140–141). Gavin represents the atypical but not unrealistic Southerners, some of whom are writers, who returned to the South after a Northern and European education, having, as Cash said, "deliberately elected to return out of a sense of duty to the South."[107] A creditable member of the upper class in Jefferson, Gavin Stevens nevertheless reveals some of the reasons for the failure of that class to exercise positive, effective leadership and thus to serve effectively the cause of truth and justice they espoused: his Southern romanticism and rhetoric are symptomatic of his limited grasp of reality and his acceptance of much of the Southern myth.

The De Spain family, also of the aristocracy, did not degenerate mentally like the Compsons or morally like the Sartorises but "kept a certain leaven of a stronger stock by instinctive choice" (*Faulkner in the University,* p. 119). In contrast with Gavin Stevens, who served Eula Varner without reward, Manfred dared to love and to win Eula and in consequence lost his social and financial position. Manfred had strength and courage enough to be superior to Gavin Stevens and showed fidelity without benefit of clergy. He well illustrates the romanticism and hedonism which Cash finds characteristic of the South and shows how these qualities are driven underground by community morality.

The upper classes in Jefferson in the twentieth century produced no effective leaders; the ruthless pioneer adventurers or chivalric but aggressive aristocrats had no descendants able to enlarge or even to retain their ancestral heritage. At the end of *The Mansion* the Compson estate has disappeared, the De Spain mansion has reverted to a "bedridden old woman" and her daughter, a retired school teacher, and Gavin Stevens is living on the estate his wife inherited from her father, with Hollywood-style improvements made by her bootlegger first

[107] Cash, p. 328.

husband. The one hope remaining among the "best" families, in addition to young Lucius Priest, is Charles Mallison, Gavin Stevens's nephew, of whom Faulkner said: "I think he may grow up to be a better man than his uncle; I think he may succeed as a human being."[108]

When the leading characters in Yoknapatawpha are sorted into social classes, a peculiarity in distribution appears: there are few characters who are definitely middle class, with neither pretension to gentility nor origin in the lower class. Explanations of the small part played by the middle class in Faulkner's Jefferson may be found in V. O. Key's comment on the absence of a middle class in the agrarian economy and in Cash's account of the late development of the middle class as a consequence of the growth of industry and the development of towns in the rural South; by the 1920s the middle class was "clearly marked out": "a numerous army, ranging from small property-owners, small traders and small speculators, and run-of-the-mine professional men, down through clerks, bookkeepers, schoolteachers, and white-collar people of every sort."[109] Faulkner remarked that "the middle class has been broken down. It no longer exists as a homogeneous condition recognized by everyone everywhere" (*Faulkner in the University,* pp. 188–189), but he was speaking generally. There is no evidence that it ever existed as "a homogeneous condition" in Jefferson. Although, as Myrdal observed, most Americans consider themselves middle-class, Hortense Powdermaker notes, and Myrdal confirms, that in the South white people tend to identify themselves with the aristocratic tra-

---

[108] Quoted in "The Curse and the Hope," *Time,* LXXXIV (July 17, 1964), 45. At the end of *The Mansion,* in 1946, Charles is back in Jefferson, a veteran of World War II, trained as a lawyer but still unmarried.

[109] V. O. Key, *Southern Politics* (New York: Vintage Books, Caravelle Edition, 1949), p. 240; Cash, p. 272. Clement Eaton in *The Growth of Southern Civilization* explains that the role of the middle class before the Civil War was not adequately understood until the census returns of 1850 and 1860 had been studied, in the 1940s: "the middle class in the ante-bellum South included not only the large body of yeoman farmers but also the mechanics, tradesmen, and overseers" (pp. 151, 160).

dition and do not admit to being middle class.[110] This is apparent in the actual modest economic status of the gentry in Jefferson.

The middle class in Jefferson reflects mobility both downward and upward, as well as maintenance of class level. Two members of the aristocracy, as descendants of the first settlers, have come down to the middle class in their way of life by adopting lower-middle-class occupations. Miss Eunice Habersham (*Intruder in the Dust*) was forced by the decline in family fortunes to live in the unpainted family mansion with two Negro servants and raise and peddle vegetables and chickens. Her expensive gloves and shoes were the badge of her gentility. Her gentility was equalled only by her courage, loyalty, compassion, and sense of responsibility. Not only does Miss Habersham provide a classic example of the traditional situation of an impoverished family and the loyalty of former slaves to their unfortunate masters or mistresses but she also provides a contrast with the Compsons, casting light on their failure to cope with their misfortune with dignity, energy, and integrity. Isaac McCaslin, after repudiating his McCaslin inheritance, became a carpenter and later ran a hardware store. Like Miss Habersham, he retained his social prestige without town social life.[111]

Those who have risen to middle-class status are few in num-

[110] Myrdal, pp. 670, 597; Powdermaker, p. 19; Russell Warren Howe, "Prejudice, Superstition, and Economics," refers to the rarity of middle-class thinking in the South and the prevailing peasant mentality in the country (p. 223). By removing the university, Oxford's chief "industry," from Jefferson, Faulkner also removed the portion or proportion of the middle class that depends largely on the university community for professional and business patronage.

[111] Cash devotes several paragraphs to the type represented by Miss Habersham, and its "high pride, unflinching and undismayed" (pp. 158–159). Miss Worsham in "Go Down, Moses" seems to be the same person as Miss Habersham, with the same devotion to Molly Beauchamp and her family. Apparently Faulkner decided in *Intruder in the Dust* to make Dr. Habersham one of his first settlers and continued the "history" of the family in *Requiem for a Nun*. Miss Habersham and Ike McCaslin illustrate the retention of aristocratic status despite loss of wealth and abstention from aristocratic social life (Davis and Gardner, pp. 195–196).

ber, in comparison with the great upward mobility in the social structure of the United States.[112] The Snopeses, especially Flem, are the most notable examples of those social climbers, aptly called *strainers,* who rose from the lower class and who, Cash said, were regarded with pride and admiration by the less fortunate.[113] Among the Snopeses there are clearcut distinctions. Flem, the perfect strainer, devotes his energies to attaining all the outward symbols of economic success and respectability, but his basic insecurity motivates the abstemious behavior which Dollard cites as typical of his kind.[114] But economic success and active membership in the Baptist church did not suffice to admit him to the ranks of the gentry.[115] Senator Clarence Snopes had a specious political success and remained impossibly crude and vulgar. In contrast with Flem, Wallstreet Panic Snopes and Admiral Dewey, his younger brother, won respect by their success in a wholesale grocery and did not aspire above their middle-class station. Typical Snopeses who improved their status by their own efforts or through Flem's influence failed to retain their middle-class status in Jefferson. The most disgraceful examples are Byron Snopes, bank embezzler, and Montgomery Ward Snopes, purveyor of pornography. Cash's account of the rise of poor whites and its effect on both the ruling class and the submerged masses sounds like a history of the Snopeses.[116]

[112] John Dollard's "Southerntown" has a large number of people who have risen to the middle class (p. 95).

[113] Cash, p. 227.

[114] Dollard, p. 78. Flem's "respectability" labels him as middle class, in contrast with the freer conduct of aristocrats like De Spain (Davis and Gardner, pp. 74–75, 76–77).

[115] Dollard emphasizes the fact that, to belong to the aristocratic upper class, one has to "have a certain kind of memory of the past and to hold a certain role in the eyes of others with similar memories" (p. 79). Ralph McGill's description of the "small-town rich man" who is the "real enemy," the "malignant rural miniature" of the robber barons, fits Flem remarkably well, from the "repellent and hard" manner and the home which sustained "the legend of the South as a place of many mansions" to his business and community activities (pp. 161–164).

[116] Cash, p. 168. *Snopes* seems to be Faulkner's own inspired coinage, but it has a parallel and possible origin in Ransy Sniffle, in Augustus

In attitudes, occupation, and way of life Jason Compson had
more in common with the shrewder, more successful Flem
Snopes than with the rest of the Compsons. Since Mrs. Compson reiterates that Jason resembles her family, the Bascombs,
of whom we know little except for her brother Maury, one
might infer that they were middle class and perhaps lower
middle class, unsuccessful strainers except for the marriage of
one of their clan to a gone-to-seed Compson. Maury's chimer-
ical schemes and his epistolary style suggest that the Bascombs,
if the truth were known, might furnish a parallel to the
Micawbers, with their pretensions to middle-class status despite financial incompetence. Jason's subordination of every
humane consideration to keeping up appearances is like
Flem's "respectability," in contrast to the genuine gentility of
Miss Habersham. Jason's treatment of Negroes shows his lack
of aristocratic feeling. In Jason, the family dwindles out into
middle-class mediocrity from which it had broken away by
the attachment of the Glasgow printer to the lost cause of
the Stuarts. The Compsons first were middle-class gamblers,
then vulgar rich imitators of the genuine aristocrats. With
the collapse of the family fortunes through General Compson's apathy, the family returned to the middle-class mediocrity from which, by a stroke of luck, it had emerged. Jason
represents the new middle class, with no prospect of realizing
his dreams. Cash describes his type: "Every trader, every clerk,
every bookkeeper, committed to the illusion of free and un-
limited opportunity, was engrossed in dreams or schemes
whereunder, he felt, he would surely achieve position and
wealth for himself out of the rosy whirl about him."[117] In
1928 Jason was playing the cotton market and defrauding his
niece; in 1942 he had lost the last of the Compson Mile and
a Snopes was living in the converted carriage house (*The
Mansion,* p. 328).

The middle class is better represented than might appear

Baldwin Longstreet's *Georgia Scenes.* In *Old Times in the Faulkner
Country* (Chapel Hill: University of North Carolina Press, 1961), John
Cullen tells about "Senator Snipes's (not Snopes) son, Hubert" (p. 81).
[117] Cash, p. 272.

from the above examples. V. K. Ratliff is really a middle-class character but he achieved a kind of classless social position. The family was of mixed Russian and poor-white origin, traced back to the Revolutionary War; a Ratcliffe was the agent at the Indian trading post before Jefferson was founded. The family of Suratt, in *Sartoris* (p. 141), was poor white; presumably both character and background carry over to Ratliff, merely the name being changed.[118] As an agent for sewing machines, radios, and television, in natural sequence, Ratliff associates in business with all social classes. But because of his shrewd intelligence and disinterested sense of civic responsibility, he mixes on terms of social equality with his social superiors, especially Gavin Stevens and Charles Mallison. He links town and country and the social classes in both and exhibits middle-class virtues and classless wisdom. Through him, the middle class is better represented than mere numbers of middle-class characters might suggest.

Furthermore, a substantial number of extras, some of whom appear in a number of different works and many of whom belong to the middle class, fill in the social class structure of the white caste. These extras may be grouped chiefly as small merchants and their clerks; office workers, especially in banks; some of the local law-enforcement personnel, such as jailers and sheriffs; professional men, including lawyers, judges, and doctors not belonging to leading families. A few examples of recurring characters in this general category will suffice. Uncle Willy Christian, the druggist in *The Town, The Mansion,* and *The Reivers* and the short story, "Uncle Willy," and Skeets McGowan, in *As I Lay Dying, Intruder in the Dust, The Town,* and *The Mansion,* represent retail merchants and clerks—though probably not typical in their personal characters. The Hamptons, father, son, and grandson, alternate terms as sheriff with Ephriam Bishop, running their farm in

---

[118] There is a connection between the two names which seems more than coincidental: according to the *Military History of Mississippi* W. T. Ratliff was a lieutenant in the First Regiment, Mississippi Artillery, and M. Surratt was Quartermaster in the Second Regiment, Infantry, of which William C. Falkner was Colonel (pp. 849, 426).

the terms when they are not in office. The reference in *The Reivers* to the third Hub Hampton, in 1961, emphasizes the significance of the official role and the family.

There are few poor whites in Jefferson. If, like Flem Snopes, they get to town, they do so by ceasing to be sharecroppers. Some may be minor law officials, such as night marshals. The planing mill in *Light in August* represents gradations from poor white to middle class: at the bottom are shiftless workers like Lucas Burch; above him potentially is Joe Christmas, in dress and manner imitating middle-class city people; Byron Bunch may have been poor white to begin with but has risen to steady middle-class status and standards by industry and self-discipline. The foreman, Mooney, and the superintendent, Simms, are in the management class. Jefferson, with few industries, has few opportunities for white working men.

The Negroes in Jefferson are, of course, the working class. The class stratification in the Negro caste is not apparent in Jefferson because the community is too small to provide enough professional and business opportunities for Negroes, limited as they would be to the patronage of their own race. Hence upper-class Negro imitation of middle-class white culture is not illustrated. Most of the Negroes in Jefferson who are individualized are servants, often in the same family in which they or their elders were slaves before the war. Association with a leading white family lends prestige to Negro servants, who are identified with the white family and like them pride themselves on successive generations in a superior status. The Sartoris servants represent the "quality" Negroes, especially Simon, who is himself a kind of status symbol as part of Colonel Bayard's aristocratic equipage, and his putative daughter, Elnora, who scorns trash and admires "quality," though perhaps without knowing she was the daughter of Colonel John Sartoris ("There Was a Queen," p. 727). The Negroes in *Sartoris* are closer to fictional stereotypes than those in later works. Simon is lustful and financially irresponsible and meets his death at the hands of a jealous rival, after spending on the mulatto servant maid the church money entrusted to him. His life-long service to the family gives him certain privileges, such as getting money from Colonel Bayard to pay back what he had "laid out," in imitation of Bayard's practice as a banker (*Sartoris,* pp. 233, 274–275). Caspey, returned from service in World War I, represents the impudent Negro service man who does not know his place; he is knocked down by Old Bayard (*Sartoris,* p. 83). Simon and Caspey present the contrast in attitude of different generations; Simon illustrates the Negro who knows his place but who also plays his role to secure lenient treatment by amusing his white master with his rascality, while Caspey adopts a role not permitted by the stereotype and suffers accordingly. Neither is a particularly worthy character.

The Compson servants, the Gibsons, in *The Sound and the Fury,* show the extremes of responsibility and irresponsibility in different generations, and are most significant in their relationships with their white employers. The family structure, with Dilsey as the center of the several generations, is typical of lower-class Negroes. Luster, as a boy assigned the tedious duty of tending the idiot Benjy, understandably seeks amusement. Each generation of young Gibsons has taken his turn at tending Benjy: Versh, T. P., then Luster. Similarly, each drives the horse. Dilsey assumes full responsibility not only for her own duties but for supervising those of her children or grandchild. Because she bears the whole burden of the Compson household, she "talks back" on occasion, especially to Jason in defense of Miss Quentin or Benjy. Treated by Jason and his mother with neither respect nor kindness, Dilsey demonstrates the traditional Negro virtues of patience and love of children plus individual competence, dignity, and deep religious fervor, qualities unrecognized by the white people whom she serves.

The good side of Negro-white relationships is seen in the foster-brother or -sister companionship when loyalties established in childhood prove lasting. Ringo and Bayard, in *The Unvanquished,* have a modern parallel in Charles Mallison and Aleck Sander in *Intruder in the Dust*; although Aleck Sander is merely the son of Mallisons' cook, his loyalty to Charles makes him willing to risk his life, not for Lucas—

"It's the ones like Lucas makes trouble for everybody"—but for Charles. Miss Habersham's motive is similar but even stronger: Molly, Lucas's wife, and Miss Habersham were the same age, both nursed by Molly's mother, one of old Dr. Habersham's slaves, and were bound by ties of genuine family feeling. (Miss Worsham in "Go Down, Moses" bears the same relationship and attitude toward Molly.)

Incidental Negroes in Jefferson, like old Job in *The Sound and the Fury,* show the free Negro without a white patron, maintaining his independence by devious self-assertion while conforming to or illustrating the stereotype. Willing to spend hard-earned money for pleasure, Job shows that Jason's inability to enjoy himself is the white man's deficiency. His responses to Jason show genuine wisdom and humor but allow Jason to feel superior; admitting that Jason is too smart for him, Job has the last word: Jason is so smart he can't even keep up with himself (pp. 248–249, 267). Old Het, in *The Town,* lives on charity and provides, she realizes, opportunity for folks to be blessed by being givers (p. 245).

Negroes as criminals or social undesirables are represented also, but always matched with their white counterparts: Nancy the dope addict and prostitute is hired by Temple Drake because they have so much in common, and Nancy tries to save the soul of Temple (*Requiem for a Nun*); Minnie works for Miss Reba, in *Sanctuary* and *The Reivers*; Joe Christmas, possibly part Negro, is a bootlegger, but so is Lucas Burch, and the customers are white men. And as Uncle Ned says about Bobo Beauchamp: "Everybody got kinfolks that aint got no more sense than Bobo" (*The Reivers,* p. 293). The execution of Butch Beauchamp, in *Go Down, Moses,* reminds one of that of Popeye in *Sanctuary.* And, as Molly repeats, it was Roth who sold his young kinsman into Egypt, showing less responsibility for Butch than Uncle Ned showed for Bobo.

Of upper-class Negroes in Jefferson, there is only one, belatedly introduced: the high school principal in *The Mansion,* "the intelligent dedicated man with his composed and tragic face," who asked Gavin and Linda to give Negroes their friendship all of the time and their help when needed but to keep their patronage until the Negroes asked for it, until the white people would want to say "Please" to the Negroes because there was a need for Negroes in the economy (*The Mansion,* pp. 224–225).[119] Not only is there no trace of the stereotype in this upper-class Negro but the sentiments he expresses as well as the language in which they are couched are very close to Faulkner's own. The degree to which Ike McCaslin falls short of an ideal appears in the other passage in which an educated Negro is introduced, in "Delta Autumn," when the young granddaughter of James Beauchamp, a schoolteacher but niece of a washerwoman, shows more depth of feeling and dignity than Ike does.

The invisible barrier between whites and Negroes may exist also between members of the same caste. Faulkner's use of the theme of isolation is well known. In terms of social class structure and place in the community, the isolation or ostracism that excludes individuals from their proper place is usually involved directly with problems of race. The nature of the exclusion varies: it may be withdrawal by the individual or ostracism by the community, open defiance of society, or desire to redeem society.

Although the Sutpen story belongs to the nineteenth century, it is of vital significance. The exclusion of Sutpen by Jefferson society, with the exception of General Compson and his wife, made the isolation and withdrawal of Judith scarcely noticeable. The stories about Sutpen fighting with his own Negroes for sport and the common knowledge that, not merely was Clytie Sutpen's daughter, but Sutpen made no attempt to conceal the fact, would increase public disapproval

---

[119] The passage (p. 223) preceding the one summarized testifies to the "simple humanity" of a "gentle and tender people," to use Gavin's terms, when their problems are not "from the passions of want and ignorance and fear" and to their knowledge that Linda, if she persisted in her efforts to help the Negroes, would be destroyed by the ignorance and superstition of the white people. The principal represents the Negro leader who "can get things from the whites" and will not lose his own power and "endanger the welfare of the whole Negro community" by ineffective aggressiveness (Myrdal, pp. 770–771).

or condemnation.[120] The story of Wash Jones well represents the identification of the poor white with the planter after the war. Although Sutpen's problems were essentially those of his relationships with the Negro race—his failure to adopt a paternalistic attitude toward them like that of the other planters, his overt fathering of a child by a Negro slave and his hidden refusal to acknowledge his fatherhood of part-Negro Charles Bon—his poor-white origin and his relationship with Wash throw light on the class structure. He defended slavery because, as Lillian Smith points out, those who rose from poor-white status had to defend what they had invested their integrity in.[121] Those who still hoped to rise or could vicariously identify themselves with the planters, as Wash did with Sutpen, also defended the system. Thus in Sutpen and Wash may be seen a symbol of the alliance between the upper-class and the lower-class whites which served to keep the Negro in his inferior status, and in the killing of Sutpen by Wash may be seen a symbol of what happens if the poor white realizes that he, like the Negro, is regarded as of less value than a fine animal.

The Burden family, as carpetbaggers, went into Mississippi to redeem the society and were rejected, the grandfather and young Calvin shot and Joanna ostracized. Joanna represents, as a type of individual, the Yankee schoolmarm and the Southern reaction to the type. In the summer of 1964 young college boys and girls went into Mississippi in somewhat the same spirit as the dedicated Northern teachers and met at best the same hostility.

Doc Hines represents the opposite extreme from the Burdens, the fanatic who hates and persecutes Negroes but preaches to them. Isolated from Mottstown by his unbalanced mind, he is forgiven by the community for "that which in a young man

[120] In Shirley Ann Grau's *The Keepers of the House* what rouses the community to viciousness and violence against the Howlands is the fact that their Negro relatives are not only acknowledged but are the legal offspring of William Howland.

[121] Smith, p. 147. Du Bois's comment that, to the poor whites, "the only heaven that attracted was the life of the great Southern planter" (*Black Reconstruction*, p. 27) was true first of Sutpen and then of Wash.

it would have crucified," his preaching to Negroes, and is being supported by Negro charity (*Light in August,* p. 299). The paradoxical actions of the Negroes are explained by G. W. Odum's comment that Negroes will assent to abuse of the Negro and by the fact that Negro compassion is stronger than resentment.[122]

Since the possibility of Joe Christmas's having Negro blood was not known in Jefferson until after the murder of Joanna Burden, his alienation was due to his own search for identity and his secret defiance of the racial code and overt rejection of association with whites of respectable standing. He would not accept food from Byron, nor, when he brought his own food, eat with the other men. The defensive mask of the Negro he wore habitually. He dressed like a white man and wore a hat. Throughout his association with Joanna Burden, who did learn of his belief that he had Negro blood, the racial etiquette was usually observed even though the primary purpose for it was soon violated. Precisely so a white man who would not sit with a Negro woman or eat with her might have sexual relations with her. Joe never came into the house by the front door, Joe always ate alone—or rejected the food because it had been set out *For the nigger,* to be eaten in the kitchen. Joe and Joanna always stood while talking. The episode in his cabin, when she sat beside him on his cot and talked to him, is the more astonishing because it is a quiet and innocent violation of the etiquette.

Unorthodox attitudes concerning race were permitted the McCaslins, perhaps because of their social prestige, perhaps because Carothers' deviation was not apparent until his death, when he willed money to his Negro descendants. Buck and Buddy, living in a cabin and putting the Negroes in the big house and freeing some of their slaves after their father died, were tolerated as eccentrics; their patriotic fervor during the Civil War was as great as if they had believed in slavery as morally right. Isaac's repudiation of his inheritance did not affect his status in the community; it is safe to say that a direct

[122] Quoted by Dollard, p. 180, footnote 5.

and active effort on his part to alter the status of Negroes or
even to ignore conventions would have aroused public feeling.
In Roth Edmonds the cycle is complete: the deviation in Buck
and Buddy and Ike is cancelled by Roth's repetition of the offense of old Carothers, that of fathering a child with Negro
blood and paying money rather than saying "My son" to a
Negro, and by Ike's condoning of Roth's action ("Delta Autumn").

VII.   *Caste and Class in Rural Society*

Three major class groups in Yoknapatawpha County are not
represented in significant numbers in Jefferson: the yeoman
farmers, the poor whites, and the Negro farm workers. There is,
moreover, no rural community which notably includes all three.
The Negroes are found chiefly on the plantations, the farmers
and poor whites in the Frenchman's Bend area. The curse and
guilt of the caste system is absent from Frenchman's Bend,
but social injustice is present in the domination of the poorer
whites by merchants and landlords.

In Frenchman's Bend, Uncle Will Varner illustrates the
merchant and landowner who controls the economic lives of
the whites, like the typical country-store keeper described by
Clark: "He was a puppet master who made his community
go through its peculiar economic dance."[123] Varner is an example of the supply merchants that Cash describes as the
real ruling class by the early 1900s, and like them was of the
yeoman farmer stock which made up the ruling class in
"primitive local communities."[124] From Varner, with his two-

---

[123] Clark, p. 53. Cash also states the role of the supply merchant (pp.
150–152). The country store and the merchants will be dealt with in
detail in the next chapter.
[124] Cash, p. 209. Hathorn's statement that land along the Yocona
River was not at first considered valuable explains why the Frenchman's

FAULKNER'S CHILDHOOD HOME

". . . the house . . . was about five hundred feet back from the street" (J. Faulkner, *My Brother Bill,* p. 14).

ROWAN OAK

". . . the house itself was still and serenely benignant" (*Sartoris*, p. 7).

FAULKNER'S FARM

"My life is farmland and horses and the raising of grain and feed"
(*Faulkner at Nagano*, p. 142).

J. R. Cofield

COURTHOUSE, OXFORD, 1862
Tents of an Illinois regiment, during Grant's occupation.

COURTHOUSE, CONFEDERATE MONUMENT,
FEDERAL COURTHOUSE–POSTOFFICE

"The stone infantryman on his stone pedestal" stared "toward the
south" (*Requiem for a Nun*, pp. 239–240).

FLEM'S MANSION

With "colyums across the front" (*The Town*, p. 342).

OFFICE OF PHIL STONE

"A one storey building of
brick trimmed with white"
(*The Sound and the Fury*,
p. 161).

COTTON GIN, OXFORD

"Draped with feathery soiled festoons of lint" (*Sartoris,* p. 168),
"the town water tank spiderlegged elongate against the blue"
(*Intruder in the Dust,* p. 115).

MONUMENT OF COLONEL FALKNER, RIPLEY

"John Sartoris' effigy lifted its florid stone gesture" (*Sartoris*, p. 304).

FAULKNER'S GRAVE

"Simple: no Sartoris man to invent bombast to put on it" (*Sartoris*, p. 374).

COLLEGE HILL PRESBYTERIAN CHURCH
One of "the two oldest congregations in the county" (*The Town,*
p. 307).

Jones–Miller house

Graveyard, Jones–Miller house

YOKNAPATAWPHA RIVER

VIEW FROM INDIAN MOUND, SARDIS RESERVOIR

MAIN STREET, TOCCOPOLA

TOCCOPOLA

"A weathered paintless dog-trot cabin" (*The Mansion*, p. 399).

Negro cabin, Oxford

"Sagging fences gaudy with drying overalls and aprons" (*Intruder in the Dust*, p. 147).

COUNTRY STORE NEAR OXFORD

J. R. Cofield

BRONZE HEAD OF FAULKNER BY LEON KHOURY, 1965

storey house and his servants, down to the landless and destitute tenant farmer is a gradation of economic levels, from
comfort down through subsistence to privation. Not in the
Frenchman's Bend area but northeast of Jefferson are clannish
hill-dwellers who fill places in the economic chain. The Mc-
Callums own land, employ Negro servants, establish a heritage, and are friends of the Sartorises. They share the Delta
belief, cited by Key, that federal aid is "destructive of moral
fiber," as they demonstrate in "The Tall Men."[125] The Gowries, another clannish family of father and sons, engage freely
in illegal activities; they lack the rustic gentility of the Mc-
Callums and scorn the white society that scorns them. They
are like the mountaineers Cash describes, with their cultural
backwardness and hatred of Negroes.[126] A group of small
farmers in Frenchman's Bend, competent enough to be self-
sustaining though living modestly in one-storey unpainted
cabins, includes Tulls, Quicks, Bookwrights, and others who
appear in more or less minor roles in *The Hamlet* and other
Yoknapatawpha novels and short stories. The daughter of
Bookwright married Houston who acquired property and was
the only person besides Varner employing Negro help. On
the borderline, apparently, between bare subsistence and poor-
white privation are several other families: the incompetent
Res Grier whose sons are superior to their father; the luckless
Anse Bundren, whose one competent son was Cash.

The Henry Armstids in *The Hamlet,* the most bitterly poor
of the families in the area, own only one disintegrating mattress for a family of seven (*The Hamlet,* p. 361). Although
they apparently own land, their way of life is as miserable as

Bend area was settled by farmers rather than planters (p. 22). As Eaton
explains in *The Growth of Southern Civilization,* the planters could
buy the richest public lands and the yeoman "had to buy the cheaper
lands at the minimum price" (p. 155).

[125] Key, p. 243.

[126] Cash, p. 219. Faulkner's use of "Caledonia" in referring to the
Gowrie district in *Intruder in the Dust* suggests that Beat Four is a
highland fastness and that there are notable similarities between Scotland and the South (Elmo Howell, "William Faulkner's Caledonia: A
Note on *Intruder in the Dust,*" *Studies in Scottish Literature,* III [1966],
248–249).

that of the lowest of the white caste, such as Mink Snopes. Shields McIlwaine, in *The Southern Poor-White from Lubberland to Tobacco Road,* calls Anse Bundren the first important poor white in contemporary American fiction.[127] Anse certainly displays poor-white mentality, but, as a landowner, he has a slight advantage over the tenant families who are the typical poor whites. Except for caste status, these poor whites are as low socially and economically as the lowest Negro. The documentary account of tenant farmers by James Agee and Walker Evans, *Let Us Now Praise Famous Men,* could be used to illustrate Yoknapatawpha. Cash explains the poor whites as "merely the weakest elements of the old backcountry population," who were pushed back to the poorest lands and barred from advance; they were characterized by lankness, colorlessness, and indolence.[128] The swampers who appear briefly in "The Bear" exemplify the type (*Go Down, Moses,* p. 222).

Mink Snopes is the most fully developed poor-white character in Yoknapatawpha. The destitution of Mink and his family and his cabin in *The Hamlet* ("The Long Summer," p. 2) and in *The Mansion* (Chapter One) is confirmed by Cash[129] and by both pictures and text in *Let Us Now Praise Famous Men.* Mink was worse fed, clothed, and housed than Houston's hired Negroes. After selling his cotton and paying Varner his share as landlord and his "furnish" bill at Varner's store, Mink would have left only eight or ten dollars for his

[127] Shields McIlwaine, *The Southern Poor-White from Lubberland to Tobacco Road* (Norman: University of Oklahoma Press, 1939), p. 228.

[128] Cash, pp. 24–25. Mary Chesnut's description of the "sand-hill tacky," living on charity and never bettering himself, resembles Cash's picture (*A Diary from Dixie,* pp. 542–543). McIlwaine lists squatters, sharecroppers, and tenants as generally poor white, lacking material and psychological resources (p. xvii). In *The Growth of Southern Civilization,* Eaton identifies the poor whites as the victims of bad environment and enervating diseases; they might be squatters or own land; not all those who were landless were poor whites (p. 169). Poor whites were typically lacking in energy and industry and felt inferior but "had a striking personal pride" (pp. 169, 170).

[129] Cash, pp. 24–27.

year's work. He was that much better off than those who re-mained in debt to the landlord. Lacking the upper-class white patrons which Negroes might have, the poor whites had only the advantage of caste in competition with Negroes and the opportunity to improve their status if they were of superior ability. But even when Mink picked cotton for a Negro, he was treated with the respect due the white caste (*The Mansion,* pp. 400–403).

Three patterns of poor-white lives can be distinguished in Yoknapatawpha. Mink Snopes is the poor white whose physical and mental limitations make him unable by his own un-aided efforts to rise above his destitution. Physically stunted and mentally a child, except for a kind of shrewd cunning, Mink may well reveal effects of inadequate diet. Flem is the second type, the one who can achieve economic success in terms of his own limited scope and can to all outward appear-ances attain middle-class respectability, but who lacks intel-ligence and imagination enough to find other than economic satisfaction in life. Of such men whose fathers had been share-croppers there were, Cash says, "precious few." Cash describes the pattern of success of those few, beginning at the bottom, and the accompanying "constant elevation" of relatives. Relatives (like Mink) who were not elevated or were unable to maintain higher status were confirmed by one success in the family in their illusion of "free and open opportunity" and accepted their own failure as bad luck.[130] Sutpen is the third type, the poor white of physical stamina and intellectual vigor, capable of dreaming fine dreams. Sutpen, like Flem, failed to win complete acceptance by the upper class, though on his own initiative and guided by some taste for luxury he could ape the aristocratic way of life. Flem's success is more typical than Sutpen's of what a poor white can achieve, but Flem is most typical of the rapacious, materialistic opportunist rather than of any one class, except as he, like Sutpen, was goaded to effort by early degradation.

The poor whites in *The Hamlet* have few contacts with

[130] *Ibid.,* pp. 210, 168.

Negroes. Those in the McCallum-Gowrie area, near large plantations, are closer to Negro farmers and tenant farmers. One of the finest passages in *Sartoris* (pp. 343–350) is the account of Young Bayard's Christmas with a Negro family who shared with him their meager food and the Christmas treats of bananas and cocoanut. Bayard ignored racial etiquette here by insisting that the family eat with him, rather than waiting till Bayard had finished.

Most of the Negroes developed in detail are associated with the McCaslin-Edmonds family. Rider, hero of "Pantaloon in Black," rents a house from Edmonds.[131] He best exemplifies the competent Negro who adopts middle-class standards of family life, with the husband as the head and breadwinner, pledged to marital fidelity, assuming responsibility for improving living conditions. His way of life and his grief for his dead young wife destroy the stereotypes; the deputy sheriff, blinded by the stereotype, sees in Rider only animal lack of feeling.

Two Negroes of McCaslin blood, Uncle Ned McCaslin and Lucas Beauchamp, represent two contrasting ways of dealing with white society: Uncle Ned accommodates to it, Lucas defies or ignores it. In *The Reivers,* Ned is called "Uncle" by the little Priest boys because Ned, too, has McCaslin blood (p. 30). With Lucius, Ned relaxed etiquette and referred to Boon without the *Mr.* and was reprimanded by the boy, though Ned was superior to Boon in every way and Boon had Indian blood. With Boon, when Ned became a passenger instead of a stowaway, Ned acted the clown a bit, but with Miss Reba, Lucius said, he dropped both "the spoiled immune privileged-retainer impudence of his relations with Boon and the avuncular bossiness of those with me" and talked sense (p. 128). The difference between Lucius and Otis in social class is clear: Otis called Ned "nigger" (p. 143). Ned's Masonic connections exemplify the Negro's fondness for social organizations, in which Negroes are, as Myrdal remarks,

---

[131] Although Faulkner regarded Rider as a McCaslin Negro, he did not say so in the story (Cowley, p. 113).

merely " 'exaggerated' Americans."[132] This point is implicit in Lucius's comment that his grandfather is a Mason too. Ned's shrewd appraisal of Butch, the white-trash sheriff who insulted Ned and Uncle Parsham, is a fair sample of the contrast between the Uncle Remus role Ned adopted when necessary with his white inferiors and his real thoughts. To younger Negroes, somewhat to the surprise of Lucius, Ned was "Mr. McCaslin." With Lucius and with other Negroes, Ned was never Uncle Remus (p. 182). With Boss Priest and Colonel Linscomb and Mr. van Tosch, Ned was on his dignity and observed racial etiquette: he would not drink the whiskey given him until told to; the second time he merely set the glass on the mantel (pp. 285, 293).[133] His explanation of what white men's reactions would have been to Bobo throws light on the way in which the Negro can predict stereotyped responses to individual problems.

The other leading Negro character in *The Reivers,* Uncle Parsham, is so fully the patrician gentleman that Lucius as narrator refers to him as "the aristocrat of us all and judge of us all" (p. 176). The dignity and decorum of his way of life and the delicate tact with which he helped little Lucius to regain self-control made him a wholly adequate substitute for Lucius's own grandfather, and Lucius responded with equal tact, eating with Uncle Parsham and gladly sharing his bed, disclaiming the only possible reason for not doing so: his grandfather snored too and Lucius didn't mind (p. 250).

Uncle Parsham, of course, is neither a McCaslin nor an inhabitant of Yoknapatawpha County, but he is teamed with Ned who is both and he is obviously intended to exemplify the finest of the upper-class Negroes of older generations, who have successfully assimilated the best in white culture through generations of association with the best white families. Lucas

[132] Myrdal, p. 952. The fact that not only Ned and Uncle Parsham but also Boss Priest are Masons explains the hostility of the KKK to the Masons.

[133] Sarah Patton Boyle explains that a Negro could accept a drink but not sit down (p. 24). Earlier in *The Reivers* (p. 113), Minnie would not drink in a group of white people but always took her glass into the kitchen.

Beauchamp is even more exceptional than Uncle Parsham, though not than Ned, in that his white blood is acknowledged by his white relatives, he has a secure social and economic position, and he has enough of his grandfather McCaslin in him to regard few white people as his equals. Instead of accommodating as Ned does or judging as Uncle Parsham does, Lucas is inscrutable and intractable. His fidelity to Molly, symbolized by the fire on the hearth which Rider imitated, and the family portraits—in which Molly appears without a headrag—indicate his rejection of the old plantation Negro image. His way of life is otherwise fairly typical—the food is what Negroes who do not eat in white-folks' kitchens have "a chance to learn to like" (*Intruder in the Dust,* p. 13). In dress Lucas imitates his grandfather, with his beaver hat and gold watchchain and gold toothpick. The hat alone is defiance of etiquette: it should always be doffed to white folks, so Lucas always kept it on his head.[134] He omitted titles of respect even in the Federal courthouse ("The Fire and the Hearth," pp. 128–129). With upper-class white men, especially when his white relatives were near-by, Lucas could escape with only "Why, you uppity—." With lower-class white men, such behavior proved nearly suicidal (*Intruder in the Dust,* pp. 18–20).[135] And the beginning and the ending of *Intruder in the Dust* are based on Lucas's defiance of racial etiquette: for a white person to tip a Negro but not another white person is customary. When Charles tried to pay for his dinner, Lucas quite rightly interpreted the action as one of racial superiority in return for hospitality. When Gavin came

[134] Doyle explains that the hat was the chief symbol of the freed man, and that wearing it indoors and out was an assertion of manhood (*The Etiquette of Race Relations,* p. 114). The significance of Lucas's hat in itself disproves Edmond Volpe's statement in *A Reader's Guide to William Faulkner* (New York: Noonday Press, 1964), that Ned is the same as Lucas Beauchamp (p. 345); they are both the grandsons of Carothers McCaslin but are completely different in appearance and character; the first detail given about Ned is his bald skull and fringe of hair (*The Reivers,* p. 30).

[135] The fact that Lucas was eating gingersnaps in the store was a breach of racial etiquette. Negroes would usually take food or Cokes outside (Doyle, p. 146).

to the jail, Lucas said: "I'm gonter pay you" (p. 59). And at the end, when Lucas insisted on paying for the services of Gavin Stevens and getting a receipt, his action is as much a declaration of independence of patronage as was Dr. Johnson's letter to Lord Chesterfield. As Sarah Patton Boyle says: "it is the new Negro's right—one he covets—to pay for services from whites. His escape from our paternalism has real meaning for him."[136] The humor lies only in the careful counting out of the small change.

In the closed world of Yoknapatawpha County, where most of the inhabitants have lived all of their lives, and their parents and grandparents before them, even gestures are part of the elaborate ritual by which an uneasy peace is maintained: to omit the right gesture or to use the wrong one creates a sense of insecurity, especially in those who are least secure to begin with, the Negroes and the poor whites. The Snopeses may rise and still be the objects of scorn, but it is another Snopes who kills Flem, not an economic rival or victim of Flem's sharp dealings. The cumulative effect of insults or of threats to security in the everyday relationships between races is serious enough, but added to the restraints imposed upon the inferior caste is the whole structure of social and economic institutions through which the caste division runs. Social crises are the consequence of an interaction of forces which go back to the very beginning of the social history which has been reviewed and to the ideology which saturates customs, laws, and institutions.

[136] Boyle, p. 105. Davis and Gardner note that "the white group recognizes in the salesman-customer relationship an inversion of the usual colored-white relationship and is defensive about this behavior" (p. 257). Gavin's attitude toward Lucas may be both defensive and patronizing. Gavin is not otherwise represented as having Negro clients, and he tried to maintain with Lucas a personal relationship as patron rather than a professional relationship.

4

SOCIAL INSTITUTIONS
AND PATTERNS OF ACTION

1. *Cotton Economy*

RACIAL etiquette and Jim Crow laws provided the social patterns of daily life of the "authoritarian regime
in the South during which state, church, home, school,
and courts taught or defended the ideology of white supremacy and the constellation of skin-color-purity concepts
that fixed and supported it and kept the mind of the people
from questioning its 'truth.' "[1] In this statement by Lillian
Smith are listed the social institutions with which this chapter
will deal. The economic basis of the institutions, however, in
the rural South is the post-war equivalent of the plantation
system of slavery days which, as Myrdal says, built up "a
labor organization as similar as possible to slavery": the sharecropping system which came to include both Negroes and

---

[1] Lillian Smith, *Killers of the Dream* (Garden City, N.Y.: Doubleday Anchor Books, 1963), p. 180.

poor whites.[2] Like the paternalism of slavery, that of the post-war plantation owner had potentialities for good and evil in exercising the broad social and economic power revealed in the commissary ledger of the McCaslins, as Isaac McCaslin interpreted it:

. . . that chronicle which was a whole land in miniature, which multiplied and compounded was the entire South, twenty-three years after surrender and twenty-four from Emancipation—that slow trickle of molasses and meal and meat, of shoes and straw hats and overalls, of plowlines and collars and heel-bolts and buck-heads and clevises, which returned each year as cotton—the two threads frail as truth and impalpable as equators yet cable-strong to bind for life them who made the cotton to the land their sweat fell on . . . ["The Bear," *Go Down, Moses,* pp. 293–294].

Under good landlords, which probably the McCaslins were, the system offered security and profit to the workers; Ike repudiated not so much the current form of the system under McCaslin Edmonds as its origins in gross exploitation of both land and human beings. It is a system, however, of benefit only to the simple, unskilled workers and one which had to be administered "by human beings to whom it offers an un-

[2] Gunnar Myrdal, *An American Dilemma* (New York: Harper & Row, 1962), p. 224. Sections in Myrdal relevant to this chapter are: Part IV, "Economics"; Part V, "Politics"; Part VI, "Justice"; Part X, "The Negro Community." Since Lafayette County has less diversified agriculture and fewer industries than many areas in Mississippi and the South in general, the changes in agricultural economy since 1944, noted by Arnold Rose in his Postscript to *An American Dilemma* (p. xviii), may well be less evident in Lafayette County. The year 1944, moreover, marks the chronological end of all the Yoknapatawpha narratives except *The Mansion* and *The Reivers,* neither of which deals with rural Yoknapatawpha after 1944. In *Shadow of the Plantation* (Chicago: University of Chicago Press, Phoenix Books, 1966), Charles S. Johnson specifies what is covered in the "labor organization" referred to by Myrdal: "the high proportion of Negro tenantry, the almost exclusive concentration upon cotton, the crude unskilled labor in need of land and skilled supervision, the credit system and advances, the tradition of dependence upon planters on the part of the Negro tenants, and the tradition of dependence upon capital on the part of the planters" (pp. 103–104).

usual opportunity to rob without detection and punishment."[3] William Percy, in making this admission, speaks as a member of one of the best families of the old tradition; with unquestioned benevolence and integrity, he worked his plantation on a fifty-fifty sharecropping basis with his Negro workers. An economic system which, for equitable operation, requires almost superhuman virtue on the part of employers is unlikely to operate with due benefit to both employers and workers. At best, the traditional paternalistic pattern, as Myrdal observes, left little opportunity for the small farmer to prosper, since he seldom had as good land as the large plantation owner, and there was little incentive or possibility for the tenant to become independent.[4]

The real motive behind the whole economic-racial system is seldom expressed in the South; William Faulkner is one of the exceptions: he said, "It's economic."

The Southern farmer can make more money when he can have peonage to do the work. If he can keep the Negro in a position where he will be content with less food than the white, man to man, will live in worse quarters than the white, man to man, will be satisfied with inferior schooling, then he will continue to work for less pay than the white man gets. The white man in my country is afraid that if he gives the Negro any advancement, any social advancement at all, the Negro man will stop working for the low wage and then he will get less when he sells his cotton, that's all it is. But they will use religion, they will use all sorts of nonsense about the white man having been created by God better than the black man to justify this position. It's not that at all. It's purely and simply they want the black man

---

[3] William Percy, *Lanterns on the Levee* (New York: Knopf, 1941), p. 282. Even while defending the principle, Percy elaborates on the abuses of the system under inferior upstarts "on the make." His attitude toward Negroes is that of benevolent paternalism and shows appreciation of the virtues traditionally ascribed to the race. The Percys represent those whom Myrdal describes as "better than the system" of plantation economy (p. 249).

[4] Myrdal, p. 276. Myrdal is commenting on the difficulties encountered in the South by the Farm Security Administration.

to keep on working for less money than they'd have to pay a white man to do that work [*Faulkner at Nagano*, p. 129].[5]

Cotton-growing as a one-crop system has always provided wealth for a few and poverty for the many by preventing diversified agriculture which will produce food for home consumption and by discouraging the year-round industry necessary for economic betterment of the workers: quick returns from a cash crop require that maximum land be given to cotton. Thus the agricultural pattern brought into Mississippi before the Civil War, after it had ruined lands to the east, has been continued. "Must the country languish and die, that the slaveholder may flourish?" Charles James Faulkner asked, in South Carolina.[6] Almost a century later an editorial in the Oxford *Eagle* (September 19, 1935) describes cotton as always a slave crop: "one man prospered only because many men didn't get enough to eat or wear." This "tradition of human exploitation," Myrdal states, "—and now not only of Negroes —has remained from slavery as a chief determinant of the entire structure of the South's economic life."[7]

Details of the plantation tenant system are summed up in Isaac McCaslin's meditation on the ledgers:

[5] Vardaman, the Mississippi demagogue, advised controlling the "nigger" by whipping and by never paying him "more wages than is actually necessary to buy food and clothing" (quoted in W. J. Cash, *The Mind of the South* [New York: Vintage Books, 1960], p. 253). Myrdal points out that the caste system is never defended as in the interest of white people: "*in America, social segregation and discrimination will practically never be motivated in this straightforward way as being in white people's interests.*" Particularly in the South, "one is led to believe that such base and materialistic considerations never enter their thoughts" (p. 585; italics Myrdal's). John Dollard confirms the economic objective of the caste system: "a large and passive population of lower-class Negroes who are accustomed to do the most strenuous and ill-paid work" (*Caste and Class in a Southern Town* [Garden City, N.Y.: Doubleday Anchor Books, 1957], p. 202).

[6] Quoted by Frederick Law Olmsted, in *A Journey in the Seaboard Slave States in the Years 1853–1854. With Remarks on Their Economy* (New York: Putnam, 1904), p. 320.

[7] Myrdal, p. 220. He questions the statement, common in the South, that both planters and tenants are poor (p. 1252).

. . . the whole plantation in its mazed and intricate entirety—the land, the fields and what they represented in terms of cotton ginned and sold, the men and women whom they fed and clothed and even paid a little cash money at Christmas-time in return for the labor which planted and raised and picked and ginned the cotton, the machinery and mules and gear with which they raised it and their cost and upkeep and replacement—that whole edifice intricate and complex and founded upon injustice and erected by ruthless rapacity and carried on even yet with at times downright savagery not only to the human beings but the valuable animals too, yet solvent and efficient and, more than that: not only still intact but enlarged, increased . . . ["The Bear," *Go Down, Moses,* p. 298].

With less complete, unquestioned control by the plantation owner over his workers, the system would have allowed less scope for exploitation. But the owner kept all of the records; even if the worker could read and figure, he could only accept the white man's word, which, as Ike thought, imagining an illiterate Negro asking to see the ledger page, "he would have had to accept for the reason that there was absolutely no way under the sun for him to test it" ("The Bear," pp. 266–267). Although, as Myrdal explains, rural relief agencies and other federal authorities now exercise some supervision over the dealings of landowners with tenants, "the credit relations between landlord and tenant, the system of unilateral bookkeeping, as well as the legal impotence of the Negro tenants, still may enable the landlord to receive a larger share of the benefits than he is supposed to get . . . ."[8]

---

[8] *Ibid.,* p. 257. The "legal impotence" of the tenants is due not only to their lack of knowledge and means to secure legal aid but also to the facts that "the police generally take orders from the planters" and "lower courts tend to decide against the tenants" (p. 1250). The police also enforce debt peonage by allowing employers to pay court fines, imposed for petty offenses, and thus to get, as cheap labor, the Negroes whose fines they paid. As Cash observed, the landowner not only kept all the records for abjectly ignorant workers but had such power that he could "easily cow or crush any recalcitrant into submission" (p. 156). In *Deep South* (Chicago: University of Chicago Press, Phoenix Books, 1966), Allison Davis and Burleigh and Mary Gardner devote a chapter (pp. 223–231) to "Intimidation of Labor," with evidence based on instances reported by both Negro workers and white employers.

W. E. B. Du Bois explains the difference between croppers, who furnish only their labor, and those "who work the land on their own responsibility, paying rent in cotton and supported by the crop-mortgage system." The latter had some incentive. "The change from cropper to tenant was accomplished by fixing the rent."[9] Du Bois, however, states that the economic advantage still remained with the landlords and merchants. *Sharecroppers* Myrdal defines as those who receive one-half or less of the crop, cash *tenants* as those who furnish all of the work, implements, and supplies.[10]

The short-term credit system,[11] which encouraged cash crops and therefore perpetuated the vicious cycle of tenancy and soil erosion, results in debt peonage, not only of Negroes on plantations but of white farmers in other areas. This means that the worker ends the agricultural year with a deficit and nothing to live on except credit; he cannot move unless the landlord is willing.[12]

In the rural areas where most of the tenants work on small holding and are white,[13] the institution of the country store where the storeowner is also a landowner represents the whole system of tenancy and credit. The Varners and their store in *The Hamlet* epitomize this aspect of the cotton economy as neatly as the McCaslin ledgers did the plantation economy.

[9] W. E. B. Du Bois, *The Souls of Black Folk* (Greenwich, Conn.: Fawcett Publications, Premier Americana, 1961), pp. 118–119.

[10] Myrdal, p. 237. In *The Negro in Mississippi, 1865–1890* (New York: Harper Torchbooks, 1965), Vernon Wharton explains how the system of sharecropping developed as a consequence of emancipation and describes various labor systems which came to absorb both Negro and white farm labor (pp. 62–73). Much that is said about Negroes in the Reconstruction period still applies to sharecroppers. Land ownership in Lafayette County has declined and tenancy increased, according to the Oxford *Eagle* during the late 1930s. Johnson explains tenants and sharecroppers (pp. 109–112).

[11] Myrdal, pp. 232, 234.

[12] *Ibid.*, pp. 247–248, 1237, 1242, 1243. Du Bois describes such a problem in Georgia in 1890 and the effects upon the Negroes and on their living conditions (*The Souls of Black Folk*, pp. 99–100, 105–107).

[13] Myrdal emphasizes the lack of attention, in studies of the South, to the "Southern non-plantation tenant" of whom the majority are white (p. 243).

The commissary on the plantation served the same purpose as the general store in supplying the needs of the workers, at a good profit; and the plantation owners, at least in Yoknapatawpha County, might have interests in banks and thus, like the country merchant, might engage in money-lending, mortgaging, and such other profitable enterprises. Bayard Sartoris was a banker and Cass Edmonds also had "one foot straddled into a farm and the other foot straddled into a bank" ("The Bear," *Go Down, Moses*, p. 250).

As Thomas Clark says in his history of the country store, it was "as vital an institution as . . . the church and the democratic party."[14] Will Varner was the head man of Frenchman's Bend in every kind of activity including politics and the law:

He was a farmer, a usurer, a veterinarian . . . . He owned most of the good land in the country and held mortgages on most of the rest. He owned the store and the cotton gin and the combined grist mill and blacksmith shop in the village proper and it was considered, to put it mildly, bad luck for a man of the neighborhood to do his trading or gin his cotton or grind his meal or shoe his stock anywhere else [*The Hamlet*, p. 5].

Lien laws which enabled farmers to "give unplanted crops as collateral for supplies," Clark explains, served to make farmers, tenant or otherwise, debtors to the local country store owner for all of their supplies, family or agricultural.[15] No doubt the scope of Will Varner's monopolistic enterprises was not unique. Because the one-crop system did not allow much raising of foodstuff, the farmer had to buy food of the local merchant at generously marked-up prices.[16]

[14] Thomas D. Clark, *Pills, Petticoats, and Plows* (Indianapolis and New York: Bobbs-Merrill, 1944), p. 336.

[15] *Ibid.*, p. 314. In *Shadow of the Plantation*, Johnson reports a Negro tenant's account of trying to keep books and "the man" saying he went by his own books; the Negro continued: "They got you 'cause you have to carry your cotton to his mill to gin and you better not carry your cotton nowhere else" (p. 128).

[16] Lillian Smith, in *Killers of the Dream*, explains the sharecropping system as operated by the plantation owner, with a commissary in which a "high interest" was charged on the food sold on credit by the

In *The Hamlet,* the account of Varner's store and the role it played in the lives of the people as a meeting place and the source of such luxuries as crackers and cheese and sardines does not conceal the fact that it was also a monopolistic enter-prise. When Flem Snopes got control and took over handling the finances, there was no change from honest to dishonest, as Flem's unsavory character might make one suppose, but merely a change from a careless but amiable dishonesty on the part of Will or Jody Varner, with a genial way of exact-ing interest on what was sold on credit, to a strict but inhu-man accuracy in all money matters on the part of Flem (*The Hamlet,* p. 57). The ramifications of the system Faulkner stresses by his description of the weighing of the cotton and the operating of the gin and the yearly settlement with Var-ner's tenants and debtors (pp. 59–62). In his dealings in mort-gages and lending at usurious interest, anything from "twenty-five cents to ten dollars" (p. 61)—sums that suggest the financial range of the villagers' dealings—Flem was merely following the example not only of the Varners but of the whole breed of gen-eral store merchants. Clark's story of such a merchant, George Cobb, who died and went to hell, certainly sounds like a close relative of Ratliff's story of Flem and the Prince of Hell, at the end of Book Three of *The Hamlet.* The devil imprisoned George Cobb under a washpot and screamed at a visitor who wanted to look under the pot: "Don't lift that pot! We have Old Man George Cobb under there and if you let him out

---

plantation owner, who himself depended on credit from the bank, also at high interest (pp. 51–52). Ralph McGill refers to the "brutal mark-ups on every item that had been sold" in either the general store or the commissary (*The South and the Southerner* [Boston: Little, Brown, 1963], p. 160). Clement Eaton, in *The Growth of Southern Civilization, 1790–1860* (New York: Harper Torchbooks, 1961), cites 100 percent mark-ups before the Civil War (p. 206). Davis and Gardner explain the white landowners' preference for Negro tenants as due to white ten-ants' being less easily imposed on and more likely to seek legal defense; white storekeepers also preferred Negro customers to lower-class whites (pp. 266–267, 268). In *The Winds of Fear* (New York: Award Books, 1964), a novel dealing with the Mississippi Delta during World War II, Hodding Carter refers to Negro tenants "enslaved to the commissary" and unable to grow their own vegetables (p. 55).

he'll foreclose a mortgage on all hell in the first crop season."[17]

Ab Snopes, in "Barn Burning," is the best example of the white sharecropper: his story provides some useful contrasts with what would be true of a Negro in the same economic stratum. In ten years or less, Ab had lived in a dozen almost identical paintless two-room houses with his wife, his four children, and his sister-in-law. He burned a barn in revenge for being charged a dollar pound fee to get back the hog he failed to fence in. When he deliberately ruined an expensive rug of his landlord's, Major De Spain, and was charged twenty bushels of corn to pay for it, he sued De Spain because the damage charged was too high. Even after the penalty was reduced to ten bushels of corn, he set fire to the Major's barn. Since Ab appears again in *The Hamlet,* still using arson as a threat against landlords, he got away with the De Spain affair. The impossibility of a Negro opposing a landlord or retaliating in such ways and escaping alive, let alone unpunished, is obvious. Ab's record indicates that he was not a desirable tenant; according to Hortense Powdermaker, two years on one place is a good average for a Negro.[18]

Faulkner's rural characters illustrate all gradations in cotton economy, from the lazy to the industrious, from the landless to the comfortable landowner. The landless and lazy are represented by Wash Jones, in *Absalom, Absalom!* The landless and more or less industrious include, in addition to Ab Snopes and his family, Mink Snopes. Ab is soured and Mink is bitter, but both show some sense of responsibility. Those who own some land but do not make efficient use of it include Res Grier, in "Shingles for the Lord" and "Two Soldiers," and Anse Bundren, in *As I Lay Dying.* Res owns a "little shirt-tail of a farm" of "seventy acres of not extra good land" and nothing else even he would borrow, and he is always behind

---

[17] Clark, p. 330.
[18] Hortense Powdermaker, *After Freedom: A Cultural Study in the Deep South* (New York: Viking, 1939), p. 87. The account of Negro labor given is very detailed. In *Shadow of the Plantation,* Charles Johnson makes extensive use of statements by Negro workers and white employers.

in his work ("Shingles for the Lord," "Two Soldiers," "Shall Not Perish," in *Collected Stories,* pp. 34, 84, 103). He is more energetic than Anse Bundren, but even more hapless. In family background and education both the Griers and the Bundrens are superior to Mink and Ab Snopes. Addie Bundren had been a school teacher. Pete Grier had gone through high school. With poorer land but more industry, Jackson Fentry and his father just barely manage to eke out a living for themselves. Their fierce independence, which, unlike Anse Bundren's, is not merely verbal, identifies the Fentrys as the clannish, proud hill dwellers, seen in their less law-abiding aspect in the Gowries and at their best in the more prosperous and socially superior McCallums. The latter live in easy but not elegant comfort, with servants, and can afford their independence, whereas Jackson Fentry in marrying a dying woman and rearing, unaided, her child made a real sacrifice ("Tomorrow," *Knight's Gambit*). Fentry lived in the northeast corner of the county. Back in the Frenchman's Bend area are such families as the Quicks, the Tulls, and Houston who are competent owners of good land. But to the extent that these families traded with the Varners and may well on occasion have been in debt to them, they were caught in the system. The emphasis on the stunted growth of both Mink and Jackson Fentry and the descriptions of the ill-clad, ill-fed, beaten Armstids (*The Hamlet,* pp. 294–297) point to one of the most vicious consequences of the cotton economy: the failure of the farmers and tenants to raise food, their dependence on such limited staples, at marked-up prices, as meal, salt meat, and molasses, and the consequent dietary deficiencies and low vitality.[19] Mrs. Pruitt said of Jackson Fentry that he "never in

[19] *Ibid.,* p. 80; Clark, Chapters Four and Seven. Ike McCaslin's "slow trickle of molasses and meal and meat" ("The Bear," p. 293) is accurate. In *The Peculiar Institution: Slavery in the Ante-Bellum South* (New York: Vintage Books, 1964), Kenneth Stampp says: "A peck of cornmeal and three or four pounds of salt pork or bacon comprised the basic weekly allowance of the great majority of adult slaves" (p. 282). Johnson gives the same account of chief foods for Macon County, Georgia, in the 1930s (p. 100).

his whole life had ever set down to a table and et all he could hold" ("Tomorrow," *Knight's Gambit,* p. 94).

Jackson did demonstrate his ability in his few years' working in Frenchman's Bend at Quick's sawmill, one of the few kinds of wage-earning jobs available in the area. He hired a Negro to help his father and walked thirty miles to Frenchman's Bend; he made the round trip in a three-day Christmas vacation. He began with the same work and same pay as a Negro would get but by the next summer was running the mill by himself, so well that the Quicks seldom went to the mill. Rider, in "Pantaloon in Black," also worked at a mill near the Edmonds' plantation, and until his wife died they lived well on his wages, with a stove to bake in and a cake every Saturday (*Go Down, Moses,* p. 139). In Jefferson, Byron Bunch worked at a planing mill and lived simply but comfortably (*Light in August*). Those who worked for wages in the country would still have to trade with the local country store but could keep out of debt.

The changes in transportation, the development of chain stores with marked prices, and the government activities which began under the New Deal gave promise of remedying some of the worst evils. The most direct use Faulkner makes of these developments in the 1930s and early 1940s is in "The Tall Men," in which the McCallums refuse to take money for not raising cotton, but prudently learn about cattle-raising and give up the one-crop system. This rugged individualist attitude the McCallums could afford. Faulkner does not show in his fiction what federal aid, in all forms, meant to the area, from subsidies for acreage restrictions to soil conservation projects.[20] But he does include one story to suggest a de-

[20] Myrdal deals with the effects of the A.A.A. on cotton and on the sharecropping system. Mechanical cotton pickers are now in use in the Lafayette County area, displacing Negro labor in its most traditional role. Unlike the McCallums, Southern politicians, Ralph McGill said, "embraced the New Deal and its props for agriculture . . . and its patronage with all the ardor of a bridegroom" (p. 166). The ardor was reflected in the Oxford *Eagle* in the 1930s; many less well off than the McCallums were saved from ruin by payments for not growing cotton. In *"I Do So Politely": A Voice from the South* (Boston: Hough-

sirable alternative to the old general store. Wall Snopes made
the most of his schooling and used his father's indemnity
money to buy into a grocery. He opened the first self-service
grocery store in Jefferson, with a parking lot. Then he built
up a chain of wholesale groceries so that "a merchant anywhere in the county can buy jest what he needs at a decent
price without having to add no freight a-tall" (*The Town,*
pp. 148–149). Wall symbolizes the end of the country store
monopoly for those who can get to town and pay cash. But
as James Silver puts it, the leaders of Mississippi are trying
"to freeze the status quo while revolutionizing the economic
order," vainly hoping to raise a modern industrial structure
"upon the sands of segregation, minimum wages, poor schools,
anti-intellectualism, Negrophobia, meager social services, anti-
unionism, and a general policy of 'hate the federal government' "—from which Mississippi receives more than it pays
into the federal treasury in taxes.[21] There are too many Flem
Snopses and too few like Wall. And the Uncle Will Varners
and the town bankers demonstrated what Flem could do—
and let him do it.

II. *The Family*

The paternalism of the plantation system was preserved after
the Civil War not only in the economic system but also in the
concept of the family which underlies some of the darkest
and most terrible of Faulkner's dramas. Southern pride in

---

ton Mifflin, 1965), Robert Canzoneri recalls: "When Mississippi was
voting avidly for the man and his socialism, for which they now
blame him but not their empty bellies of the 1930s, I was apparently
the only boy in my class who came from a family opposed to Franklin
D. Roosevelt" (p. 124).
[21] James W. Silver, *Mississippi: The Closed Society* (New York: Harcourt, Brace & World, 1964), pp. 77, 75.

family and intense interest in genealogy,[22] combined with white supremacy ideology, necessitated guarantee of the purity of the legitimate line in upper-class white families. The cult of gyneolatry, what Carl Rowan terms "the white goddess complex,"[23] put upper-class white women on a pedestal, both before and after marriage, and hedged them around with taboos to insure the purity of the white blood and the husband's paternity of the offspring. The racial aspect of the cult stressed the white–good, black–evil moral symbolism. The term *chivalry* is so commonly used in relation to the Southern tradition in general and this aspect in particular that the origins of gyneolatry are easily traced; the romantic-medieval strain in Southern culture, influenced by the novels of Scott, is the immediate source; the ultimate source is the code of courtly love of the Middle Ages. In a racial context, with white woman at the top of the chivalric hierarchy and Negro woman at the bottom,[24] the "rule of courtly love" as defined by Denis de Rougemont, which "made of rape the crime of crimes, a felony for which there is no remission,"[25] was interpreted especially to mean rape of a white woman by a Negro man. The extravagance with which the creed of this cult is stated is exemplified by the toast of an Alabama fraternity ritual quoted by Cash from Carl Carmer's *Stars Fell on Alabama*:

"To Woman, lovely woman of the Southland, as pure and chaste as this sparkling water, as cold as this gleaming ice, we lift this cup, and we pledge our hearts and our lives to the protection of her virtue and chastity."

[22] A relevant example of Southern genealogy, for comparison with Faulkner's fictitious families, is Thomas Felix Hickerson's *Echoes of Happy Valley* (Chapel Hill: T. H. Hickerson, 1962). The author, who wrote *The Falkner Feuds,* is related to R. J. Thurmond, who killed Colonel Falkner, and the genealogy includes the Thurmond family.

[23] Carl Rowan, *South of Freedom* (New York: Knopf, 1952), p. 226.

[24] Howard W. Odum, *The Way of the South* (New York: Macmillan, 1947), p. 77; Powdermaker, p. 35.

[25] Denis de Rougemont, *Love in the Western World,* Montgomery Belgion, trans. (New York: Pantheon, 1956), p. 210.

One need not be unduly cynical to anticipate Carmer's comment, that the young man reading the toast is likely to be inebriated and to be one "among the better known seducers of the campus." William Wasserstrom quotes this toast and comments: "What Faulkner thought of this ideal and the confusion it perpetrates, he allowed Temple Drake and Popeye, Miss Burden and Joe Christmas, to illustrate; what he thought of this 'leader,' he showed in Percy Grimm."[26] Faulkner's illustrations go far beyond the characters Wasserstrom cites. The ideal has had and still retains tremendous cultural significance, however antiquated and extravagant it may be. Cole Blease, once Governor of South Carolina, said: "Whenever the Constitution comes between me and the virtue of the white women of the South, I say to hell with the Constitution."[27]

The basic cause and purpose were not only those avowed, the need to insure the sanctity of the home and the purity of the blood line; Gunnar Myrdal sums up an unacknowledged cause:

The fixation on the purity of white womanhood, and also part of the intensity of emotion surrounding the whole sphere of segregation and discrimination, are to be understood as the backwashes of the sore conscience on the part of white men for their own or their compeers' relations with, or desires for, Negro women.[28]

[26] Quoted in W. J. Cash, *The Mind of the South,* pp. 339–340, in a discussion of the cult of Southern Womanhood in the 1920s and 1930s, and in William Wasserstrom, *The Heiress of All the Ages* (Minneapolis: University of Minnesota Press, 1959), p. 149.

[27] Quoted in Cash, p. 253. The resistance in Mississippi to obeying Supreme Court decisions and federal orders regarding segregation represents the attitude of Blease, for any weakening of segregation is regarded as a threat to white women.

[28] Myrdal, p. 591. Myrdal goes on to observe that "these psychological effects" are magnified by the "puritan *milieu*" of the South. The "logic" of the caste theory, as based on "race purity," Myrdal presents on p. 58. He gives an autobiography of a white Southerner which shows the development of conventional beliefs and attitudes (pp. 1192–1194).

Rooted in this sense of guilt is the obsessive fear of retaliation from the Negro men whose homes have been invaded and women violated. The fact that these real causes are unacknowledged intensifies the emotional reactions and renders them inaccessible to reason. The cult of the "white goddess" is marked by fanaticism and violence, but the violence is inexplicable except in terms of the whole cultural complex.

The effects of the cult of pure Southern womanhood are not limited to race relations: the lives and character of women, the institution of the family, and the whole culture show its influence. The authoritarian paternalism of the white man toward his women reduced them to slavery; as Mary Chesnut bitterly remarked, "All married women, all children and girls who live on in their father's houses are slaves."[29] Howard Odum notes the paradox that the same culture which placed woman "on the highest possible pedestal" at the same time refused her such basic rights and privileges as education and interest in vital social institutions and movements.[30] Lillian Smith elaborates the point of the "culturally stunted" women, on their "lonely pedestals" with their men elsewhere, made to equate "innocence, virtue, ignorance, silence," forced into lives of "sexual blankness" which was "God's way," pushing

[29] Mary Boykin Chesnut, *A Diary from Dixie* (Boston: Houghton Mifflin, Sentry Edition, 1961), p. 486. Mrs. Chesnut gives an example of paternal tyranny in the Chesnut family: a father forbade his daughter to marry the man she loved; she spent forty years in her room, with every luxury but freedom, "but neither party would give in" (p. 535). In *A Social History of the American Family*, Vol. II (New York: Barnes and Noble, 1960), Arthur W. Calhoun notes the contrast between exaggerated "surface respect" for women in the South and obvious "degradation of the sex": "Gallantry to woman was the gallantry of the harem" (p. 323). The Southern attitude, of course, reflected to an extreme degree a national trend. In "The Cult of True Womanhood: 1820–1860" (*American Quarterly*, XVIII [Summer, 1966]), Barbara Welter shows how that trend was manifest in women's magazines and in gift books: "Woman . . . in all her roles accepted submission as her lot" (p. 162), and "Purity was as essential as piety to a young woman, its absence as unnatural and unfeminine" (p. 154).

[30] Odum, pp. 77, 138.

sex "out through the back door as a shameful thing never to be mentioned."[31]

In Faulkner, the consequences of the cult as it stunted or ruined the life of women by forcing them into accepted patterns or into self-destructive rebellion are clearly illustrated. Miss Emily Grierson was victim of a father with whom her relationship is pictured by townspeople as a tableau, Miss Emily "in white in the background, her father a spraddled silhouette in the foreground, his back to her and clutching a horsewhip" ("A Rose for Emily," *Collected Stories,* p. 123). No wonder she was still single at thirty and later had to kill her man to keep him. In real life, there was no tyrant father and the unsuitable match ended in a successful marriage. Faulkner's deviation from fact adds to the significance of Emily's story. In *The Unvanquished,* Drusilla rejected woman's role until forced into conventional marriage. Narcissa Benbow took as her model the conventional and phony image of the pure white woman, only to reveal the impurity beneath (*Sartoris, Sanctuary,* "There Was a Queen"). Minnie Cooper was driven to desperation by the "idle and empty days" of a "nice" unmarried woman who lacked occupation, intellectual interests, and social position: her fantasies took the form implicit in the cult of the pure white woman ("Dry September"). Elly, younger but equally bored, did not stop with fantasy and was not repelled by Paul's Negro blood ("Elly").[32] Caddy Compson openly rebelled and was de-

---

[31] Smith, pp. 123, 124, 122, 123. In *The Southern Temper* (Garden City, N.Y.: Doubleday, 1959), William Peters gives an account of gyneolatry and its consequences (pp. 191–200) and cites Sarah Patton Boyle and Lillian Smith among women leaders against racism and segregation (p. 32). He ascribes their sympathy with Negroes as related to their own struggle to free themselves from minority status (p. 33).

[32] Elly destroyed both Paul and herself. Lillian Smith refers to reports, unverified, that a few white women were killed by male relatives for having sexual relations with men of Negro blood (p. 104). The patterns in Faulkner's women characters of conformity to and rebellion from the cult of the Southern Woman are discussed at length in my article, "William Faulkner and the Southern Concept of Woman," *Mississippi Quarterly,* XV (Winter, 1961–1962), 1–16.

stroyed; her destruction was a factor in that of her daughter, Miss Quentin (*The Sound and the Fury*).

Marriage did not solve the problems of women brought up according to the cult. Ellen Sutpen, the butterfly, exemplifies the women who were unable to face the realities of their lives and who, at the cost of all wifely and motherly qualities, acted out the role into which they were cast. Isaac McCaslin's wife overcame only once her physical shame, her desire for property being stronger than her shame; after one failure to beget a child, Ike was doomed to be childless ("The Bear," *Go Down, Moses,* pp. 312–314). Faulkner's explanation of Ike's wife as believing that "sex was something evil . . . to be justified by acquiring property" suggests the Calvinist ethics of capitalism (*Faulkner in the University,* p. 275). Mrs. Compson, wearing mourning because Caddy had kissed a boy, forcing the pregnant Caddy to marry Herbert Head, perfectly exemplifies the women Lillian Smith mentions who closed "the path to mature genitality" to their sons and daughters and who established a police state in the home which drove some men to drink.[33] The only cause for wonder regarding Mrs. Compson is that she ever had four children and that, so far as we know, drink was the only sin to which she drove her husband. Mr. Compson's lack of ambition and his cynicism may well have been due to Mrs. Compson's deficiencies as a wife, but there is no direct evidence.

With women as individuals emotionally and intellectually restricted by the psychological equivalent of Chinese foot-binding, with children brought up by such mothers, indoctrinated in the cult from early childhood, the whole culture was affected. Joe Shaw sums up the corollary of the cult, the *unspoken* tradition of the past: "Sex relations with a Negro wench seemed to be a sort of puberty rite of the southern gentry, much as getting a driver's license is today."[34] Negro

[33] Smith, pp. 133, 131.
[34] Joe Shaw, "Sociological Aspects of Faulkner's Writing," *Mississippi Quarterly,* XIV (Summer, 1961), 151–152. This point is confirmed by Calhoun (II, 294–295). South African apartheid is more consistent in legally banning all interracial sexual relations between whites and colored races.

women were sacrificed to protect white girls. Faulkner confirms these consequences of the cult of Southern womanhood, in Mr. Compson's account of the three kinds of women: "ladies, women, females—the virgins whom gentlemen someday married, the courtesans to whom they went while on sabbaticals to the cities, the slave girls and women upon whom that first caste rested and to whom in certain cases it doubtless owed the very fact of its virginity," because girls of the young man's own class were "interdict and inaccessible" and courtesans "inaccessible because of money and distance" but the house servants were at hand and the slave girls in the fields were available if the young man merely told the overseer to send a certain one to him (*Absalom, Absalom!*, pp. 109-110).

The worst effects of the cult, however, were that it exalted white women by debasing white men and that it demanded human sacrifices, not merely the sacrifice of the emotions and intellect of the white women, but the sacrifice of the bodies of Negro men. The statement by Vardaman, quoted by Albert D. Kirwan, is only one of many similar ones by Vardaman, equalled by other white-supremacy politicians in Mississippi: "We would be justified in slaughtering every Ethiop on the earth to preserve unsullied the honor of one Caucasian home."[35] Lillian Smith sums up what Southern men did "in the name of *sacred womanhood,* of *purity,* of *preserving the home*":

lecherous old men and young ones, reeking with impurities, who had violated the home since they were sixteen years old, whipped up lynchings, organized Klans, burned crosses, aroused the poor and ignorant by an obscene, perverse imagery describing the "menace" of Negro men hiding behind every cypress waiting to rape "our" women.[36]

[35] Albert D. Kirwan, *The Revolt of the Rednecks: Mississippi Politics, 1876–1925* (Lexington: University of Kentucky Press, 1951), p. 147. Kirwan observes that Vardaman consistently held this view through thirty years of politics and that on this point all other white politicians in Mississippi agreed with Vardaman.

[36] Smith, p. 126.

Southern culture was "strong in the institutional power of the family," as Odum stated,[37] but, with the typical Southern paradox, the strength of the white family was founded on the weakness of the Negro family and the evidence of the actual decay of Southern families was ignored. Joe Shaw, referring to the Southern creed of the upper class's divine right to rule, generalizes with Faulkner's works in mind: "The occurrence of a few idiots, dipsomaniacs, homosexuals, frequent illegitimacy, a bit of fratricide, and a slight touch of incest in the best families does not seem to dim this view."[38] In the white family, the effects of the white-goddess cult were intensified by the fact that many children had Negro nurses as second mothers, which, Lillian Smith observes, made the Oedipus complex seem simple: the child's conscience was tied to the white mother and its pleasure feelings to the col-

---

[37] Odum, p. 74. Colonel W. C. Falkner expressed praise of marriage which will serve to illustrate not only the Southern but the Falkner tradition:

> The marriage ceremony was an invention
>   For which we our God should bless—
> It heals our woes and makes us happy,
> And makes little ones call us papa.
>
> It supplies the world with population
>   Without which we would be awful;
> It does all this, besides it makes copulation
> A virtue, when under circumstances lawful.

(From "The Siege of Monterey," quoted by Donald Duclos in "Son of Sorrow," a Ph.D. dissertation [University of Michigan, 1962], p. 87.) The threat of a population explosion from excessive virtue is ironically countered, by pure coincidence, by William Faulkner's statement that over-population is a serious problem and that one way to cope with it might be to pass a law that "woman can't have but one child like she can't have but one husband" (*Faulkner at West Point*, p. 87).

[38] Shaw, p. 151. This account of Faulknerian families helps to explain why one familiar aspect of family life in the South, hospitality, is so meagerly represented in Yoknapatawpha that discussion of it would be irrelevant. Calhoun notes that hospitality in the South might be limited to family and close friends but that twenty to sixty relatives might gather for such special occasions as Christmas.

ored one, setting up a polarity of pure and impure.[39] The consequence was, she states, sometimes sadistic feeling toward all women and the centering of attention on male companions. We are not told enough about mother-child relationships in the McCaslin and McCallum families to be sure that this explains why the men lead lives largely without women; but the effect is there, whatever the cause. Faulkner referred to his Negro foster mother, with whose children he slept. Any latent aversion to mixing came with maturity and appeared only in connection with the economy (*Faulkner at Nagano,* pp. 168–169). The Faulkner family is a better example of the favorable aspects of the family tradition than any family in Yoknapatawpha, except the Priests in *The Reivers.*

The Negro family, in contrast to the strongly patriarchal white family, was typically a matriarchy, like that of the Gibsons under Dilsey. Lucas Beauchamp and Rider, who imitated him, are unusual in being so clearly the heads of their families. The rarity of Negro men seeking revenge against the white men who threaten the Negro marriage and family is well explained in the episode when Lucas challenges Zack Edmonds: few would, like Lucas, risk the rope and coal oil ("The Fire and the Hearth," *Go Down, Moses,* p. 58). The reversal of male and female roles in the family, the contrast between the unity and security of the white family and the broken homes of the Negro, the destruction of the Negro man's self-respect by his inability to defend the sanctity of his home and to support his family—all adds up to an ironic reversal of the white family ideal, a reversal which is due largely to the cult of Southern womanhood and the principle on which it is based. Du Bois bitterly sums up the way in which Negro women and Negro homes have been sacrificed:

[39] Smith, p. 113. Calhoun suggests that when it was the custom for white babies to be suckled by Negro nurses, that fact might partially explain the sex-tastes of Southern men (II, 285), a point relevant to the story of Roth in "Delta Autumn," as Calhoun's discussion of the "psychology of arrogance" is relevant to Roth as a child in "The Fire and the Hearth" (p. 286).

The red stain of bastardy, which two centuries of systematic legal defilement of Negro women had stamped upon his race, meant not only the loss of ancient African chastity, but also the hereditary weight of a mass of corruption from white adulterers, threatening almost the obliteration of the Negro home.[40]

Isaac McCaslin was appalled by what he read in the ledgers: he did not even begin to read the whole story.

The McCaslin-Beauchamp family and the Sutpens illustrate how the white and colored children of the white father might grow up on the plantation together, in two castes: these families are unusual only in the relationship's being recognized by the white members, "challenging unspoken penalties," as Odum says, for the naming of the fact which, unnamed, could be ignored.[41] The distinction of the McCaslins is clear in the public, legal recognition of the relationship. The Sutpen situation is unusual in that Clytie lived with Judith, her half-sister, but observed caste distinctions. After the death of Judith, Clytie assumed responsibility for young Jim Bond and ultimately for her half-brother, Henry, when he returned. Hers is the most intimate relationship with white kin. Sarah Patton Boyle states the fact baldly: "in life's most intimate relationship there never had been segregation in the South . . . ; these were white men's own sons and daughters, sisters and

---

[40] Du Bois, p. 20. In Calhoun's terms, "The master's right of rape wiped out female honor" (II, 294). Under slavery, the illegality of Negro marriage and the impossibility of maintaining family relationships set a pattern of weak family ties which was difficult for free Negroes, still subject to white aggression, to overcome. As Canzoneri notes, Negroes are maligned as disdaining marriage, but married Negroes are denied *Mr.* and *Mrs.* before their names in newspapers (p. 71). As an editor, Hodding Carter used titles of respect in his paper, but in *The Winds of Fear* he represents a Negro professor writing up social notes for the white newspaper and erasing *Mrs.* before a woman's name (p. 142).

[41] Odum, p. 140. Mary Chesnut describes this pious ignorance, in an account of a man who kept his part-Negro offspring "in full view," and provided "handsomely" for them in his will. "His wife and daughters, in their purity and innocence, are supposed never to dream of what is as plain before their eyes as the sunlight. . . . They profess to adore their father as the model of all earthly goodness" (p. 122).

brothers, cousins, uncles and aunts against whom they built segregation walls."[42]

Proof of the gulf between professed beliefs and action lies in these rejected offspring of the white men; in the words of W. E. B. Du Bois: "The rape which your gentlemen have done against helpless black women in defiance of your own laws is written on the foreheads of two millions of mulattoes, and written in ineffaceable blood."[43] The most notable example in Yoknapatawpha of the mulatto rejected by the father, the one taken as an allegory of the South, is that of Charles Bon and Sutpen, of whose relationship Faulkner said: "It was a manifestation of a general racial system in the South," the epitome of "a constant general condition" (*Faulkner in the University*, p. 94). Miscegenation is the self-created horror Southern men seek to efface from their consciousness by the whole elaborate system which is designed to prevent Negro men from doing to the white race what the white race has done to the black and which is based on the unproved assumption that Negro men desire to do so.[44] Miscegenation is thus both the cause of the white-goddess concept, rooted as it is in the guilt-ridden phobia of the whites, and one effect of it; bringing up white women to equate sexuality and sin inhibits the women and drives their husbands to seek sexual experience outside marriage. The segregation laws which protect white women cause the "perennial increase of mulattoes," according to Sarah Patton Boyle, who lists the factors responsible for the effect: "the lure of forbidden fruit," nostalgic childhood memories of Negroes, economic pressure which

[42] Sarah Patton Boyle, *The Desegregated Heart* (New York: Morrow, 1962), p. 69. According to Calhoun, often most of the master's children had slave mothers and these children and their children would be whipped by the overseers (II, 295, 296, 301).

[43] Du Bois, p. 86.

[44] The fact that miscegenation in the South is due almost wholly to relations between white men and Negro women is unquestioned: e.g. Myrdal, p. 589; Powdermaker, p. 181. Dollard gives numerous specific examples and concludes that concubinage and miscegenation continue but that there is social pressure to conceal the extent (pp. 142–143). Faulkner's story of Elly, a white girl taking the initiative with a man with colored blood, is a startling departure from convention.

drives Negro women to prostitution, greater secrecy because of segregated housing, and security against forced marriage.[45] And the results of amalgamation affect only the Negro race: the slightest trace of Negro blood is sufficient for a person to be considered a Negro.

The rejected children of white-Negro relationships are the most significant and some of them the most tragic group in Faulkner's fiction. The McCaslins and the Sutpens provide the chief examples. The McCaslin ledger records the deeds of a fairly scrupulous man, in that Carothers McCaslin not only assumed responsibility for his Negro offspring but was willing for the relationship to be known after his death: it was cheaper to will them money than to say "My son to a nigger" ("The Bear," *Go Down, Moses,* p. 269). Ike McCaslin expressed the power the white man had over a Negro slave, a power little changed after freedom because the lower-class Negro women and men dare not defend themselves when the white man controls both the economic system and the law:

. . . that evil and unregenerate old man . . . could summon, because she was his property, a human being because she was old enough and female, to his widower's house and get a child on her and then dismiss her because she was of an inferior race and then bequeath a thousand dollars to the infant ["The Bear," p. 294].

Old Carothers was at least a widower and did at least bequeath the thousand dollars, in these respects being morally superior to many who exercised the same power. The exceptional horror in the story of Carothers is that he probably had a child by

---

[45] Boyle, p. 161; Calhoun, III, 38. Myrdal notes that illegality of interracial marriages protects the white man and thus increases miscegenation, to the added disadvantage of the woman. Wharton's statement that interracial marriages were legally prohibited in Mississippi after 1876 and that "such marriages were declared to be 'incestuous'" (p. 229) raises the question of the possible realistic basis for such a law, which did not, of course, end miscegenation, whether incestuous or not. The stories of Charles Bon and Judith and of Roth and the Girl, though the relationship was remote, illustrate the possibilities. In *Southern White Protestantism in the Twentieth Century* (New York: Harper & Row, 1964), Kenneth Bailey notes that "the general rules of kinship, mating, and incest which prevail among southerners prevail among hundreds of millions around the world" (p. 159).

his own daughter ("The Bear," pp. 267–271). All of the descendants of Tomey's Turl and Tennie Beauchamp are Beauchamps, denied their birthright and the McCaslin name as the direct descendants through the male line, while the Edmonds family, descendants through Carothers' daughter, own the plantation after Isaac McCaslin repudiated his inheritance. The Beauchamps may well have white blood. In view of Hubert's Negro mistress and his general character, it is likely that he had relations with other slaves; the Beauchamp name might be a token of Beauchamp blood. In *The Reivers,* Faulkner adds Uncle Ned McCaslin to the Negro descendants of Carothers (p. 31). The story of Roth Edmonds and the granddaughter of James Beauchamp adds an example of miscegenation in which the white man can escape forced marriage but in which there is love on both sides, as much love as Roth is capable of ("Delta Autumn," *Go Down, Moses*). The future of the son of Roth and the girl augurs ill, whether he lives in the North or South.[46]

The caste barrier between blood relatives who are also foster brothers is illustrated in the stories of Lucas Beauchamp and Zack Edmonds and their sons, Henry Beauchamp and Roth Edmonds. Lucas acted like a man, not a subservient "good" Negro, when he challenged Zack and in so doing risked the rope and coal oil. Saved by a misfire from killing Zack, Lucas was left with the question: "How to God . . . can a black man ask a white man to please not lay down with his black wife? And even if he could ask it, how to God can the white man promise he wont?" ("The Fire and the Hearth," *Go Down, Moses,* p. 59). The impossibility of a comparable question entering any white man's mind about any Negro suffices to show caste differences.

Not only is the story of Charles Bon the tragic story of the rejected son but it also "sums up the fundamental Southern

[46] Elnora, the one example of miscegenation in the Sartoris family, possibly but not probably did not know that Colonel John Sartoris was her father. She is proud of being one of several generations, slave and free, serving the Sartoris family ("There Was a Queen," *Collected Stories,* p. 727).

anxiety: to the racist's question, 'would you want your sister to marry one,' Faulkner adds, 'when he may also be your brother?' "[47] The crowning horror is that, in *Absalom, Absalom!*, the questions are really reversed: first, "Would you want your sister to marry your brother?" To this the answer apparently was *Yes*. Then came the question: "If he had Negro as well as Sutpen blood?" The answer was a pistol shot. The fact that apparently incest is regarded with less horror in the South than sexual relations or marriage between a white woman and a man with Negro blood, even if imperceptible to the eye, is patent in *Absalom, Absalom!* and implied in other stories by Faulkner which involve incest. Incest is the oldest, the most universal taboo: Bronislaw Malinowski calls the rules of incest "the most widely spread and most rigidly enforced qualification to marriage."[48] Before examining Faulkner's use of the incest theme in *Absalom, Absalom!* and other works, the connection between incest and the Southern family tradition bears investigation.

Much less obvious and familiar than miscegenation in Southern culture, incest is of significant incidence in the South. In collecting bills in Tennessee mill towns, Ralph McGill learned about incest, of two cases of a father having a child by his own daughter.[49] Despite the difference in social status, the Tennessee men being apparently poor whites, the story of

[47] "The Curse and the Hope," *Time* (July 17, 1964), 46. Davis and Gardner cite an instance in which the girls in a family committed incest with the father and had Negro men. "It is significant to note from this interview that the incest situation was viewed with less horror than infraction of the caste sex taboo" (p. 30). Robert Penn Warren points out that "most of the Negroes in Faulkner—certainly those (including the problematical Christmas) who have significant roles—are of mixed blood. Waiving the fact that, even in the period treated by Faulkner, the infusion of white blood among Negroes was widespread, there remains the fact that Faulkner's theme of the rejected 'brother' is at the very center of his drama and the character with mixed blood is mandatory" ("Faulkner: The South, the Negro, and Time," in *Faulkner: A Collection of Critical Essays,* Robert Penn Warren, ed. [Englewood Cliffs, N.J.: Prentice-Hall, 1966], p. 263).

[48] Bronislaw Malinowski, *Sex, Culture, and Myth* (New York: Harcourt, Brace & World, 1962), p. 28.

[49] McGill, pp. 61–62.

Carothers McCaslin and Tomey leaps to mind. The "incredulous (and shocked) speculation" of General Compson that the child at Charles Bon's grave might be Sutpen's by his daughter Clytie (*Absalom, Absalom!,* p. 201) provides a hypothetical parallel to Carothers and Tomey.

Incest between father and daughter is less common in Faulkner than incestuous feeling between sister and brother. This theme was chosen by Andrew Lytle, another Southern novelist, who explained his choice of it as a theme inherent in the Southern social and family system. His explanation of the psychological factors involved should exonerate both Lytle and Faulkner of the charge of inventing unnatural horrors. In "The Working Novelist and the Mythmaking Process," Lytle emphasizes the family as the institution best expressing Southern culture. To support his statement that "incest was a constant upon the Southern scene" he cites his knowledge of "whorehouses where too many of the girls had been ravished by fathers and brothers," and expresses his belief that "incest of the spirit" was "a spiritual condition which inhered within the family itself," citing his own family as evidence. "It was clearest in the county family, where the partial isolation meant an intimacy and constancy of association in work and play which induced excessive jealousy against intrusion from the outside."[50] For the Sutpens, this isolation was intensified by two opposite but complementary psychological patterns: Thomas Sutpen's glorification of the dynasty he was founding as part of his Grand Design and the failure of the community aristocrats to receive the Sutpens into their society. Henry is credited with his father's megalomania when Shreve imagines him justifying the marriage of Judith with their half-brother, Charles Bon, by saying: "But kings have done it! Even dukes!" (*Absalom, Absalom!*, p. 342), thus arrogating to the Sutpens the violation of the taboo reserved for royalty.

The Henry-Judith-Charles relationship seems to involve incest of the spirit between Judith and Henry and homosexual

---

[50] Andrew Lytle, "The Working Novelist and the Mythmaking Process," *Daedalus*, LXXXVIII (Spring, 1959), 331.

love of Henry for Charles, climaxed by Henry's promotion of
a marriage between Judith and Charles that would be incestuous. Judith obeyed Henry, when Henry defied his father,
"because of that relationship between them—that single personality with two bodies both of which had been seduced
almost simultaneously by a man whom at the time Judith had
never seen" (pp. 91–92). How and why Judith was seduced
in absentia is explained by Henry's feeling for Charles and
for Judith: since Henry's love for Charles had homosexual elements, Judith must have seen Charles "with exactly the same
eyes that Henry saw him with" (p. 95). Henry, in love with
both Charles and Judith, seduced Judith for Charles so that he
could vicariously satisfy his love for both of them. He and
Judith had a rapport like that of two people "who had been
marooned at birth on a desert island: the island here Sutpen's
Hundred; the solitude, the shadow of that father" (p. 99)
whom the town and the Coldfield relatives had not accepted.
In his pride in his sister's virginity, Henry imagined "the pure
and perfect incest": the vicarious "taking that virginity in the
person of the brother-in-law" whom he would like to "metamorphose into, the lover," and by whom he would choose to
be despoiled if he could "metamorphose into the sister, the
mistress, the bride" (p. 96). This is how Mr. Compson imagined it was.

Henry's realization that Bon was his half-brother changed
this vicarious incest into actual incest between Bon and Judith
should they marry. Culturally but not instinctively Henry rebelled against incest; rationalizing his incestuous instincts, he
might have seized on justification by royal precedent. But
cultural influence proved stronger than instinct when Henry,
having condoned incest, could not condone marriage between
his sister and their part-Negro half-brother—though his father's daughter by a Negro slave was a member of the Sutpen
household. Henry shot Bon; as Quentin-Shreve imagined Bon
saying to Henry: *"So it's the miscegenation, not the incest,
which you cant bear"* (p. 356). The fact that so much of this
story is filled in by the imagination of the narrators strength-

ens its validity as representing cultural concepts and attitudes.[51]

The incest theme in the Sutpen story gains significance in relation to the story of Quentin Compson in *The Sound and the Fury*: Quentin understands Henry, or his imaginative creation of Henry, because of his own incestuous attachment for his sister Caddy. Quentin tells the Sutpen story to Shreve in January and in June commits suicide in despair over Caddy's loss of honor, first in her promiscuous sexual relationships with several men and finally in her marrying Herbert Head when pregnant with another man's child. Andrew Lytle's explanation of the brother-sister relationship as a search for innocence applies more fully to Quentin (not to Caddy) than to Henry. The desert-island analogy quoted above suggests also the Garden of Eden myth which Lytle relates to his own novel, *The Velvet Horn*:

The brothers and sister . . . withdrew from the stresses of formal society in an effort to return to the prenatal equilibrium of innocence and wholeness. This is an habitual impulse, the refusal to engage in the cooperating opposites that make life. It is also as illusory as any Golden Age, and forbidden by divine and human law. Therefore, it is the grounds for one of the oldest forms of search and conflict. The symbol for this is incest.[52]

This explanation fits Quentin, as Lytle's statement about the South fits the Compsons: "the defeated are self-conscious." W. J. Cash confirms the effect of defeat and economic decline as "a growing inclination to withdraw . . . from a world grown too dangerous; to shut away the present and abandon the future . . . to retreat behind their own barred gates and hold

[51] The story of Charles Bon's son, Charles Etienne, returns to the theme of miscegenation and the rejected child. In defiance of the culture which assigned him, delicate and gently reared, to an inferior caste, he married a barbaric black woman.

[52] Lytle, p. 331. The children in *The Velvet Horn* were suddenly orphaned; Quentin and Caddy were without a father's constructive guidance and a mother's love.

commerce with none save the members of their own caste."⁵³
Edwin Burgum describes the specific situation in the Compson
family: "In a family on the defensive against the world, knit
close by its own morbidity, to be capable of falling in love
must mean the bitter folly of falling in love with one's own
sister."⁵⁴

Although these are the most significant examples of the incest theme in Yoknapatawpha, several others should be mentioned. Drusilla, in the episode with her step-son, Bayard, in
The Unvanquished (p. 174), is an incipient parallel to Phaedra, with Bayard more cooperative than Hippolytus. The
abhorrence with which this specific incestuous relationship is
regarded is expressed by Denis de Rougemont in his comment
comparing the story of Tristan with that of Phaedra: "Public inclination . . . continued to side with Tristan against King
Mark, with the seducer against the deceived husband; but it
could never have sided with an incestuous couple."⁵⁵ Analo-
gously, public opinion elsewhere than in the South can more
easily side with Othello than with Francesco Cenci. The suggestion of incestuous feeling on the part of Horace Benbow
for his sister Narcissa in *Sartoris* anticipates, in date of publication of the novel, the story of Quentin and Caddy; moreover, Narcissa is the outward embodiment of the Southern
ideal woman: Narcissa dressed and behaved in accordance
with the ideal Horace expressed of her pure serenity. The
theme of incest is repeated in *Sanctuary* in Horace's feeling
for his stepdaughter, Little Belle, the reverse of the Drusilla-
Bayard situation. In the original version of *Sartoris*, *Flags in
the Dust*, and in the unpublished galleys of *Sanctuary*, Horace
Benbow was a more fully developed character and his incestuous feeling was clearly revealed.

The themes of incest and miscegenation Faulkner used with
relative frequency, in the stories of his upper-class families⁵⁶;

⁵³ Cash, pp. 157–158.
⁵⁴ Edwin Burgum, *The Novel and the World's Dilemma* (New
York: Oxford University Press, 1947), p. 210.
⁵⁵ De Rougemont, p. 203. Drusilla's marriage was a concession to
Southern conventions concerning women, not a matter of her personal
choice.
⁵⁶ Ralph McGill's experience indicates that incest occurred also

he did so, it seems, to reveal characteristic aspects of Southern family life and to suggest the more universal significance of attitudes toward life and toward other human beings reflected in the traditional Southern paternalistic family, founded upon and nourished by white supremacy concepts and gyneolatry.

III. *Organized Religion*

The church in the South is the bulwark of the paternalistic concepts upon which the social institutions are founded and is a force of reactionary conservatism. As it was in the days of slavery, when Negroes were taught that patience and submission were their Christian duty, the church still uses religion, John Dollard says, "as a mechanism for the social control of Negroes" by negating the value of physical welfare in this world.[57] Religious liberalism, like every other kind, has been dead in the South since before the Civil War. In the beliefs of McEachern, in *Light in August,* may be seen the "Protestant theology of the sixteenth century and the Dissenting moral code of the seventeenth" which Cash says made up the "intellectual baggage" of the Southern frontier.[58] In the New South as in the Old South, described by Francis Butler Simkins, "religious conservatism" still triumphs over "eigh-

---

among lower-class whites, a fact confirmed by Davis and Gardner (p. 30). A fictional instance is suggested in Harper Lee's *To Kill a Mocking Bird.* Miscegenation also was not limited to the upper class. Though poor whites had an antipathy toward Negroes, the father of Mink Snopes's wife, a boss in a convict labor camp, lived with a quadroon woman (*The Hamlet,* p. 241). The fact that this was a lumber camp is interesting, in light of the statement by Davis and Gardner that a "criticism of sawmill whites was that they violated caste taboos" (p. 268). Homosexuality as a parallel to incest in isolated plantation families is suggested in Buck and Buddy McCaslin—Buddy "should have been a woman to begin with" (*Go Down, Moses,* p. 272), and perhaps also in the McCallum family and in the Sartoris twins, John and Bayard.

[57] Dollard, p. 248.
[58] Cash, p. 56.

teenth-century tolerance and skepticism."[59] Nineteenth-century science as represented by Darwinism was banned in Mississippi by anti-evolution laws, and in the 1960s, according to James Silver, "shibboleths taken from Social Darwinism, imperialism, and hallowed Anglo-Saxonism, deepen the bankruptcy of today's rationalization in Mississippi."[60] At the root of the terror of new ideas revealed in the hostility toward the Northern schoolmarms after the Civil War and toward the Northern college students in Mississippi in recent years, hostility to the point of murder, is theology of an earlier century. Similar theology has similar effects in South Africa. This theology of hate and authoritarianism which supports closed societies is at the root of what Faulkner condemns in organized religion in Mississippi. He affirmed his faith in God but added: "I think that the trouble with Christianity is that we've never tried it yet" (*Faulkner at Nagano,* pp. 23–24). He might well have agreed with William Percy: "Not science but the Christian sects are causing the death of religion."[61] The landscape of Yoknapatawpha as envisioned by Charles Mallison was punctuated by church spires: "he remembered the tall slender spires which said Peace and the squatter utilitarian belfries which said Repent and . . . one which even said Beware but this one said simply: Burn" (*Intruder in the Dust,* p. 157).[62] He remembered none which said Love.

For love and human brotherhood are not the chief ideals in the dominantly puritanic and fundamentalist Southern branches of the leading white denominations. The split in those denominations into Northern and Southern branches

[59] Francis Butler Simkins, *The South Old and New (1820–1942)* (New York: Knopf, 1948), p. 75.

[60] Silver, p. 23.

[61] Percy, p. 315.

[62] William Van O'Connor in "Protestantism in Yoknapatawpha County," commenting on this passage, says that Faulkner seemed to say in his stories that Protestantism makes Peace hard to experience and that the Calvinist heritage has "a terrifying willingness to say 'simply: Burn.'" O'Connor is probably right in saying that Faulkner made a mistake in identifying the religion of the Burdens as Unitarian. (In *Southern Renascence,* Louis D. Rubin, Jr. and Robert D. Jacobs, eds. [Baltimore: Johns Hopkins Press, 1953], pp. 156, 161.)

took place before the Civil War because the South supported slavery. The strongly Calvinistic element in the Southern branches of the Baptist, Methodist, and Presbyterian churches is due to the theology brought into the South by Scotch settlers or from New England.[63] W. J. Cash related Southern religion to the "triumph of the evangelistic sects": "From the first great revivals onwards, the official moral philosophy of the South moved steadily toward the position of the Massachusetts Bay Colony."[64] Much of the similarity between Faulkner and Hawthorne is explained by the survival in the South of religious doctrines and moral attitudes characteristic of the earlier days in New England. Faulkner is most critical of the Calvinistic denominations in the South, but as a Southerner he shows an awareness of evil and a moral intensity which hark back to the theological climate of Massachusetts.

The God of the Old Testament, not of the New, was the model for the paternalistic society and family in which white men claimed authority: this God was not only the prototype of paternal authority but "became the mighty protagonist of ambivalence," as Lillian Smith learned in her childhood.[65] The Calvinist doctrines of original sin and predestination and the Puritan strict code of behavior and distrust of pleasure as sinful, especially sexuality and drink, imposed upon Southerners a way of life contrary to the natural hedonism which Cash observes as a major element in the Southern character.[66] The grimness and dullness of the lives of many of Faulkner's characters are derived from the repressive influence of religion

[63] Harold J. Douglas and Robert Daniel, "Faulkner and the Puritanism of the South," *Tennessee Studies in Literature,* II (1957), 3. This study gives a better account of Calvinism than of Calvinistic elements in Faulkner's own attitudes or in his works.

[64] Cash, p. 59. Cash specifies the Southern Methodist trend toward Calvinism (p. 84). Clement Eaton states that the religious orthodoxy of the South was due to the "Great Revival of 1800–1805" which "changed the religious atmosphere of the age" and was the beginning of Methodist and Baptist dominance. "By 1830, there were few deists or free-thinkers left in the Southern states" (p. 14).

[65] Smith, pp. 72, 71. Myrdal observed the Old Testament emphasis (p. 458).

[66] Cash, p. 59.

and are relieved by outbreaks of violence. Lillian Smith describes how the South, like Calvin, "bent every little wire in childhood and pinched it to a predestined shape," and how families like her own were "firmly triangulated on sin, sex, and segregation."[67]

Most comforting to those who regard themselves as the leaders in the South is the Calvinist view that class distinctions reflect divine will and that the Old Testament law of retribution, of reward and punishment on earth, still prevails. As Cash expressed it, in referring to employers and strikers in the South: "Heaven apportions its reward in exact relationship to the merit and goodness of the recipient."[68] The prevailing authoritarian, fundamentalist, Calvinistic dogma of the chief Protestant denominations shores up the entire caste and class system of the South.

This effect of Protestant influence is revealed in Faulkner's works. William Van O'Connor observes it in *Absalom, Absalom!*, which he speaks of as "having its origin and center in Faulkner's belief that the Protestant or puritan spirit is one of the most significant factors, even the key factor, in the tragedy of Negro and white relationships."[69] The contrast between Charles Bon and Henry Sutpen stresses the sophisticated, Latin view of Charles, that an octoroon mistress, with or without marriage, is no barrier to marriage with a white woman, and Henry's inflexible puritanic principles, his shock, not at the mistress but at the marriage. To Charles, Mr. Compson conjectured, Henry's reaction was "a fetish-ridden moral blundering which did not deserve to be called thinking" (*Absalom, Absalom!*, p. 93). Despite his being born of "one long invincible line of Methodists" (p. 340), Henry was not appalled by incest or by miscegenation involving a white man and a Negro woman. But a marriage ceremony between a white man, as Henry at first supposed Charles to be, and a Negro woman or between a technically Negro man and a

[67] Smith, p. 79. James Silver refers to Ross Barnett as "firm in the knowledge that 'God was the original segregationist'" (p. 43).

[68] Cash, p. 359.

[69] O'Connor, in *Southern Renascence,* p. 158.

white woman was unthinkable. The religion of the South would support the principles which kept Sutpen from acknowledging Charles as his son and which impelled Henry to shoot Charles. In *Light in August,* Calvinism provides the theme as stated by O'Connor: "rigidity of spirit as opposed to the need for acceptance of human fallibility and the need for pity and sympathy."[70]

The meddling of "respectable" church-goers with the private lives of others aroused Faulkner's ire. The story of "Uncle Willy" is that of a gentle dope-addict who is driven to suicide by the church women who try to reform and rehabilitate him and consequently deprive him of all that makes life bearable. The point of view, that of a fourteen-year-old boy, gives a special twist; he regards as admirable and even enviable an old man for whom life holds nothing but the needle and the friendship of a few boys who enjoy his drug-store ice cream. But the self-righteousness of the women, their blindness to the human virtues as well as the vices of Uncle Willy, remains appalling, even when one discounts the admiration of the narrator. Narcissa Benbow and the other "Christian" women who hound poor Ruby Lamar and her ailing baby from one place to another while she waits for her husband's trial are another even more appalling example of the "good" people of Jefferson (*Sanctuary*). Cora Tull, with her sanctimonious self-righteousness, is a rare example in Faulkner of religiosity used for humorous effect (*As I Lay Dying*).

Faulkner indicates the denominational pattern of religion in Yoknapatawpha County and has Charles Mallison outline its history: "ours was a town founded by Aryan Baptists and Methodists, for Aryan Baptists and Methodists," he begins, then indicates other denominations which became subordinate

[70] William Van O'Connor, "Protestantism in Yoknapatawpha County," *Hopkins Review,* V (1952), 31 (a slightly different version of the article in *Southern Renascence*). In "*Light in August*: The Calvinism of William Faulkner" (*Modern Fiction Studies,* VIII [Summer, 1962]), Alwyn Berland describes Calvinism as "the institutional belief that elevates righteousness above love, that accepts depravity as the natural condition of man, that suggests a strong measure of predestination" (p. 159).

to the two chief ones, founded to establish a tyranny "in which
to be incorrigible and unreconstructible Baptists and Methodists" (*The Town,* pp. 306–307). In Yoknapatawpha as in the
South, the Baptists and Methodists are most important.[71] The
Baptists are not only the most numerous in Mississippi but are
the most bitterly attacked by Faulkner. He questions whether
the "bucolic, provincial Southern Baptist" believes in God, and
he ascribes the warped and twisted emotional condition of
Southern Baptists to spiritual starvation, to lives without
beauty or pleasure (*Faulkner in the University,* pp. 173, 189–
190). Horace Benbow was indignant at the hypocritical "good"
people of Jefferson, who bought whiskey from Lee Goodwin,
then "jumped on him" when he was down. It was the Baptist
preacher who took Goodwin for a text when Goodwin was
awaiting trial for a crime of which he was innocent. Horace
interpreted the intent of the sermon:

Not only as a murderer, but as an adulterer; a polluter of the
free Democratic-Protestant atmosphere of Yoknapatawpha county.
I gathered that his idea was that Goodwin and the woman should
both be burned as a sole example to that child; the child to be
reared and taught the English language for the sole end of being
taught that it was begot in sin by two people who suffered by fire
for having begot it [*Sanctuary,* pp. 123–124].

[71] Harold F. Kaufman, "Mississippi Churches: A Half Century of
Change," shows the distribution of denominations, including Lafayette
County, and shows that Southern Baptists are strongest in Mississippi
and that church membership in Mississippi is among the highest in the
nation (*Mississippi Quarterly,* XII [Summer, 1959], 105–135). William
Percy lists in Greenville, Mississippi, 53 Baptist churches, 18 Methodist,
one Episcopal and one Catholic, plus a scattering of others. A relevant
article is: Robert N. Burrows, "Institutional Christianity as Reflected
in the Works of William Faulkner," *Mississippi Quarterly,* XIV (Summer, 1961), 138–147. In Chapter XVIII of *The Negro in Mississippi,*
Wharton gives a good account of the growth of separate Negro
churches in Mississippi after 1865. The scope of Kenneth K. Bailey's
thoroughly documented study is indicated in the title: *Southern White
Protestantism in the Twentieth Century* (New York: Harper & Row,
1964). Erskine Caldwell's *Deep South: Memory and Observation* (New
York: Weybright and Talley, 1968) deals with both white and Negro
religion and a variety of sects. He notes that the "extreme conservatism"
of fundamentalist Protestants "is in keeping with the traditional sharecropper plantation system, the segregated racial pattern, states rights,
and one-party political domination" (p. 55).

Aunt Jenny's comment is "They're just Baptists." When one considers that Faulkner no doubt had actual parallels for Flem and Clarence Snopes as active members of the Baptist church —Ross Barnett, for example—one begins to understand Faulkner's attitude.[72] Flem's rise to respectability is realistically accompanied by his Baptist affiliation in Jefferson and his becoming deacon, a pattern of social-religious activity which Kaufman showed to be characteristic of economic success in Southern towns.[73]

In Yoknapatawpha County, the Methodists seem most prominent in Frenchman's Bend. The Varners were Methodist (*The Town*, p. 344), and one assumes that Faulkner chose with deliberation the name of Whitfield, the minister, descendant of the first one in the area. Whitfield is both a rustic Arthur Dimmesdale, in *As I Lay Dying,* saved by Addie's death from confessing his sin, and a vigorous, self-reliant minister, firm in faith, in "Shingles for the Lord." One assumes that Wesley Snopes is also Methodist. As a revival song leader, he was caught in a cotton house with a fourteen-year-old girl and tarred and feathered (*The Mansion*, p. 71).

Charles Mallison's account of the first Presbyterian church in the area (in fact built at College Hill in 1842) as reflecting the culture and refinement of that denomination in the Old South[74] is basically accurate. But, as Charles notes, the Presby-

---

[72] *The Town,* p. 359; *The Mansion,* p. 304; Silver, p. 44. In James W. Webb and A. Wigfall Green, *William Faulkner of Oxford* (Baton Rouge: Louisiana State University Press, 1965), Calvin Brown quotes a remark made by Faulkner at a baseball game in which there was a Baptist team: " 'I don't know what church God belongs to, but I know he isn't a Baptist because he permits the other sects to exist' " (p. 46). Robert Canzoneri refers to his father's opinion that some ministers "are Baptists only because they knew they could never make Pope" (p. 176).

[73] Kaufman, p. 128. Cash makes a similar point of the South in general, in a passage that might be a description of Flem Snopes except that Flem did not pass his free evenings "in making most unholily merry" (pp. 227–228).

[74] Simkins, p. 77. The Presbyterians continued the same qualities in the New South (p. 316). William Faulkner was married in the College Hill Church; see illustration.

terians and the Episcopalians were "usurped and dispossessed" by the Baptists and Methodists (*The Town*, p. 307). Gail Hightower, the chief Presbyterian, is obviously not typical (*Light in August*). Hightower's loss of authority may reflect Charles's remark on the dispossession of the Presbyterians and also may suggest the loss of leadership of the clergy. Hightower's meditation on Protestant music is the key to the whole paradox of Southern religion and its relation to other social institutions and to the action of individuals and mobs:

Listening, he seems to hear within it the apotheosis of his own history, his own land, his own environed blood: that people from which he sprang and among whom he lives who can never take either pleasure or catastrophe or escape from either, without brawling over it. Pleasure, ecstasy, they cannot seem to bear; their escape from it is in violence, in drinking and fighting and praying; catastrophe too, the violence identical and apparently inescapable. *And so why should not their religion drive them to crucifixion of themselves and one another?* [p. 322].

To balance the inertia of Hightower, Byron Bunch represents the earnest Christian, living puritanically but acting out of Christian charity and a sense of responsibility, involved despite himself in the needs of Lena and of Joe Christmas.

As might be expected, considering the eminence of the Episcopalian church in the East and its consequent aristocratic, enlightened character, Faulkner's most admirable, least fanatic characters are Episcopalians: Granny Millard, presumably the Sartorises, Gavin Stevens, and the Mallisons (*The Unvanquished*, p. 153; *The Town*, p. 342). Granny lived by a strict code; when all seemed fair in war and she departed from it, she accepted the responsibility for her own actions, not looking on herself as an instrument of the Lord but as a sinner, with the sins of others on her conscience (*The Unvanquished*, pp. 155–156, 167–168). She paid with her life. Brother Fortinbride, the Methodist serving during the war in the Episcopal church, is presented with sympathy. And Granny brought up Bayard so that he had courage to refuse to kill his father's slayer ("An Odor of Verbena," pp. 246–247).[75]

An obvious implication of Faulkner's treatment of religion is the lack of liberal leadership among the clergy in times of social crisis. This reflects the actual situation in which, as Ralph McGill says, "the Christian church has been either in retreat or standing afar off wringing its hands in an agony of spirit and guilt."[76] The explanation is significant; in churches where the congregation have authority over the minister, deviation from Southern orthodoxy results in the minister's losing his position.[77] Churches like the Episcopal where there is a hierarchy allow more freedom of expression and the congregation are more receptive to liberal views.[78] The implications in relation to Faulkner's attitudes toward Protestant denominations are clear: he favored that one in which opinion is most enlightened and least Calvinistic but regarded organized religion as lacking in true Christian leadership.

The influence of puritanic Protestantism is clearly seen in distinctive aspects of Southern individuals and society. Prohibition survived until 1966 in Mississippi. Myrdal explains that prohibition was directed at the Negro and remarks that he saw more hard drinking in Mississippi than anywhere else;

[75] The Episcopal church in Jefferson referred to by Charles Mallison (*The Town*, p. 306) has its original in St. Peter's in Oxford, built in 1851. William Faulkner's daughter was married there, and the rector of St. Peter's conducted Faulkner's funeral service. The comparatively minor position of the Episcopalian church in Mississippi is one of the significant differences between the Tidewater aristocracy, who were largely Anglican, and the leading families of Mississippi (Cash, p. 58).

[76] McGill, p. 286. McGill's chapter, "The Agony of the Church," explains the prevailing attitudes against which the clergy can make little progress. The hate organizations, he remarks, "employ God and Christ somewhat as cosmic bellboys" (p. 270).

[77] Silver quotes a minister as saying, "In Mississippi a Christian minister is free only as long as he is willing to run and bay with the pack" (p. 59). Of 28 young Methodist ministers who published a statement in January, 1963, "Born of Conviction," affirming liberal beliefs, ten had left Mississippi by summer and at least six had been sent to more liberal urban churches (p. 58).

[78] McGill states that Roman Catholic and Episcopal churches, not being split into Northern and Southern divisions, have less trouble from laymen (p. 276).

he quotes Will Rogers: "Mississippi will hold faithful and steadfast to prohibition as long as the voters can stagger to the polls."[79] Constant lawbreaking by a large part of the adult population and the fact that the state collected taxes on bootleggers' stock scarcely inculcated respect for the law or for the sincerity of those who supported prohibition. In a letter to the Oxford *Eagle,* September 8, 1950, with sustained irony Faulkner disclaimed being a proponent of legal beer and avowed himself "as much an enemy of liberty and enlightenment and progress as any voting or drinking dry either in Oxford." He referred to "the long and happy marriage between dry voters and illicit sellers," and objected, without irony, "to ministers of God violating the canons and ethics of their sacred and holy avocation by using, either openly or underhand, the weight and power of their office to try to influence a civil election."[80] The McCallums who make bootleg liquor, the Joe Christmases who sell it, and the Linda Snopeses who buy it offer overt evidence of prohibition in Yoknapatawpha. The plot of part of "The Fire and the Hearth" involves Lucas Beauchamp's still. But a good deal of the social life in Yoknapatawpha gives no idea that the leading citizens are actually all lawbreakers and that the official view of alcohol is that it is the road to damnation. A similar split between avowed personal principles and actions is apparent, constituting what Cash calls "the old cleft in the Southern psyche,"[81] in the Gowries' observing the Sabbath by postponing the lynching

---

[79] Myrdal, pp. 457–458.

[80] Reprinted in *Essays, Speeches, and Public Letters,* Meriwether, ed., pp. 209–210. Bailey gives an account of the part played by Southern clergymen, unanimous on the prohibition issue, in defeating Al Smith in the campaign of 1928 (Chapter 5). Lillian Smith tells how her father won the fight for prohibition by bribing his mill workers (pp. 22–23). V. O. Key, in *Southern Politics,* explains how the blackmarket tax on illegal liquor sales operated (p. 233). Robert Canzoneri neatly sums up the situation that prevailed: "Mississippi's liquor laws provide so obvious an illustration of pervasive hypocrisy that even the most disinterested summary runs the risk of being discounted as caricature" (p. 115).

[81] Cash, p. 136. Cash's analysis of the "two currents of Puritanism and hedonism" in Southern society throws light on one of the chief paradoxes of the South (pp. 136–137).

until Monday and, despite Sabbath piety, leading lawless lives. The facts about Wild Bill Sullivan, the "King of the clans" and patriarch of Sullivan's Hollow, in which 350 of 450 pupils were Sullivans, exceed anything in Faulkner. Wild Bill and his brothers lived under "laws that his people wrote with cold lead from hot pistol barrels," but they went to church every Sunday.[82] William Percy described Sullivan's Hollow: "than which there is no more blood-spilling, moonshine-drinking, tobacco-spitting nest of outlaws in all the South."[83]

This suspension of Christian conscience in public actions is alarming enough, but Percy quotes a clergyman as saying that those who have been saved believe that "when you are certain of salvation you may do what you like."[84] Certainty of salvation and certainty of white superiority seem allied. Faulkner presents several characters who reveal this conviction in its most extreme and vicious form, regarding themselves as absolved of personal responsibility because they are instruments of divine will. Four of the characters in *Light in August,* that most sweeping exposure of Calvinism, reveal this aberration: Joanna Burden, Mr. McEachern, Doc Hines, and Percy Grimm. They will be discussed in relation to violence as a pattern of action, but the source of their violence is Calvinistic religion.

In contrast with the religion of white people, that of the Negroes is presented sympathetically in Yoknapatawpha. As the Civil War caused a split of Protestant denominations into Northern and Southern bodies, it caused the establishment of separate Negro churches, often the same denominations as the white, with Baptists and Methodists popular. The emotional demonstrations which often distinguish Negro from white worship are a survival from white religious revivals of

[82] The Oxford *Eagle* (June 30, 1932), in reporting the death of Wild Bill.

[83] Percy, p. 194. Faulkner refers to Sullivan's Hollow in "Mississippi" (in *Essays, Speeches, and Public Letters,* Meriwether, ed. [p. 33]); he mentions the clannishness of the families, their feuds, and their hostility to revenue officers and Negroes.

[84] Percy, p. 314.

the eighteenth and nineteenth centuries.[85] In the account of Dilsey at the Easter service, in *The Sound and the Fury,* IV, sincerity and depth of feeling characterize preacher and congregation, and the expressions of emotion are reverent. The faith of Dilsey and of Nancy, in *Requiem for a Nun,* is contrasted with the weakness, selfishness, and viciousness of those whom they serve, the Compsons and Temple Drake, who were nurtured in the Southern upper-class tradition.

For both races, especially on the lower social and economic levels, religion provided drama and excitement. "Orgiastic religion," Cash observes, and violence were the only pleasures that could be practiced openly.[86] Lillian Smith, recalling white revivals of her childhood, said: "Guilt was then and is today the biggest crop raised in Dixie, harvested each summer just before cotton is picked." But sin and hell and the wrath of God, not love of God and the brotherhood of man, were preached, and, believing in original sin created within the individual soul, they "stubbornly refused to assent to the possibility that culture had had any role in its creation."[87] Thus

[85] Powdermaker, p. 232. The description of a Negro service in Harper Lee's *To Kill a Mocking Bird* (Philadelphia: Lippincott, 1960) and the account of the meeting of the missionary society, discussing foreign missions and their servants and congratulating themselves on their Christianity, provide useful parallels to Faulkner's treatment of religion and should be footnoted by Canzoneri's account of the experiences of his sister, a missionary in Nigeria, and of Nigerians in the United States, with the Mississippi Baptists (Chapter XIV). Excellent accounts of Negro revival services are given by Dollard, who notes some aspects which are not European in origin (pp. 226–242), and Wharton (Chapter XVIII), who deals with the development of Negro churches in Mississippi. Stampp points out the strong similarity between Negro and white revivals and concludes that the religion of Negroes and poor whites was "strikingly similar" in the ante-bellum South (pp. 375–377). Caldwell says: "the worship of God among Negroes, no matter how fervent in belief and reverent in attitude, has never approached the religious excesses of white Protestants of the many evangelical sects" (p. 51). Johnson makes the same point (pp. 151–152).

[86] Cash, p. 136.

[87] Smith, pp. 87, 89. Her account brings out the emotional and dramatic qualities experienced and the characteristics of the preachers who, though they "preached asceticism . . . with the libertine's words,"

institutional religion set up defenses against critical examination of the culture, strengthened the patriarchal, authoritative
pattern in family and state, and sanctioned the caste system.
Faulkner's denunciation of such religion is based on its lack
of Christianity.[88]

IV. *Politics*

In a sparsely populated rural county, politics follow the same
pattern as religion: Baptist fundamentalists are likely to pre-
dominate in both secular and religious government. Because
Mississippi is the most rural Southern state and has the highest
proportion of Negro population, in Mississippi, more than in
any other Southern state, the pattern of a rural county is repeated in that of the state. As V. O. Key states, "the beginning
and the end of Mississippi politics is the Negro," a fact which
serves to explain why "Mississippi only manifests in accentu-
ated form the darker political strains that run throughout the
South."[89] Faulkner's one significant use of a political campaign, in *The Mansion,* introduces the essential institution of
Mississippi politics and presents its dominant characteristics.

---

were sincere. Caldwell explains how the revival season fitted into the
laying-by season in cotton growing, the only time of year when
farmers could spend days in town with their families (p. 105). Bailey
explains that revivals "fulfilled vital needs in southern society. They
brought hope to many who knew little of hope and release to many
who knew little of release" (p. 24). Since 1940, he says, "Accounts of
revival meetings remained a conspicuous feature in most Southern
Baptist papers" (p. 155).

[88] Logically, education and the schools should follow religion and
the churches, but Faulkner seldom deals with institutional education.
Wharton, in Chapter XVII, discusses the growth of Negro education in
Mississippi after the Civil War, initiated largely by missionaries from
the North, and the development of public education for both Negroes
and whites. Davis and Gardner deal with education of Negroes.

[89] V. O. Key, *Southern Politics* (New York: Vintage Books, Caravelle
Edition, 1949), p. 229.

The farcical conclusion, however, may tend to obscure the realities of the issue and the parallels between Clarence Snopes and actual Mississippi politicians.

The disfranchisement of the Negro that took place after the Civil Rights Bill of 1875 was declared unconstitutional has had the most complete and lasting effects in Mississippi, the state which V. O. Key says "undoubtedly has harbored the most unrestrained and most continuous advocates of white supremacy."[90] By excluding Negroes from the Democratic primary, and continuing to do so in effect after the Supreme Court in 1944 declared the white primary unconstitutional,[91] Mississippi held to the tradition of white superiority. Myrdal's statement in *The American Dilemma* (1944) that Mississippi probably had the fewest Negro voters, according to Ralph Bunche's estimate "only a few hundred 'good' Negro aristocrats and school teachers," is confirmed in Arnold Rose's Postscript to the 1962 edition of *An American Dilemma*: "the only state where they were almost systematically excluded from the polls . . . was Mississippi."[92] James Silver states that usually less than five percent of the Negro voting population is allowed to register. Since a voter applicant is required "to read and write *and* interpret any section of the state constitution" (the satisfactory interpretation being judged by the white registrar) and to be "of good moral character and have his name and address published in a local newspaper for two weeks,"[93] it is easy to understand why few Negroes dared try to register and why few who did try succeeded in meeting the qualifications. Faulkner's reference to Negroes voting in Jefferson does not indicate proportional numbers voting and may

90 *Ibid.*, p. 233, footnote 8.
91 *Ibid.*, p. 625. The campaign in *The Mansion* is in the summer of 1945 (p. 306).
92 Myrdal, pp. 488, xxxix. Davis and Gardner note that the taboo on Negroes' voting is exceeded in strength only by that on intercaste sexual relations (p. 260).
93 Silver, pp. 86, 87. Facsimiles of two applications, white and Negro, are given, showing that "in precisely similar situations" the white citizen was registered and the Negro disqualified (p. 106). Davis and Gardner observe that destruction of caste anonymity is a strong deterrent to Negro registration (p. 285).

suggest that their choice of candidates is limited as well as injudicious: "even Negroes passing beneath the balconies and into the chancery clerk's office to cast ballots too, voting for the same white-skinned rascals and demagogues and white supremacy champions that the white ones did . . ." (*Requiem for a Nun*, p. 47).

In reality, little choice may be offered between candidates on the issue Faulkner names. The one-party system gives control to white supremacists: rival candidates from the time of L. Q. C. Lamar through that of Leroy Percy and down to the last election for governor in Mississippi have been agreed on white supremacy. As James Silver puts it: "There can be no real debate on issues for *there is no issue beyond the supremacy of the white man,* no continuity in the existence even of factions, no competition between recognizable groups."[94] The opportunistic tactics of Clarence Snopes will seem less incredible if this fact is remembered.

Clarence as a politician exemplifies the way in which the political power of poor whites is used to keep Negroes politically impotent. As we shall see, violence and intimidation of Negroes was a behavior pattern with Clarence from his early youth. This same kind of violence could be and is used to keep Negroes from voting,[95] and is most likely to be used by the poor whites like the Snopeses who are in economic competition with Negroes and who resent the paternalistic relationship that sometimes prevails between upper-class whites and Negroes but not between upper-class whites and poor whites.

[94] *Ibid.,* p. 20. The power of the Mississippi press and the effectiveness with which the two extremist Jackson papers manipulate the news in the interests of "racial, economic, political, and religious orthodoxy" is dealt with by Silver (pp. 28–35). In *The Way of the South,* Odum cites the example of an editor of "an important industrial publication" who published "literally hundreds of falsehoods about individuals, institutions, and movements when the facts could have been verified," with statements ranging from "libel to naïve misunderstanding," without being discredited and in fact being "rewarded by election to the board of trustees of his state university" (p. 205). Faulkner deals too little with the press to warrant its inclusion as a separate topic.

[95] Myrdal describes the forms violence and intimidation take (p. 485).

(Sutpen was himself a poor white; his patronizing Wash Jones in *Absalom, Absalom!* is not typical.) William Percy's description of the "sovereign voter" who put and kept Vardaman and, even worse, Bilbo in power sounds like a group picture of the Snopes clan: "They were the sort of people that lynch Negroes, that mistake hoodlumism for wit, and cunning for intelligence, that attend revivals and fight and fornicate in the bushes afterwards. They were undiluted Anglo-Saxons."[96] Carl Rowan explains the strategy used by the upper-class white to keep the Negro in the gutter without staying there himself to hold the Negro down: "he was keeping the Negro in the gutter by duping the poor white into staying there and holding him."[97] The Clarence Snopeses are only too willing to do the holding.

And they are aided by the Mississippi Constitution, as revised in 1890 for the avowed purpose of "crushing out the manhood of the Negro citizens,"[98] successfully achieving its purpose by becoming "the instrument and shield of fraud."[99] Thus, although the constant cry against federal civil rights legislation is that mores and folkways cannot be changed by stateways,[100] the stateways of Mississippi were designed to mold folkways, to make a white man feel contaminated by the proximity of a seated Negro in a public place, and have succeeded in the conditioning process. The corrupt state legislature through which the constitution achieves its effect, as

[96] Percy, p. 149.

[97] Rowan, p. 149. The gutter analogy was originated by Booker T. Washington. The essence of the poor white's motivation, upon which politicians capitalize, is summed up in a statement by a poor white quoted by Russell Warren Howe; he objected to integration because "it'd mean a nigger beat'n me f'r a job jus' because he could do it better" ("Prejudice, Superstition, and Economics," *Phylon*, XVII [1956], 220). Faulkner explains that the KKK draws most heavily from the unsuccessful poor whites who fear the economic rivalry of the Negroes who can beat them at their "own poor game"; their only superiority is their white skin (*Faulkner in the University*, p. 223).

[98] Quoted by Charles E. Silberman in *Crisis in Black and White* (New York: Random House, 1964), p. 23.

[99] Quoted by James Silver (p. 17) from the editor of the Port Gibson *Reveille*.

[100] Myrdal, p. 462.

described by James Silver, makes the inclusion of a Clarence Snopes among their number seem terribly possible.[101]

The relation of economic to political power is epitomized by Uncle Billy Varner, just as he epitomized the economic monopoly of the rural merchant.[102] Uncle Billy, as a kind of rustic king-maker, used his influence over the voters, by means of his "diffused usurious capacity for blackmail," to get Clarence elected constable in Varner's "own private Beat Two," then Beat supervisor, then county representative at Jackson (p. 297).[103] After he "translated" Clarence to the upper house of the state legislature—and to C. Egglestone Snopes—it began to look terrifyingly possible, to Gavin Stevens and Ratliff, that Uncle Billy, "by all the mutually compounding vote-swapping Varners of the whole congressional district" (p. 297), could send Clarence to Washington. Uncle Billy's name was all the platform Clarence needed (though he devised one for himself). Uncle Billy's patronage was not, however, due to his admiration for Clarence's sterling character but rather to a desire to get rid of a source of irritation and provide, at public expense, for an incompetent whom otherwise he and the Snopeses might have to support (pp. 301, 310). At the Varner's Mill picnic Uncle Billy planned to tell the people whom to vote for (p. 313). And there, as easily as Uncle Billy elevated Clarence, he cast him down. Such is the power of the man to whom everybody owes money.

Clarence represents the most vulgar, stupid, unprincipled, hypocritical kind of white-supremacy demagogue. He is rendered more believable by a few facts about Mississippi's Bilbo

[101] Silver refers to the legislature which convened in January, 1962 (pp. 47–49). Robert Canzoneri quotes Shelby Foote as saying that "Ross Barnett was not the first Snopes to live in the governor's mansion" (p. 80).

[102] The story of Clarence's political career and the primary campaign which ended it is given in Chapter Thirteen of *The Mansion*. All page numbers given in the account of Clarence are to *The Mansion* unless otherwise specified.

[103] "Beats" are county districts. Faulkner switches beat numbers, interchanging Beat Two and Beat Four in Lafayette County terms. The "tough" Beat of the Gowries is really Beat Two, not Four; the Frenchman's Bend area is really Beat Four, not Two.

and Vardaman. The popularity of Vardaman and Bilbo among lower-class and poor whites is reflected in Yokna-patawpha by proper names: in addition to Vardaman Bundren there are two sets of twins named Vardaman and Bilbo, I. O. Snopes's sons and old Gowrie's. William Percy explains why the people loved the "pert little monster, glib and shameless, with that sort of cunning common to criminals which passes for intelligence": "They loved him not because they were deceived in him but because they understood him thoroughly; they said of him proudly, 'He's a slick little bastard.' "[104] These dema-gogues who dished out the "racial hog slop," aided by preach-ers and editors, Lillian Smith feared more than she feared their followers, the ignorant and stubborn rural folk who still had a conscience.[105] Bilbo, who had done some Baptist preach-ing, defended himself against the charge of racial and religious intolerance by piously declaring himself for "every damn Jew from Jesus Christ on down."[106] Bilbo made less of a campaign issue of white supremacy than did Vardaman, who pro-nounced the Negro to be "a lazy, lying, lustful animal which no conceivable amount of training can transform into a toler-able citizen."[107] Clarence's career is rooted in racial antagonism and facilitated—in addition to Uncle Billy's influence—by his knowledge of voters' reactions.

Clarence, like many Mississippi politicians, was a Baptist and a Sunday School teacher, though perhaps untypically frank in admitting to Horace Benbow: "I'm putty liberal my-self. I aint hidebound in no sense . . ." (*Sanctuary*, p. 199).[108]

---

[104] Percy, p. 148. A political novel, *No Place to Run* (New York: Viking, 1959), has a politician-hero, Gene Massie, who resembles Clar-ence Snopes in many respects and who is referred to by his admirers as "a slick little bastard." The author, Philip Alston Stone, was Faulk-ner's godson and the son of Phil Stone, the literary mentor of Faulkner's youth; the scene is recognizably Oxford.

[105] Smith, pp. 150, 153.

[106] Quoted by Key, p. 243, footnote 31.

[107] Quoted by Kirwan, p. 146.

[108] In *No Place to Run*, Gene Massie during his campaign teaches his old Sunday School class at the Baptist church, and orates eloquently on prohibition, though neither religious nor abstemious in private. (The popularity of prohibition with politicians may be explained by the

Clarence began as the leader of a gang which terrorized Negroes and women. As constable he became the defender of public peace and beat up Negroes, not on principle as before but to see "how far his official power and legal immunity actually went" (p. 300) and how strong he was. He was a "goon" before the term was invented and kept the Klan alive as long as it served his purpose. Then he became its enemy to win the votes of "the literate and liberal innocents" (p. 302) who thought that "decency and right and personal liberty would prevail simply because they were decent and right" (p. 302). And he did destroy the Klan, only to become a Silver Shirt, a more durable organization than the "county-autonomous Klan." He used "the emotions of religion or patriotism" (p. 303) to gain political support and took up first Huey Long's "soak the rich" policy, referring to the rich in other states, and then that of opposition to organized labor. For his own advantage he used all of the federal relief agencies of the Depression and "all the other agencies created in the dream or hope that people should not suffer," and supported them in a voice "full of racial and religious and economic intolerance" (p. 306). His personal sliminess and filth are more apparent in *Sanctuary,* in his encounters with Horace Benbow, than in the largely summarized account in *The Mansion.*

Clarence's opponent was Devries, a World War II colonel, graduate of the University of Mississippi, who commanded a Negro regiment and did it well:

. . . being a Southerner, he knew that no white man understood the Negroes and never would so long as the white man compelled the black man to be first a Negro and only then a man, since this, the impenetrable dividing wall, was the black man's only defense and protection for survival [p. 308].

---

temperance lobby's "powerful but unacknowledged allies in the bootleggers" [Key, p. 235].) The opponent of Massie was Jamieson, a fanatic who really believed in the hate talk Massie used merely for votes. Jamieson resembled an Old Testament prophet and was "a fierce and vengeful hater," urging that Negroes be killed rather than be allowed to vote or attend white schools (*No Place to Run,* p. 233).

He returned to the front for the third time, after being decorated for valor, and won the Congressional Medal of Honor. Devries, carrying a wounded sergeant, was saved by an Arkansas fieldhand after Devries had rescued a part of a battalion trapped by a barrage; Devries insisted on having his last medal dug out of his locker, said to the fieldhand, "Lift me up, you big bastard," and pinned the medal on the Negro (p. 309). Campaigning with a "tin leg," with nothing to recommend him except his war record, Devries was running against Clarence Snopes in the primary. He could count on the votes of "the heirs of the same uncoordinated political illusionees innocent enough to believe still that demagoguery and bigotry and intolerance must not and cannot and will not endure simply because they are bigotry and demagoguery and intolerance" (p. 309). Such a candidate, Lillian Smith asserts, could "swing the decent voters in the state to his side" but "the politicians in a southern state will not gamble on there being a majority of decent people."[109] Devries, though an exception in that he did so gamble, proved the truth of Myrdal's statement: "All over the South it is dangerous for a candidate to be accused of friendliness to the Negro."[110] Clarence simply stressed the reason why Devries won the Medal of Honor: he was saving one Negro and was saved by another. Clarence let the people embroider the facts until Devries was supposed to have chosen to save a Negro and to have left a white boy to die. Thus before the primary "Clarence was already elected":

. . . that Medal of Honor which the government had awarded Devries for risking death to defend the principles on which that government was founded and by which it existed, had destroyed forever his chance to serve in the Congress which had accoladed him [p. 312].

On this record and with these principles his defeat in most rural areas and many urban ones in Mississippi would be insured.

[109] Smith, p. 175.
[110] Myrdal, p. 476.

Clarence Snopes was defeated, but not by popular support of his rival's superior principles and character; he was defeated by the machinations of an "anonymous underhanded son-of-a-gun" and two small boys and a pack of dogs, and a bit of blackmail based on the principle that to be made ridiculous is as potent a threat as one encounters. Uncle Billy Varner withdrew his support and Clarence retired from politics. By himself, Clarence "would have wound up having every rabies tag in Yoknapatawpha County counted as an absentee ballot" (p. 319). But Uncle Billy refused to have his district represented by "nobody that ere a son-a-bitching dog that happens by cant tell from a fence post" (p. 319). The political significance of the success of Devries in winning the primary is simply that in Mississippi politics the qualifications of candidates are irrelevant and that any son of a bitch can prove more influential than an advocate of the principles on which the United States was founded. The significance as Charles Mallison and Gavin Stevens saw it is that we must "learn how to trust in God without depending on Him. In fact, we need to fix things so He can depend on us for a while" (p. 321). But in Mississippi, the sentiments behind that statement find little endorsement in pulpit, press, legislature, or court.

The small and politically impotent group who voted for Devries on the basis of principles and Gavin and Charles and the "anonymous underhanded son-of-a-gun" Ratliff are fictitious evidence of a liberal element in the population which, in Oxford, was represented by Faulkner and by such university professors as James Silver.

James Silver quotes a statement given him by William Faulkner to be used as the introduction to *Three Views of the Segregation Decisions*: Faulkner reduces the question to "whether or not white people shall remain free" and continues:

We accept contumely and the risk of violence because we will not sit quietly by and see our native land, the South, . . . wreck and ruin itself twice in less than a hundred years, over the Negro question.

We speak now against the day when our Southern people who will resist to the last these inevitable changes in social relations,

will, when they have been forced to accept what they at one
time might have accepted with dignity and goodwill, will say,
"Why didn't someone tell us this before? Tell us this in time?"

Silver then adds the words of Gavin Stevens as "a firm basis
for 'standing up to be counted' ": "Some things you must
never stop refusing to bear. Injustice and outrage and dishonor
and shame. No matter how young you are or how old you
have got. Not for kudos and not for cash: your picture in the
paper nor money in the bank either. Just refuse to bear
them."[111]

Faulkner as a liberal spoke out through his fiction and
James Silver as a liberal speaks out in meetings, articles, and
books, and on television. Both of them, when heard and understood by fellow townsmen, incurred abuse and threats. The
nature and plight of the Southern liberal are pertinent here
in relation to Faulkner's fiction: how the liberal is represented
and what place and effect he has in his society.

By removing the university from Jefferson, Faulkner removed from Yoknapatawpha one of the chief sources of liberal
opinion in the state, but one in which freedom of speech and
freedom of dissension are limited and from which many liberals have departed. In Jefferson there is no group of liberals,
but we do have Gavin Stevens, an intellectual and liberal, and
Ratliff, a liberal, and young Charles Mallison, growing up
under his uncle's influence. (Devries is a liberal but appears
only in *The Mansion* and plays no part in town life.) Gavin
Stevens is humane and kindly, but despite his goodwill he

[111] Silver, pp. xii, xiii. The situation of the liberal in the the university
and the state is discussed and exemplified by Silver throughout the
book. He resigned from the University of Mississippi and left the state.
Gavin Stevens resembles his creator in being more interested in law, as
will be apparent in the next chapter, than in politics. Faulkner's close
friend, W. McNeill Reed, said that "William was not at all interested
in politics, even on behalf of his uncle" ("Four Decades of Friendship,"
in *William Faulkner of Oxford,* James W. Webb and A. Wigfall Green,
eds. [Baton Rouge: Louisiana State University Press, 1965], p. 182).
Faulkner's inclusion of the political career of Clarence Snopes is more
significant, in light of his lack of interest in politics, than is the absence
of other political figures in Yoknapatawpha. In *Faulkner: A Biography*
(New York: Random House, 1974), Joseph Blotner revealed that, contrary to his usual indifference to politics, Faulkner supported Adlai
Stevenson as candidate for president; Blotner quoted Faulkner as saying
that Stevenson lost because he "had three strikes against him: wit,
urbanity, and erudition" (p. 1622).

clings to stereotypes; Charles and Miss Habersham, not Gavin, saved Lucas by being willing to believe he might be telling the truth and might be innocent (*Intruder in the Dust*). Gavin expends his energies in talking and ineffectually fighting Snopesism. He does not go into politics or show any active interest in improving the legal system. His spare time he spends translating the Old Testament back into classic Greek (*Knight's Gambit*, p. 207). In his long speech in *Intruder in the Dust* (pp. 153–156), which has mistakenly been taken to represent Faulkner's opinion, Gavin refers to the Negro as Sambo and defends the right of the South to set him free; he defends the South in resisting the North, but he does not question the right of Sambo to be free—sometime. The weakness of Gavin is that he does nothing but talk to Ratliff and Charles and that his liberal ideas are vitiated by conflicting traditional attitudes. He treats Lucas with amused condescension, when Lucas first says "I'm gonter pay you," and when Lucas finally does so (*Intruder in the Dust*, pp. 59, 244–247), Gavin regards him, not as he would a white man of equal dignity, and his elder, but as he would a child to be humored with tolerant amusement. In *The Mansion* Gavin and Ratliff both support Devries, but only Ratliff is able to do anything about it. Gavin knew the way in which Clarence Snopes was put into office and kept there for years; he despised Clarence and the whole Snopes tribe. But as a lawyer, a member of a leading family, known and respected throughout the county, he did nothing, though doubtless he could have won the political support of not only the innocents who favored Devries but of the country people whom he knew and with whom he could communicate.

Faulkner's ideal was not the people who privately entertain the right ideas; he said: "What we need are people who will say this is bad and I'm going to do something about it, I'm going to change it" (*Faulkner in the University*, p. 246). The novelist does something about it by writing novels; the history professor does something about it by teaching, speaking, and writing; the lawyer does something about it by carrying his liberal views into the courtroom and going into politics, as Atticus Finch did in *To Kill a Mocking Bird*. Gavin Stevens is a realistic Southern liberal in a small town, deficient in his understanding of people and ineffective in the real world (*Faulkner in the University,* pp. 140–141); he is reluctant to become totally committed and involved. He is not a mouthpiece for Faulkner, despite their sometimes similar views. There are too few liberals in the South who share Gavin's ideas, and, like Gavin, they are not active enough to make a breach in the closed society. To do them justice, it must be remembered that, in this society, to stand up to be counted may mean literally to be a target.

v. *The Legal System*

The frequency with which the jail and the courthouse are scenes in the Yoknapatawpha fiction and the prominent role of the lawyer, Gavin Stevens, indicate Faulkner's concern with the problems of crime and punishment and justice. Like every other social institution in Mississippi, the legal system is cleft by caste, and the human facts of stories of crime and punishment are likely to have distinctly racial aspects. Obviously the police system and the courts and the prisons are the social institutions upon which depends the preservation of the caste system, and obviously in a society in which religion can subserve that system and Jim Crow laws be enacted, the legal system will be devised to promote white man's justice: all are equal before the law—if their skins are white. Or, as George Orwell put it in *Animal Farm,* "Some are more equal than others." "In the administration of justice in the South today," Malcolm Parsons says, "resistance to change is most prominent in a continuing tradition of violence and in the reflection of the color caste line in the courts."[112] And the passage of sixty

[112] Malcolm B. Parsons, "Violence and Caste in Southern Justice," *South Atlantic Quarterly,* LX (Autumn, 1961), 458.

years in Mississippi has made just this difference, according to Christopher Jenks: "white Mississippi today feels obliged to pretend" that Negroes are protected by the law, whereas in 1904 the white man felt it his right to treat Negroes as he pleased. Now, if a sheriff "shoots a Negro he must claim that the prisoner was 'trying to escape.' "[113] Since the judicial system serves to enforce the caste system it must, like caste, operate on what Myrdal calls a basis of "consistent illegality."[114]

In the legal system also the plantation pattern is visible: by tradition, the police are watchdogs over Negroes. As Carl Rowan discovered in Georgia, "any white man who decides to be is a policeman, where a Negro is involved."[115] The police are more a threat than a protection to Negroes, and police brutality to Negroes is taken for granted. Sheriffs and deputies, especially in small towns, are likely to be petty politicians. By nature they are hostile to Negroes, because, as Myrdal says: "The average Southern policeman is a promoted poor white with a legal sanction to use a weapon."[116]

Concern for votes on the part of a sheriff is illustrated in "Pantaloon in Black": the sheriff and deputy allowed the Birdsongs to take Rider out of jail and lynch him because

[113] Christopher Jenks, "Mississippi: When Law Collides with Custom," *The New Republic,* CLI (July 25, 1964), 15.

[114] Myrdal, p. 536.

[115] Rowan, p. 127. Myrdal says that the Negro in the South is at the mercy of any white person (p. 530) and that any white man will be supported by the police (p. 537). Davis and Gardner say that planters commonly judge and punish Negroes (p. 46).

[116] Myrdal, p. 540. Silver says: "Every lawmaking body and every law enforcing agency is completely in the hands of those whites who are faithful to the orthodoxy" (p. 151). Davis and Gardner's point that law officials are elected on the basis of ability to control Negroes (p. 288) is exemplified in the central situation in Carter's *The Winds of Fear.* V. O. Key says that the sheriffs' lobby is powerful and keeps the state out of prohibition enforcement; bootleggers might back sheriffs' candidates (p. 235). Davis and Gardner (p. 291) and Canzoneri (p. 117) say that arrests concerning alcohol usually involve Negroes and poor whites: as Canzoneri says: "One law for white, one law for black" (p. 120). In *The Winds of Fear,* the marshall, chosen "to keep the niggers in their place," although known to be "a mean man and a killer," is paid off by a bootlegger to allow a "good nigger" to have a monopoly on supplying Negroes with liquor.

"There's forty-two active votes in that connection" (*Go Down, Moses,* p. 155). Obviously the sheriff did not expect to lose non-Birdsong votes by letting Rider be lynched.

Faulkner tends to soften the realities to the extent of having more officials who are fairly decent than brutal ones.[117] The successive Hub Hamptons are the most prominent sheriffs in Jefferson: the job is passed on, by the electors, from father to son, each Hampton alternating with another sheriff and running his farm when not in office (*The Mansion,* p. 370). In *Intruder in the Dust* the current Hampton is on excellent terms with Gavin and Miss Habersham and treats Lucas Beauchamp decently, even picking up his hat for him before Lucas had a chance to (p. 44). He acts sensibly and quickly in investigating the story of Charles and Miss Habersham. But, amply confirming Myrdal's description of the Southern policeman, Faulkner both illustrates and analyzes the type which is more common. Butch, in *The Reivers,* treats not only Negroes but women with scorn and brutality, and is shrewdly sized up by Uncle Ned as a man with a little boy mind whose badges and pistol have gone to his head and who became a law official so that he could carry the gun: "some day it gonter shoot something alive before he even knowed he aimed to" (pp. 185–186). Boon sums him up as "that tin-badge stallion" (p. 195). Miss Reba knows the type, the small-town constable who could show Pharaoh or Caesar a few things:

. . . he dont give a damn about the sheriff of the county nor the governor of the state nor the president of the United States all three rolled into one. Because he's a Baptist. I mean, he's a Baptist first and then he's the Law. When he can be a Baptist and the

---

[117] A mild instance of police brutality toward Negroes is found in *Light in August,* when the sheriff beats a Negro with a belt "buckle end outward" until the Negro tells who lived in the Burden cabin (p. 256). Faulkner's generic description of deputy sheriffs is in *Wild Palms,* outside the Yoknapatawpha fiction but pertinent to it: "the indelible mark of ten thousand Southern deputy sheriffs, urban and suburban—the snapped hat brim, the sadist's eyes, the slightly and unmistakably bulged coat, the air not swaggering exactly but of a formally pre-absolved brutality" ([New York: Vintage Books, 1964] p. 293).

Law both at the same time, he will. But any time the law comes conflicting up where nobody invited it, the law knows what it can do and where to do it [p. 210].

This was Faulkner's last portrait of the small-town law official. One would be tempted to suggest, if one did not know the dates of *The Reivers* and of Faulkner's death, that Ross Barnett sat for the portrait in Oxford, in the fall of 1962. The prevailing attitude, however, of Faulkner's law officials is exemplified in the statement of the sheriff in Mottstown when Joe Christmas was arrested, wanted for murder of a white woman: "I have no more sympathy with nigger murderers than any other white man here. . . . But it is my sworn oath, and by God I aim to keep it. I dont want no trouble, but I aint going to dodge it" (*Light in August*, p. 311). To the extent that brutality seems uncommon, Faulkner seems to give a more favorable general impression of sheriffs' actions than one might expect, but he shows the other side of the picture in Butch, who is brutal even when he is not dealing with criminals.

Like Butch, police tend to see Negroes in terms of racial stereotypes: Butch calls Uncle Ned "Uncle Remus" and gets an Uncle Remus act in response; he also attaches wise-cracking epithets to the others: Boon is "Sugar Boy" and Lucius "Lord Fauntleroy" (*The Reivers*, p. 177). The contrast between the reality and the stereotype is the whole point of "Pantaloon in Black," in which the deputy interprets the desperate, suicidal grief of Rider as evidence that "they aint human . . . ; when it comes to the normal human feelings and sentiments of human beings, they might just as well be a damn herd of wild buffaloes" (*Go Down, Moses*, p. 154). In this instance, Rider had killed a white man and had not tried to escape—he had virtually committed suicide. But the law officers allowed him to be lynched by the Birdsongs, kin of the dead man, and reported Rider's death, "at the hands of a person or persons unknown" (p. 154). Faulkner lets the reader imagine the consequences of such judgment according to stereotype in the treatment of other Negroes. Myrdal reports that "probably no group of whites in America have a

lower opinion of the Negro people and are more fixed in their
views than Southern policemen. To most of them no Negro
woman knows what virtue is . . . and practically every Negro
man is a potential criminal."[118] Mr. Lilley, in *Intruder in the
Dust,* comes of the same stock as most of the local law officials.
Gavin Stevens explains him: "All he requires is that they act
like niggers. Which is exactly what Lucas is doing: blew his
top and murdered a white man—which Mr. Lilley is probably
convinced all Negroes want to do—and now the white people
will take him out and burn him"—and Mr. Lilley is ready to
help (p. 48). Ironically, Gavin is judging by stereotype too.

The consequence of this control of law agencies by the white
people is a racial split in arrest of suspects and gathering of
evidence: the Negroes aid fugitive Negroes and try to avoid
any dealings with the law.[119] For example, in *Light in August*
(p. 256), the Negro, until beaten, denied knowing about the
cabin. (The Negro woman, in *Light in August* [p. 288], who
gave information about Joe thought he was without question a
white man.) Similarly, white people refuse to testify against
other whites in serious cases. James Silver cites a case in which
after a Negro was "shot to death at midday in front of a courthouse" for having been " 'messing around' in politics," no one
was ever brought to trial: the judge "gave the reason: no
white man would testify against another for murder of a
black man."[120]

[118] Myrdal, p. 541.

[119] Myrdal, p. 525. Myrdal also notes that arrested Negroes become
heroes to their people and that whites would rather punish ten innocent Negroes than let one guilty one escape. Charles Silberman explains lack of cooperation with police and says: "there is hardly a
Negro community in the United States which does not regard the local
police with suspicion, if not with hate" (p. 51). The truth of this
statement has been proved repeatedly by riots in Northern cities, as
well as Southern.

[120] Silver, pp. 90–91. Davis and Gardner note that white men must
be ready to maintain caste superiority, by physical violence if necessary
(pp. 45, 57). Canzoneri cites repeated murders of Negroes by a white
man who was never arrested (p. 72). Dollard, dealing with white caste
solidarity, points out that a white man will turn against a Negro
friend who commits a crime against a white man but will defend a
white man in trouble (pp. 64–65).

At every stage, from testimony to sentence, justice in the courts operates on caste principles, depending not only on the race of the defendant but also on the race of the victim in cases of injury or death. The situation described by George W. Cable after the Civil War still in large measure prevails: "the colored man's [testimony] was excluded by law wherever it weighed against a white man"; Myrdal says of the present: "Greater reliance is ordinarily given a white man's testimony than a Negro's."[121] A crime committed by a Negro against a white man receives a more severe penalty than the same crime by a white man against a white man; the same crime committed by a Negro against a Negro receives a less severe penalty. Similarly, a white man receives a more severe penalty for a crime against another white man than for the same crime against a Negro. There is double discrimination involved: the more severe penalties imposed for crimes of Negroes against whites protect whites against Negroes; the less severe penalties for crimes by either whites or Negroes against Negroes leave Negroes open to aggression by both races and imply that Negroes are not worthy of being judged by the same moral standards as white men. Myrdal confirms what one would assume: "the Southern Negro community is not at all happy about this double standard of justice. . . ."[122]

One reason for Negro resentment at this discrimination which seems to favor them by leniency is that it gives im-

[121] George W. Cable, *The Negro Question* (Garden City, N.Y.: Doubleday Anchor Books, 1958), p. 57; Myrdal, p. 550. Myrdal notes that this "follows an old tradition in the South, from slavery times, when a Negro's testimony against a white man was disregarded" (p. 550). The layman's view, expressed by Sarah Patton Boyle as "you knew that no judge or jury would take a Negro's word against a white's" (p. 31), is the thesis of Harper Lee's *To Kill a Mocking Bird*: the word of the trashiest poor white, Ewell, weighs more than that of a respectable Negro, Robinson, whose employer is a character witness for him. Robinson's testimony is supported by evidence that he was physically unable to commit the crime. The jury found him guilty because to believe him would be to suspect the Ewell girl of making advances to a Negro, an unthinkable suspicion. Robinson was found guilty of rape, with no medical evidence to support the charge, and was sentenced to death; he was shot while trying to escape.

[122] Myrdal, p. 551.

munity to Negroes who court the favor of whites and enjoy white patronage. The paternalism apparent in other Southern social institutions extends to the legal system.[123] It might be relatively mild, like automobile owners paying the fines, for drunkenness, of the best auto mechanic in town if they needed his services (*The Town,* p. 68). It might be wholly acceptable, in both legal and human terms: Miss Habersham showed her loyalty to Lucas Beauchamp, the husband of her foster sister, by helping to secure the evidence of his innocence, not by enabling him to escape the consequences of guilt (*Intruder in the Dust*). William Doster gives an example of how the patronage system was too likely to work: his greatuncle in Georgia kept paying fines for a drunken Negro because the Negro "knew his place," but ran another Negro off the plantation because he did not wear the "mask" of the good Negro.[124]

If a Negro is arrested and has no white man to aid him and cannot afford a good lawyer, he is unlikely to get a white lawyer who will take the case and not prejudge it; Negro lawyers are scarce, even in urban centers, and may be barred from courts.[125] The perfect example in Faulkner of the prob-

[123] Myrdal states: "To the patriarchal traditions belong also the undue importance given white 'character witnesses' in favor of Negro offenders" (p. 551). Dollard says that a Negro who enjoys white patronage "may have extraordinary liberty to do violent things to other Negroes" (p. 282). Cash states that "even the murder of another Negro" would be unpunished if a white patron testified for the Negro, who would otherwise receive the lightest sentence for second degree murder or manslaughter (p. 425). In light of these statements, the fanatic devotion of the jury in *To Kill a Mocking Bird* to the white-goddess complex is the more significant.

[124] William Doster, "William Faulkner and the Negro," Ph.D. dissertation (University of Florida, 1955), p. 19. In Carter's *The Winds of Fear,* Catfoot, a "good nigger," is rewarded by a monopoly as bootlegger to Negroes.

[125] Myrdal discusses the usual exclusion of Negroes from juries in the Deep South (p. 549). His chapter on "Courts, Sentences, and Prisons" is a basic source on those topics. Parsons deals with both the exclusion of Negroes from juries and the difficulty Negroes have in getting lawyers (pp. 464–465). In "Timid Lawyers and Neglected Clients" (*Harper's Magazine* [August, 1964]), Daniel H. Pollitt deals with the scarcity in the South of lawyers who take racial or civil rights cases. He illustrates

lem of a Negro in getting legal services is that of Lucas Beauchamp in *Intruder in the Dust*: Gavin Stevens, a liberal lawyer, not ill-disposed to Lucas, was so certain of Lucas's guilt on the basis of circumstantial evidence which perfectly fitted the stereotype of Negro crime that, his personal knowledge of Lucas to the contrary notwithstanding, he advised Lucas to plead guilty and spend the rest of his life in prison (pp. 59–65). Lucas's failure to say "mister" to or of white people is one reason why his guilt is assumed: an "uppity nigger" is capable of any crime. Gavin is not an ideal character, but he is the most nearly so of upper-class professional men in Jefferson; his reaction, therefore, must be assumed to be the most favorable Lucas could expect. A prejudiced judge and an all-white, prejudiced jury may confront a Negro even if he has a good lawyer; the jury is likely to include lower-class whites who are more apt to be prejudiced than a lawyer or a judge. As Atticus Finch pointed out to the jury, just before it proved its prejudice and pronounced an innocent man guilty: "A court is only as sound as its jury, and a jury is only as sound as the men who make it up."[126] This kind of miscarriage of justice is not illustrated in Yoknapatawpha but is foreshadowed in the situation of Lucas if he had come up for trial.

When a prisoner is judged guilty and sentence pronounced, the color of his skin, and that of his victim in crimes of violence, determines the severity of the sentence. Crimes of Negroes against Negroes are leniently punished; consequently such crimes are frequent, because, as Hortense Powdermaker explains, the Negro takes the law into his own hands, since from the legal system he cannot expect justice or defense:

---

by the case of Mack Lee Parker, accused of rape, who could find no lawyer and was lynched (as Lucas Beauchamp would have been without Charles Mallison and Miss Habersham), contrasted with that of Byron de la Beckwith, charged with the murder of Medgar Evers, who had three attorneys (p. 84).

[126] *To Kill a Mocking Bird*, p. 218. A comparison of Atticus Finch with Gavin Stevens shows the latter to be less courageous and more prejudiced. Faulkner never shows Gavin defending a Negro in a situation of racial tension.

"The prospect of immunity perhaps leads him unconsciously to vent against another Negro the rage he is unable to direct against the white men who have wronged him."[127] This is precisely the motivation of Jesus, when Nancy fears he will kill her, in "That Evening Sun." On the other hand, a crime committed by a Negro against a white person may be punished by a penalty never exacted from a white person for the same crime. Rape is, of course, the most obvious example. Carl Rowan and Sarah Patton Boyle both state that no white man ever got a death sentence for rape,[128] though many Negroes have had "the extreme penalty" invoked. Conversely, the very concept of rape of a Negro woman by a white man is practically unheard of; a white man quoted by Sarah Boyle expressed the stereotyped idea: "A Nigra girl is always a little bit willing—especially if the man's white." The same man considered rape of a white woman by a Negro man as sodomy.[129]

Comparison of some of the crimes and penalties in Yoknapatawpha shows the double standards. In *Sanctuary,* Lee Goodwin, a white man, was on trial for murder as well as rape; the rape was medically proved and was peculiarly unnatural and horrible. Lee was innocent but was convicted on perjured evidence and lynched. Will Mayes, a Negro, was

[127] Powdermaker, p. 174.

[128] Rowan, p. 176; Boyle, p. 150. Parsons confirms this statement as of 1959 but cites a later instance in South Carolina of a white American soldier sentenced to death for raping a Negro woman and an instance in Florida of a Negro convicted of raping an elderly white woman and being sentenced to life imprisonment, not death. Parsons also gives a detailed account of the trial, conviction, and sentence of four white men to life imprisonment for the rape of a Negro college girl, in Tallahassee, Florida, in 1959. The all-white jury reflected the sentiment of the white community that the four should be tried and convicted quickly because if the rapists went unpunished no white women would be safe from retaliation. The evidence Parsons shows of change does not show the general situation in the South and is irrelevant to Mississippi during the period Faulkner deals with.

[129] Boyle, pp. 152, 151. The lapse of more than a hundred years has had little effect: "In Mississippi, when a male slave was indicted for the rape of a female slave, the state Supreme Court dismissed the case on the ground that this was not an offense known to common or statute law" (Stampp, p. 347).

lynched merely on rumor, when no crime had been committed ("Dry September"). Mink Snopes, a poor white, was convicted of the murder of Houston, another white man, on valid evidence, and served his sentence (*The Mansion*). Lucas Beauchamp, a Negro, was arrested on circumstantial evidence as the killer of Vinson Gowrie, a white man, and was in great danger of being lynched before he could be brought to trial. Rider, in "Pantaloon in Black," was guilty of killing Birdsong, a white man, and was lynched before being brought to trial. The crime of Mink was premeditated murder, but there was no mob reaction against him; the killing of Vinson Gowrie was apparently unpremeditated and that of Birdsong was completely impulsive, but each brought forth a lynching mob, and in the latter case a lynching took place.

Faulkner deals more with the jail in Jefferson than with the penitentiary at Parchman, where Mink Snopes served his sentence. The jailers and prison warden in the Yoknapatawpha fiction are superior to those who have made Mississippi prisons notorious.[130] The story of Joe Christmas is marked by absence of police brutality and shows the concerted efforts of sheriffs and jailers to protect the prisoner, a man assumed to be a Negro guilty of murder and of sexual relations with a white woman which, of course, could not conceivably be voluntary on her part. Jailers are represented by Mr. Tubbs, in *Intruder in the Dust,* who protects Lucas because he has taken an oath of office and will do the best he can but does not like the chance of being "killed protecting a goddamn stinking nigger" (p. 54). Will Legate helps Tubbs by sitting with a double-barreled shotgun in sight of the street, guarding Lucas because Sheriff Hampton paid him five dollars to do so (p. 53). Finally Miss Habersham and Margaret Mallison sit opposite the jail

---

[130] Wharton gives an account of the system of convict leasing in Mississippi which applied almost entirely to Negroes and which from 1876 to 1888 scattered convicts over the state, "in great rolling cages or temporary stockades, on remote plantations or deep in the swamps of the Delta, the convicts . . . completely at the mercy of the sub-lessees and their guards" (p. 239). The system ended in 1894, when establishment of a prison farm was authorized.

door with their mending, making the code of Southern womanhood serve the cause of justice (p. 138).[131] The worst aspects of the Mississippi prisons and prison camps and convict leasing are not reflected in the Yoknapatawpha fiction. Since Faulkner is using Oxford as his basis for Jefferson, his source material may realistically provide him with law officials somewhat superior to many. Only an investigation of Oxford itself would indicate whether or not Faulkner softened the local truth. He included two accounts of executions, neither in Mississippi: those of Popeye in Alabama (*Sanctuary*, p. 308) and of Samuel Worsham Beauchamp in Joliet, Illinois ("Go Down, Moses," p. 374). These two aptly illustrate the statement James Silver makes of the penitentiary at Parchman: "The only integrated chair was located in the state penitentiary."[132] One might add that in *this* chair a Negro has a better chance of being accommodated than a white man has.

The consequences of the inequitable legal system are apparent in the high crime rate, particularly among Negroes, who are able to work off their frustrations and repressions by aggression against other Negroes. The general disrespect for law, fostered by prohibition, becomes a normal aspect of the society: sociologists, Myrdal points out, "will be inclined to formulate a general societal law of 'the futility of trying to suppress folkways by stateways.' Lawlessness has then received the badge of scientific normalcy."[133] The forces of law are more energetic in opposition to threats against the "folkways" of white supremacy than they are against the "folkways" of violence which characterize the South and particularly Mississippi.[134] The preservation of the caste line throughout social

[131] This activity may be symbolic of the activity of the Southern Association of Women against Lynching which Cash says "has addressed itself particularly to destroying the idea that lynching serves for the protection of Southern Womanhood" (p. 311).

[132] Silver, p. 85.

[133] Myrdal, p. 525.

[134] The paradox of the Mississippi insistence on states rights and supposed fear of a strong federal government and the actuality of a "strong centralized state government" is brought out by Canzoneri: "In Mississippi local government advocates have given the governor an enlarged Highway Patrol and power to send it as a police force into

institutions but especially in Southern courts is a major cause of the persistence of violence in Mississippi from frontier days to the present.

VI.   *Land of Violence*

Sanctuary made William Faulkner notorious as a novelist of violence. Violence in this and later Faulkner novels is the outward manifestation of emotions and attitudes rooted in the caste system and fostered by the Southern tradition and by the social structure and institutions which have already been discussed. The realistic aspect of the violence in Yokna-patawpha can best be evaluated in relation to social context and to types and examples of violence offered by that society. The general fact of violence Faulkner affirmed in response to a question about the literary reason why he did not use the Ku Klux Klan:

The spirit that moves a man to put on a sheet and burn sticks in your yard is pretty prevalent in Mississippi, but not all Mississippians wear the sheet and burn the sticks. That they hate and scorn and look with contempt on the people that do, but the same spirit, the same impulse is in them too, but they are going to use a different method from wearing a nightshirt and burning sticks [*Faulkner in the University,* p. 94].

Faulkner also puts into the words of Doc Peabody, in *As I Lay Dying,* a theory about the land which explains the people, in terms which recall the theory of Taine, and explains "Dry

---

any county or city without invitation and against the will of the local authorities and local populace" (p. 169). Although the state police were not in Oxford in September of 1962 against the will of local authorities, they made no effort to prevent or control violence, not even to the extent of aiding citizens who appealed to them for protection from the riotous mob.

September": "That's the one trouble with this country: every-thing, weather, all, hangs on too long. Like our rivers, our land: opaque, slow, violent; shaping and creating the life of man in its implacable and brooding image" (p. 44).

Lillian Smith sums up the forms and the consequences of violence in the South in a statement which applies to Faulk-ner's fiction:

Wasting of land, wasting of natural resources, lawbreaking, vigi-lante groups, bootlegging of whiskey in prohibition counties, group violence, fist-fights, became southern characteristics. This acceptance of violence has piled up statistics which tell us that the southern region has proportionately the most murders, as well as the most churches, the most poverty, the highest rate of illiter-acy, lowest wages, poorest health, most eroded soil of any section of our nation.[135]

In Mississippi, the pioneer tradition and the plantation tradi-tion which began almost simultaneously with it have never died out: violence as part of those traditions remains part of the myth and hence is tolerated and even cherished, to lend excitement to a dull life. Consequently violence is not con-trolled by social institutions. Myrdal comments on the fact and the cause: "Thus the opportunistic disrespect for law, order and public morals has a complicated causation and a deep-rooted history in the South. The tradition is today still part of the way of life and as such is often patriotically cherished as distinctively Southern."[136] As is frequently true of Mississippi, statements made about a much earlier period still apply to a remarkable degree. George W. Cable wrote of the "outrageous vices" of the plantation system: "shameless hard drinking, the carrying of murderous weapons, murder, too, and lynching at its heels, the turning of state and county prisons into slave

[135] Smith, p. 184.
[136] Myrdal, p. 451. To support his point Myrdal quotes Cash's *Mind of the South* and Rupert B. Vance's *Human Geography of the South* (1932).

pens, the falsification of the ballot, night riding and whipping."[137] At the present time there is, Louis Rubin says, "no place like Mississippi" for "the tension between tradition and change" which creates many of the paradoxes and contributes to the violence. He testifies to the fact that Faulkner's novels "are directly concerned with the actual events of Mississippi life" but not, naturally, with "typical people and typical situations."[138] As it becomes increasingly difficult to sustain the myth, based on the plantation tradition, violence ensues, as it did after the Civil War. As a perceptive article on Faulkner in *Time* puts it: "they were violent, partly from the strain of sustaining this myth, partly from fear that if the myth was once cracked, at any point or in any context, the whole perilously maintained social structure would collapse."[139] The enrollment of James Meredith in the University of Mississippi was such a point: the myth was rampant and the violence extreme.

The violent individualism of the frontier and of the plantation survives and is most apparent in the common custom in the South of carrying weapons and in the acts of violence which result from the low regard for human life and the handiness of deadly weapons. Although the examples in Faulkner which leap to the mind include Lucas Beauchamp, who was not dressed for Saturday without his pistol (*Intruder in the Dust*, p. 226), and John Powell, to whom the pistol he earned and got on his twenty-first birthday was "the living symbol of his manhood" and as such "he must have it with him" (*The Reivers*, p. 7), carrying weapons is a Southern

[137] Cable, p. 20. The same characteristic kinds of violence are noted by Odum (p. 140) and by J. W. S. Nordholt (*The People that Walk in Darkness* [New York: Ballantine Books, 1960], pp. 55–56). Jay B. Hubbell in *Southern Life in Fiction* (Athens: University of Georgia Press, 1960) compares Yoknapatawpha County and Cable's Louisiana with "the darker aspects of Mark Twain's picture of disorder and violence" (p. 833).

[138] Louis D. Rubin, Jr., *The Faraway Country: Writers of the Modern South* (Seattle: University of Washington Press, 1963), pp. 68, 69.

[139] "The Curse and the Hope," *Time*, LXXXIV (July 17, 1964), 44.

custom, not a Negro custom. It is supported by its respectable past in the tradition and by the atmosphere of apprehension shared by whites and Negroes.[140]

The legend of Colonel Falkner and its fictitious version in the killing of Colonel Sartoris provide examples of violence due to this custom. Whatever the precise facts were of the shooting of Colonel Falkner, he had been accustomed to carry weapons and in Ripley before the Civil War had killed two armed men who had confronted him. All three deaths were basically due to this custom on the part of all the men involved.[141] Although feuding and moonshining are associated chiefly with mountain people, the instances cited indicate that feuding was general. The prestige status of the duel of revenge, which Bayard Sartoris refused to engage in ("An Odor of Verbena"), lent status to feuding, which often had similar provocation.

The strong family feeling which nourished revenge duels and feuds also, as has been explained, nourished the cult of Southern Womanhood, with the consequent obsession with sex which underlies most lynchings. Thus the institution of the family breeds two kinds of violence. Not only does religion contribute to violence by emotionalism which, as Myrdal said, appealed "to fear and passion," but religious leaders do not

[140] The most picturesque sidelights on this fondness for weapons are provided by Clark's account of weapons sold in country stores (pp. 129–130). Myrdal ascribes much violence to the Southern custom of carrying weapons and to the general acceptance of violence (pp. 560, 1346). Powdermaker stresses apprehensive fear as a factor in the custom of carrying weapons (p. 351). Johnson says that whites disapprove of Negroes' having guns and hunting (p. 181).

[141] In *Sartoris* (p. 23) and *The Unvanquished* (p. 266), Colonel Sartoris was shot when for the first time he went unarmed. (See Appendix E for details of the shooting.) The legendary version, in which both men were on the street, is closely paralleled by an incident in Yazoo City, reported in the Oxford *Eagle* (April 3, 1930): the mayor of the town shot the editor of the Yazoo *Sentinel* on Main Street and then committed suicide. A repeated pattern in shooting fatalities reported in the *Eagle* is illustrated in a Lafayette County incident. The defendant said: "We had a little round, probably he cussed and I cussed him; he put his hand under his coat and I shot him" (December 10, 1936). Both men had gone after a cache of liquor before the shooting.

take a stand against violence.[142] The sadistic use of physical
cruelty in the name of religion, illustrated in the beatings
McEachern gave Joe Christmas, and the treatment given by
Doc Hines to wife, daughter, and grandson, Joe, in *Light in
August,* is epitomized in the guiding principle of Calvin
Burden in dealing with his own family: "I'll beat the loving
God into the four of you as long as I can raise my arm" (*Light
in August,* p. 213). Violence as a tool in politics, especially for
the intimidation of Negroes, has continued from the Reconstruction period, when Colonel John Sartoris shot the two
Burdens, until the present, when the "Mississippi plan—the
use of the riot as a political instrument"—was demonstrated
on the University of Mississippi campus in 1962.[143] Violence
continues in Mississippi because those in power do not want
to stop it. General lawlessness has been encouraged by prohibition laws which were widely and openly violated, by
inequality of castes before the law, by police brutality, and
by the encouragement, through lenient penalties, of Negro
aggression against Negroes and white aggression against
Negroes. Violence is inherent not only in "the total attitude
that mistreatment of the Negro was not wrong, and in the
action patterns of physical brutality," in the words of George
W. Odum,[144] but in the resistance to change that regards all
of the customs of the Southern past as worthy of perpetuation.

The dullness and poverty of the lives of people like Mink
Snopes and Jackson Fentry, the lack of adult recreations
except drinking and hunting and fishing for those who have
time and means—few parties, picnics, dances[145]—help to explain why any excitement in the community is a welcome
diversion. Puritanical disapproval of pleasure stops short of
disapproval of the emotional orgies of revivals and mob
violence. The country store which provides a social center
for country dwellers is also likely to be the scene of violence,

[142] Myrdal, p. 563. Odum noted that revivals came to be "a fanning
breeze for the fires of bigotry and intolerance" (p. 170).
[143] Silver, p. 13.
[144] Odum, p. 144.
[145] Myrdal, pp. 562, 563, 1435.

as in the near-killing of Lucas Beauchamp (*Intruder in the Dust,* pp. 18–20) and the actual killing of Vinson Gowrie. Clark says of the country store: "Everything of importance that ever happened either occurred at the store or was reported there immediately," the happenings including shootings, thrashings, and drunkenness.[146] Faulkner includes the country store as one source of diversion but omits others, such as county fairs, Fourth of July and other holiday celebrations, and camp meetings.[147] Yoknapatawpha County is even poorer in distractions from a life of physical and spiritual poverty than was Lafayette County, before the days of cars, good roads, radio, and television which now alleviate the tedium for all but the most abjectly poor.

The deeds of violence in Faulkner's fiction range from suicide to lynching and usually are related to causative factors inherent in the specific kind of society. Local events in Oxford and the vicinity furnish examples far more extreme and horrible than anything Faulkner presented, directly or by suggestion. Although Faulkner's literary technique in dealing with violence is not under consideration here, one characteristic must be noted: by discontinuity and narrative ellipses Faulkner avoids complete blow-by-blow descriptions of the most violent and horrible incidents. And if one is curious as to what Faulkner could have used and what details he could have presented, James Silver presents "a classic example" of a lynching "as a means of social control" in Mississippi in 1928.[148] Similar accounts, equally revolting, are likely to comment on suppression of unprintable details. Caste patterns in deeds of violence are often apparent, either genuine differences

[146] Clark, p. 32.

[147] Simkins has a chapter on sports in the New South (pp. 300–310) which is useful in showing the comparative recreational deprivations of even the upper-class characters in Yoknapatawpha County. The episode of John Sartoris's balloon ascension (*Sartoris,* pp. 72–73) is recalled by Narcissa; apparently a balloon ascension from the Square in Oxford was a regular feature of the county fair, according to John Faulkner (*My Brother Bill,* p. 4). Faulkner omits the county fair and direct presentation of this feature of it.

[148] Silver, pp. 85–86.

or differences in the eye of the beholder blinded by stereotypes, like the deputy in "Pantaloon in Black."

The most striking instance of this caste difference has a basis in statistical fact. Isaac McCaslin, in reading the family ledger, comes on the series of entries concerning the drowning of Eunice: "Drownd herself"—"Who in hell ever heard of a niger drownding him self"—"Drownd herself." Isaac solves the mystery when he comes to the entry about the birth of a son to Eunice's daughter six months later: Eunice did drown herself, because her daughter Tomey was to have a child by Tomey's father, Carothers McCaslin. ("The Bear," *Go Down, Moses,* pp. 267–270). From the fact that Negroes do have a very low suicide rate[149] an explanation is deduced to strengthen the stereotype of the happy, contented Negro. The comment on a Negro suicide reported in the Oxford *Eagle* (December 24, 1936) confirms what one could infer: "a rare tragedy among the life-loving, cheerful Southern colored race." Eunice's suicide was motivated by Southern incest. Nancy Mannigoe attempted suicide while under the influence of drugs, an addiction which may illustrate Myrdal's point that "immoral and perverted tastes" are catered to among Negroes and illegal sale of narcotics is "much simpler" in Negro districts.[150] The jailer's conventional view of Negro suicide was not upset, "because a nigger full of cocaine wasn't a nigger any longer" ("That Evening Sun," *Collected Stories,* p. 291). Quentin Compson's suicide was motivated by Southern gyneolatry and incestuous impulses. Young Bayard and Uncle Willy both deliberately destroyed themselves through violence, in airplane crashes. Uncle Willy could not face the life the church ladies would force upon him by taking away the drugs and drink that made his dull and lonely life bearable. Bayard was driven to show his reckless courage in the Sartoris pattern because of the psychic wound he suffered in the death of his twin brother and because he lacked the inner resources and constructive impulses which might have allowed him to face life

[149] Myrdal, p. 982.
[150] *Ibid.* p. 977.

without John. The pattern of wild recklessness in Bayard's behavior is partly Sartoris, but the story of Uncle Willy provides a non-Sartoris parallel in an old man.

Despite the obsession of the South with rape of a white woman by a Negro, there is only one example of unquestionable rape in Faulkner and that is the unnatural rape of Temple Drake by Popeye, a white man and an outsider (*Sanctuary*). Gowan Stevens and Temple herself are the Southerners, brought up in the upper-class tradition. Gowan by his drunkenness and irresponsibility and Temple by her disobedience of both university rules and family injunctions are responsible for Temple's being where she had no business to be: at a bootlegger's hideout. (Since this happened in 1929, prohibition was not a state affair.) The significant aspect of the public reaction to the horrible story, falsely naming Lee Goodwin as guilty of both the murder of Tommy and the rape of Temple, was the utter absence of any thought that Temple could be other than the completely pure and innocent victim. (The consequence of that acceptance of the Southern concept of womanhood will be dealt with later.) As a picture of the times in American universities, *Sanctuary* shows the "swinish drunkenness, eternal and blatant concern with the theme of sex, and promiscuity in one degree or another" which Cash describes.[151] In the South, the revolt against tradition was greater in degree because of the puritanical mores.

Temple's rebellion against puritanism and Southern restrictions upon the conduct of women is paralleled by two Southern women who resort to murder to escape from the role society offers them. Miss Emily Grierson, victim of a tyrannical father and of family pride, poisons the man whom she cannot keep and who represents her matrimonial last chance, not a very eligible one for a Grierson ("A Rose for Emily"). The apparent necrophilia is an atypical touch. In "Elly," Elly plans to have Paul cause the death of her grandmother to prevent her parents' learning of the affair with Paul and of his Negro blood. Elly takes the initiative with Paul throughout,

---

[151] Cash, p. 339.

even to asking him to marry her, despite her knowledge of his origin and her training as a "nice girl" in Jefferson. The dullness of her prospective life with the eligible suitor is obvious; the attractions of life with Paul seem to be chiefly sexual. Elly succeeds in causing the deaths of Paul and her grandmother and probably her own. By comparison with Elly and Miss Emily, Nancy, the Negro woman who committed murder, had an unselfish motive and, Nancy being just an ignorant, unfortunate Negro, a greater excuse (*Requiem for a Nun*).

Nancy's mercy killing of Temple's baby to save Temple and the older child from the consequences of Temple's leaving her husband has a kind of parallel in Wash's murder of Milly and her new-born daughter before the sheriff and his men come to arrest him for the murder of Sutpen ("Wash"). (His death at the hands of Major De Spain and the sheriff is virtual suicide.) The murder of Milly and the baby follows Wash's killing of Sutpen for a motive inherent in the class system, the motive which made Sutpen as a boy conceive of his Grand Design: the desire to be regarded as a human being with human dignity. Wash killed Sutpen for denying Milly and the daughter Milly had borne to him the treatment he gave an animal: "too bad you're not a mare. Then I could give you a decent stall in the stable" ("Wash," *Collected Stories,* p. 535). Wash as a poor white had seen the bitter truth behind the illusion of caste superiority and white solidarity: the upper-class white man scorns both Negroes and poor whites, but flatters poor whites into serving his purposes. The earlier murder in the Sutpen family, that of Charles Bon by Henry, was motivated by caste feeling, the refusal to let a man with Negro blood marry his white half-sister, though he might marry her if he were merely her all-white half-brother. Thus the deeds of violence in *Absalom, Absalom!* are based on class and caste hostility.

Mink Snopes murdered Houston for a reason somewhat comparable to Wash's: he forgave Houston the fact that Varner sided with Houston, because rich people had "to stick together or else maybe some day the ones that aint rich might take a notion to raise up and take it away" from them.

What Mink could not forgive was "that-ere extry one-dollar pound fee" which was a downright insult (*The Mansion,* p. 39). This murder was premeditated, in part because Mink was too poor to own a pistol and ammunition and had only his grandfather's old shotgun and some shells so old they might not fire. Mink's second murder, even more premeditated —for thirty-eight years—was also an assertion of manhood in the old revenge pattern. Flem had not come to the aid of Mink after he murdered Houston and had tricked Mink into an attempt to escape from prison which had increased his sentence. Mink's code of honor bears some resemblance to those behind duelling and family feuding. His unwavering resolution to kill stems from a society in which killing is an honorable way to prove one's manhood.

By comparison the murder of Vinson Gowrie by his brother Crawford, with Lucas Beauchamp tricked to appear as the murderer, is unnatural and despicable, and was so regarded by the Gowries and the rest of Beat Four (*Intruder in the Dust*). Crawford was covering up his theft of lumber and was, so he thought, getting rid of Lucas as the only other person who knew about the theft. His murder of Jake Montgomery was intended to conceal that of Vinson. With no personal animosity but with the hope of sharing loot with Mink, Lump Snopes also threw suspicion on a Negro by claiming the Negro had borrowed Mink's gun, and planned to intimidate the Negro into confession (*The Hamlet,* pp. 236–237). Thus Crawford Gowrie and Lump Snopes act on similar assumptions about Negroes as good suspects. Crawford Gowrie reached depths of iniquity unusual in Yoknapatawpha County because his premeditated deed was fratricide and had a mercenary motive.[152]

[152] An even worse instance of cold-blooded repeated murders occurred in Taylor, in Lafayette County, in 1935. A prosperous farmer, a church and school officer, shot his first wife for her insurance and claimed it was an accident. (There is some similarity here to "An Error in Chemistry," in *Knight's Gambit.*) His second wife he burned up in a car, another accident. He then married an eighteen-year-old girl. When a neighbor expressed suspicion of the deaths, in revenge the murderer burned the neighbor's house. He was charged with arson,

Lucas was suspected of the murder of Vinson Gowrie on circumstantial evidence and his character as an "uppity nigger." He almost did commit a murder, a white-man's kind of murder, when he challenged Zack Edmonds out of jealousy and was saved from killing him by a misfire. Had Zack not had a sense of family loyalty—as well, no doubt, as personal feeling for Lucas—Lucas might have suffered for the attempt the rope and coal oil that he expected to suffer if he killed Zack ("The Fire and the Hearth," *Go Down, Moses*, pp. 57–59).

The murder of Joanna Burden by Joe Christmas is the most sensational and the most Southern in its superficial features, the murder of a white woman by a Negro man, with a razor as weapon. The killing had a fairly close parallel in Oxford. A Negro delivered a message to a woman from her husband who was in jail. To frighten him away she threatened him with a revolver, but he disarmed her and cut her throat with a razor, almost decapitating her. He was captured and jailed. That same night he was taken from the jail and lynched. The complicated motives in the story of Joe Christmas and Joanna Burden, the problems of the mulatto being matched by those of an ostracized woman and complicated by the religious fanaticism to which Joe had been subjected and which Joanna threatened him with, have no parallel in the apparently unmotivated actual crime.[153] This well exemplifies how Faulkner transformed what he did base on actual happenings.

---

new evidence on the deaths was discovered, and he was convicted of murder and given a life sentence. He committed suicide in prison. On trial at the same time in Oxford was a Negro who had shot a white man. While the jury was out, seventy-five men overpowered the jailer and three deputies, took the Negro from jail, and lynched him in the courthouse yard. Faulkner's uncle was a lawyer for the white defendant (information from issues of the Oxford *Eagle*, 1932–1937).

[153] In *Old Times in the Faulkner Country* (Chapel Hill: University of North Carolina Press, 1961), John Cullen tells about this event: a boy at the time, he was one of the posse which pursued the Negro, Nelse Patton, and he helped to capture Nelse (pp. 89–97). The Oxford *Eagle* which gave an account of the murder and lynching published a letter from 118 colored people, including four ministers, denouncing lawlessness and lynching but expressing readiness to aid "in capturing and

The hunting down of the murderer with a posse was a usual feature of such cases. The man-hunt or the milder tarring and feathering usually involves racial or sexual elements or both. Faulkner uses a comic version in "Was," with Tomey's Turl, never in danger of anything but not getting to see his sweetheart, clearly at an advantage. But the use of hunting terms— "He's going to earth. We'll cut back to the house and head him before he can den" (*Go Down, Moses,* p. 18)—recalls the inhuman coursing of Negroes with dogs for sport. Reference is made in "A Justice" to the Indians running Negroes "like you would a fox or a cat or a coon" (*Collected Stories,* p. 345). The man-hunt is part of the narrative pattern in the Indian story, "Red Leaves," in "Pantaloon in Black," and in *Light in August.* Faulkner focuses on both the pursuers and the fugitive. Lillian Smith explains the fun in the man-hunt, "with no more thought given the running, frightened human being than to a running, frightened animal."[154]

Such a hunt might be the prelude to a lynching by the captors of the fugitive, or the lynching might take place after the prisoner was jailed. Lynching is the most characteristically Southern kind of violence, with a psychological importance out of proportion to the number of cases; fear of lynching hangs over the heads of Negroes and contributes to the tension between Negroes and white people. Usually lynching is

---

punishing such criminals," who should receive "quick and severe punishment" (September 17, 1908). Whether this indicates Uncle Tomism or an unusual and sincere cooperativeness of the local Negroes with the law it is difficult to say. The crime was certainly "uncalled for and unjustifiable," as the statement from the Negroes said.

[154] Smith, p. 140. The man-hunt goes back to the pursuit of runaway slaves. Dollard describes a man-hunt in which the fugitive was shot resisting arrest (pp. 328–329). Calvin Brown sees in the recurrent man-hunt pattern in Faulkner's fiction a reflection of the paper-chases he took part in with Faulkner. Elements in Faulkner's treatment of the man-hunt which may be due to this influence are: the trial of man against man (the dogs in Faulkner never prove of real use); the accurate account of "a peculiar kind of exhaustion" which Brown experienced; the equal feeling for the hunter and the hunted, and the ritual or game element in the hunt, with the performance judged on its own merits ("Faulkner's Manhunts: Fact into Fiction," *Georgia Review,* XX [Winter, 1966], 390–393).

related to both sex and caste, sometimes to only one. As Myrdal points out, lynching is but one of many kinds of extra-legal violence in the South, and the other types are more common and their bad effects greater. He goes on to identify lynching as a small-town custom, more common in poor districts, and analogous to witch-hunting in its emotional atmosphere and sadistic elements.[155] The theory behind lynching, in its modern Southern form, is that only by lynching "could the full expiation of the horrible crime be exacted," to quote the Oxford *Eagle* in a report of a lynching of two Negroes who killed a white man (February 11, 1904). Lynching is performed by the lower classes but condoned by the upper. Of all acts of violence it affords the most complete release from the dullness of a life of poverty: Lillian Smith speaks of "the privilege of lynching" as given to rural whites "as a ritualistic reward for accepting so meekly their design for living," and explains that the lynched Negro becomes "a receptacle for every man's dammed-up hate, and a receptacle for every man's forbidden feelings."[156] Lynching is not considered murder, and the lynchers go unpunished, suffering not even community loss of status: Lillian Smith states that a white girl could have a Coke in the drugstore with a known lyncher, but if she drank a Coke with a young Negro doctor she would be run out of town or even killed.[157] An item in the Oxford *Eagle* (September 24, 1925) is typical: the sheriff recognized no members of a crowd of 400 lynchers and no arrests were made.[158]

Strictly speaking, a lynching involves a group and a victim; the vital point is that the mob confers anonymity. The best-

[155] Myrdal, pp. 560–562. Parsons notes that since 1935 lynchings have been almost exclusively of Negroes and in the South. He gives as reasons for the decline of lynching the influence of upper-class leaders, who fear federal intervention, and the swift and sure legal penalty against those who violate the code of white supremacy (pp. 460, 463). Peters (p. 35) and Bailey (pp. 39–40) give credit to activity of women and church groups against lynching.

[156] Smith, p. 142.

[157] *Ibid.*, p. 82.

[158] Myrdal states that the local police often support lynching (p. 562) and cites protection of lynchers as an example of caste solidarity.

known instance in Faulkner of the lynching pattern of pursuit
and violent, extra-legal death, the story of Joe Christmas, is
not a lynching. But the death of Joe Christmas is a perfect
example of a ritual slaying, with Percy Grimm as the officiating
priest: the castration and Percy's words to the dying Joe, "Now
you'll let white women alone, even in hell," show the object-
lesson aspect of the killing.[159] When one recalls the age of
Joanna, the length and nature of the relationship between
Joe and Joanna, and the fact that she was a social outcast, this
view of Joe's crime as the violation of white Southern Womanhood would be ridiculous were it not so appalling. The most
appalling aspect is that Percy Grimm regards himself as the
instrument of God, the pawn being moved by the Player, and
speaks in the "clear and outraged" voice of "a young priest"
(*Light in August,* p. 406).

Faulkner's comments on Percy Grimm are particularly
enlightening. He created Percy before he had ever heard of
Nazi Storm Troopers: the type is found "in all countries, in
all people," but "there are probably more of him in the White
Citizens Council than anywhere else in the South" (*Faulkner
in the University,* p. 41). Cash's analysis of the Klansman
mentality brings out the peculiarly Southern version of the
universal type and especially well fits Percy Grimm, born too
late to be a hero in World War I. The Klan followed "the
ancient Southern pattern of high romantic histrionics, violence,
and mass coercion of the scapegoat and the heretic":

. . . here was surcease for the personal frustrations and itches.
. . . But also the old coveted, splendid sense of being a heroic
blade, a crusader sweeping up mystical slopes for White Supremacy, religion, morality, and all that had made up the faith
of the Fathers; of being the direct heir in continuous line of the

---

[159] Myrdal notes the scapegoat or object-lesson role of the Negro
victim (p. 677). Davis and Gardner note that a Negro may provoke
violence by a small offense when white hostility is already aroused:
"The Negro victim then becomes both a scapegoat and an object lesson
for his group. He suffers for all the minor caste violations which have
aroused the whites, and he becomes a warning against future violations" (pp. 48–49).

Confederate soldiers at Gettysburg . . . of participating in ritualistic assertion of the South's continuing identity . . . .[160]

"Dry September" exemplifies lynching by a small group under a leader. This lynching combines the sex and race elements
and illustrates violence as a consequence of dullness and the
tensions due to weather. The killing of an innocent man on the
basis of mere rumor makes this the most terrible such episode
in Faulkner. The inability of Hawkshaw, the barber, to secure
a rational response from McLendon, even in view of the
tenuous grounds for any action—no crime or even breach of
racial etiquette had occurred—is the most significant detail in
suggesting the psychology of the lynchers. George B. Leonard,
senior editor of *Look*, described the expressions on the faces of
redneck segregationists gazing at Negroes at an integrated
beach as the unseeing "hypnotic fascination," without violence
or even horror, that is token of "the inability to make sense
from the information presented to the senses."[161] The fate
of Will Mayes is perfectly possible when the unsupported
word of a white woman is given such weight, and, as Dollard
says, "the whole matter is charged off to the sexual aggressiveness of the Negro men."[162] That white women are not
necessarily innocent is illustrated in two news items almost
sixty years apart. In 1906, after a Negro in Little Rock was
sentenced to death, the white woman who testified that he
assaulted her signed a statement that her testimony was false;
a stay of execution was refused by the governor but granted
by the supreme court. In 1962, in Columbus, Mississippi, a
young white woman reported that a Negro attempted to rape
her but admitted it was a hoax after a lie detector test indicated the innocence of the man, "held in an undisclosed
jail because of strong feeling against him."[163] After she spread

[160] Cash, pp. 345–346.
[161] George Leonard, "A Southerner Appeals to the North," *Look*,
XXVIII (August 11, 1964), 15, 16.
[162] Dollard, p. 170.
[163] The Oxford *Eagle*, July 19, 1906; Jackson *Clarion Ledger*, October
19, 1962. Brutality by small groups short of lynching is illustrated by

the rumor that cost Will Mayes his life, Miss Minnie Cooper attended the movies with her sympathetic friends.

In both "Pantaloon in Black" and *Intruder in the Dust,* lynching groups are headed by relatives of the white man who was killed; in "Pantaloon" Rider is taken from the jail and lynched, the event which seemed imminent in *Intruder.* Race but not sex was involved. Full-scale community lynching took place after the trial of Lee Goodwin, with mutilation of Goodwin before burning him with coal oil, for his supposed rape of Temple. He was innocent, and Temple, who perjured herself in letting him be convicted, apparently did not give him another thought. The potential horror of the consequences of the white-goddess complex is best seen in "Dry September" and *Sanctuary.*

Intruder in the Dust best exemplifies the situation before racial lynching by a large mob: the gathering of the crowd, the arrival of sheriff and prisoner at the jail, the security precautions at the jail. Most of all, the white crowds and the complete absence of Negroes give the atmosphere. Charles Mallison's observation of the loss of individuality in the mob parallels George Leonard's observation quoted above: "a Face; not even ravening nor uninsatiate but just in motion, insensate, vacant of thought or even passion: an Expression significant-less and without past" (*Intruder in the Dust,* p. 182). The curious title "Intruder in the Dust" is brought to mind by a passage in Lillian Smith's *Killers of the Dream*: the resistance to change and to outside interference—"always the Outsider did the evil"—caused the alienation of reason and caused to be "labeled as 'intruder' all moral responsibility for our acts."[164]

The resistance to change and outside interference has been increasing since Faulkner wrote *Intruder in the Dust.* No discussion of group violence in Yoknapatawpha County can

---

the intimidation of Hightower's Negro servants, the man being whipped, and the beating of Hightower until he was unconscious (*Light in August,* p. 62).

[164] Smith, p. 197. In the novel, *intruder* could refer to the body of Montgomery in the grave of Vinson Gowrie and to the violators of the grave of Vinson.

now omit mention of group violence in Lafayette County less than three months after William Faulkner died. Faulkner's moral convictions were dramatized in his fiction and explicitly expressed in his non-fiction. In "Mississippi," fact and fiction merge and the fictitious names—Jefferson, Boon Hogganbeck, and Colonel Sartoris—mingle with the real ones, Mammy Caroline and "Master Murry" Falkner. In his third person protagonist, Faulkner presents his own feelings for the land he loved intensely, despite the faults he hated. What he hated most of all was injustice and intolerance, specified in a catalogue of caste discriminations against the Negro in the law, in education, in religion, in politics, in employment.[165] Gavin Stevens in *Intruder in the Dust,* Faulkner told Malcolm Cowley, represented the best Southern liberals, not the author.[166] Certainly Gavin's hysterical defense of the South and Sambo—a term Faulkner did not use in his own voice—resembles nothing in Faulkner's non-fiction except his plea for the South to be allowed time to put into effect the Supreme Court decision about integration in the schools and one statement, unfortunately widely quoted, about choosing Mississippi against the United States, which Faulkner emphatically and publicly disclaimed, as not representing his reasoned judgment.[167] Certainly Gavin never showed the concern for education of all children which was a recurrent theme in Faulkner's speeches and public letters.[168] Like Gavin, Faulkner hoped that the South would take the initiative and correct its own injustices. The degree to which this hope was delusive is apparent in Faulkner's prediction on July 2, four days before his death, that any trouble at the university over Meredith's admission would be "because of the people out in Beat Two who never

[165] Reprinted in *Essays, Speeches, and Public Letters,* p. 37.

[166] Malcolm Cowley, *The Faulkner-Cowley File: Letters and Memories, 1944–1962* (New York: Viking Press, 1966), pp. 109–110.

[167] In *Essays, Speeches, and Public Letters*: "A Letter to the North," pp. 86–91; Letters to the Editor of *The Reporter,* p. 225; to the Editor of *Time,* p. 226.

[168] *Ibid.*: "Address to the Southern Historical Association," pp. 146–151; letters to the Editor of the Memphis *Commercial Appeal,* pp. 214–216, 218–222.

went to the University or never intended to send their children
to the University." He explained the election of Ross Barnett
as due to the "Beat Twos" in all the counties throughout the
state.[169] (Beat Two in Lafayette County becomes Beat Four
in Yoknapatawpha County and is inhabited by people like the
Gowries.) Faulkner was spared the realization that the
"trouble" was caused by university students themselves and the
elements in the population which they represented, and that
the trouble continued long after the riot. The genuineness of
Faulkner's interest in aiding Negroes as individuals was evident in his establishment of the Faulkner Foundation to
administer a scholarship fund for the education of promising
young Negroes who could help to educate their own people.[170]
His desire to help the Negro people he expressed to Earl
Wortham, a Negro blacksmith in Oxford. Mr. Wortham said:
"One day he told me he was writing books, and he says,
'Well, I tell you, you all is good people and all, and I'm going
to try to prepare a way for it to be easier on you than what
it has been.' So far as what that meant, I don't know."[171]
Faulkner's readers should know. Faulkner was spared the
knowledge that the power of federal troops was required to
enable one colored native of Mississippi to complete his education at "Ole Miss." And the way was not "easier" for James
Meredith.

For the reader of Faulkner, living through the weeks before
and after the riot in Oxford in 1962 was like living in a
Faulkner novel, except that Faulkner never presented violence
on such a scale, with national forces and national attention
centered on the local scene. All of the social causes of violence
herein discussed were evident. The issue was segregation in
education: enrollment of James Meredith was a threat to
Southern womanhood and the system of social inequality
designed to protect the home. The church failed to assume
leadership in the weeks before the crisis; the most courageous

[169] J. Aubrey Seay, in Webb and Green, pp. 193–194.
[170] W. McNeill Reed, in Webb and Green, p. 186. The fund has not,
in practice, been limited to Negro students (p. 187).
[171] In Webb and Green, p. 168.

stand was taken by the Episcopal clergymen in Oxford, who were bitterly reviled in the local press. The political maneuvering of Ross Barnett, the Governor, and Paul B. Johnson, the Lieutenant Governor, was obvious: Barnett's popularity rose notably but he could not succeed himself, and Paul Johnson succeeded Barnett as Governor. That the leaders of the state wanted violence was obvious to anyone on the spot, reading Southern papers. The police system, including highway police and sheriffs and deputies from other areas, was aligned against the federal forces and deliberately allowed the mob to form and failed to make any attempt to maintain control and prevent violence. A systematic campaign of deception laid the blame for the riot on the marshals and not on the mob violence. The day after the riot there was rioting in the Square in Oxford in which Negroes of the town who ventured out and Negro members of the armed forces were attacked. That day, just as in Faulkner's fiction, most Negroes took cover: Negro employees were absent from the university campus and the next day were brought to work by white staff members. The entire episode was a practical demonstration of the " 'Mississippi plan'—the use of riot as a political instrument,"[172] turned now against the federal government instead of against local and state Republican rule as during the Reconstruction.

The paradox of the South may be represented in two recollections of the time of the riot. Through the quiet evening air of September 30 in Oxford floated the tones of a church carillon playing "Love Divine, All Love Excelling" and "How Firm a Foundation"; at that very time a mob was gathering around the Lyceum and the U.S. marshals stationed there, where the riot broke out a couple of hours later. In the Oxford *Eagle* for October 11, 1962, John Cullen, author of *Old Times*

[172] Silver, p. 13. Statements about the riot are based on personal observation in Oxford and current accounts in Mississippi newspapers; they are confirmed by eye-witness accounts by both James Silver and Russell H. Barrett, *Integration at Ole Miss* (Chicago: Quadrangle Books, 1965), and by Walter Lord, *The Past That Would Not Die* (New York: Harper & Row, 1965). James Meredith's own account is given in *Three Years in Mississippi* (Bloomington: Indiana University Press, 1966).

in the Faulkner Country, expressed his rage at a statement
by Oxford clergymen calling on Mississippians to make
October 7 a time for repentance: Cullen asked what "the
citizens of Oxford" have done that they should repent and
asserted that citizens were "stabbed in the back" for standing
up for their rights. (Only the rights of white citizens were
ever considered.) The statement of the ministers acknowledged guilt in the "formation of the atmosphere" which
permitted the riot. In the same issue of the *Eagle,* the memory
text for the Sunday School lesson is: "Truly I perceive that
God shows no partiality" and the lesson is on the theme of
the fatherhood of God: "And as a father, God shows no
partiality to any of his children." The split in the Southern
psyche is distressingly evident.

   The examples of violence previously provided by his own
community, as well as the riots in Oxford and more recent
events in Mississippi, confirm the high incidence of violence
in Mississippi and the causes of it as represented by Faulkner.
In his handling of violence Faulkner made much less use of
physical brutality toward those inferior in class and caste and
of the physical suffering of those subjected to brutality than
the social facts, during and after slavery, would have war-
ranted. The reason may be conjectured—he wished to emphasize the moral aspects of violence: the destruction of
individual integrity when a man becomes one of a mob or
otherwise abdicates his personal judgment and feelings in
blind conformity to rigid orthodoxy; the destruction of human
dignity and self-respect that is less tolerable than physical
suffering and that will make a violent death an eligible choice
to a Lucas Beauchamp or a Wash Jones. In dealing with violence, Faulkner selected his characters and incidents with care,
used them with great technical restraint, and through them
revealed truths about Southerners and human nature that
could not be shown without the dramatic intensity to which
violence contributes.

5

THE CREATOR
AND HIS CREATION

THE world of Yoknapatawpha as it appears in the whole body of the fiction is presumably known to all of the characters, whose separate lives and visions form the total vision. One inhabitant of Yoknapatawpha, however, is missing in the pageant: unlike Fra Lippo Lippi, the artist did not depict himself, with an *iste perfecit opus*. After Faulkner began *Sartoris,* Maurice Coindreau believed, "he no longer lived in our world" but only appeared there: "his true domain was the town of Jefferson and Yoknapatawpha County. . . . With the odds and ends of reality offered by Oxford, Ripley, and the history of his family as a basis, he had begun to build his imaginary city and to people it with inhabitants."[1] After *Sartoris,* the first novel, apparently, about which he deeply cared,[2] Faulkner, as he roamed the streets of Oxford or stood on a corner of the Square, either watching and listening or

---

[1] Maurice Coindreau, "The Faulkner I Knew," *Shenandoah,* XVI (Winter, 1965), 32–33.

[2] Edith Brown Douds, in *William Faulkner of Oxford,* James W. Webb and A. Wigfall Green, eds. (Baton Rouge: Louisiana State University Press, 1965), p. 52.

too deeply absorbed in his own thoughts to heed familiar faces, moved between the two worlds of Oxford and Jefferson, responsive to whatever in his observations of the tangible world could be transmuted into the world of his own creation.

In addition to the logic which is inherent in Faulkner's material and the vision with which he contemplated his material, Faulkner's distinctive genius was responsible for the shaping of the Yoknapatawpha world. That rare type of creative imagination brought into being in his own mind a society peopled by characters who compelled him to tell their stories. Because his characters took on independent life, Faulkner could not plan his fictional series as a whole but had to work, except for *Snopes,* with one story at a time, often growing out of a picture or an idea spontaneously conceived:

It's an idea that begins with the thought, the image of a character, or with an anecdote, and even in the same breath, almost like lightning, it begins to take a shape that he can see whether it's going to be a short story or a novel. Sometimes, not always [*Faulkner in the University,* pp. 48–49].

Such involuntary lightning flashes are characteristic of what seems to be Faulkner's intuitive, imaginative art, derived from and directed by psychic sources inaccessible to volition and reason.

This imaginative creation of a whole society is what Faulkner most admired in Balzac's "intact world of his own." The unity it lends to Faulkner's works is more than the sum of the interrelationships between the various stories; behind his works looms a world having an independent existence. This world of the imagination is a reflection of the actual world but incomplete, revealed and illuminated by the selective creative impulse rather than invented. Each portion so selected and revealed then becomes part of the reality of the fictional world as well as part of the legend of its inhabitants. Thus Yoknapatawpha mirrors Lafayette County: a historical reality underlies myth which is invested with the authority of history, and neither the reality nor the myth is embraced in its entirety by any inhabitant. Like that of the ordinary person, the imagination of the creative artist seizes irrationally upon what is personally meaningful, but only the creative artist like Faulkner can recreate a reality and a myth from what is given. As an imaginative construct, idiosyncratically composed of matter selected from a given body of factual material, the myth of Yoknapatawpha has its artistically unrealized parallels in the consciousnesses of inhabitants of Lafayette County, in the fragmentary reflections and conceptions of their total world.

These fragmentary reflections when unsystematically arranged in works of art pose difficulties for the reader. Claude-Edmonde Magny compares Faulkner with Balzac, referring to recurrence of characters and overlapping of stories:

All this suggests the idea of a *total* world, which one can scarcely have an idea of, and which it is certainly impossible to understand when one knows only one or two of its parts; which moreover seems to have existed fully, at once, in the mind of the author, which is found thus placed (involuntarily and no doubt unconsciously) with regard to this universe, and "from the good side" in relation to him, when we, alas! see only the wrong side of the tapestry—a miserable situation and one which the author very often forgets, absorbed as he is in his vision and entirely taken by the effort to bring it up to date, just as it is, and without having the time to apply himself to setting it straight for us and to rendering it intelligible to us.

She also points out that Faulkner, like Balzac, makes the reader cooperate with the creator and supply the blanks between the parts of characters' lives which are filled in by the author, like supplying the shadows necessary to the painter.[3] One purpose of this study of Yoknapatawpha County and its people has been to aid the reader by helping him to see the whole tapestry from the right side.

The world of Faulkner's creation is not only a microcosm of the South, it is not only the universal scene of "human

[3] *L'Age du Roman Américain* (Paris: Éditions du Seuil, 1948), pp. 231, 235. (Translation by this writer.)

beings in conflict with their nature, their character, their souls, with others, or with their environment" (*Faulkner at Nagano*, p. 156)—to Faulkner it was "a kind of keystone in the universe . . . if it were ever taken away the universe itself would collapse." Faulkner expected his writing career and Yoknapatawpha to end together: "My last book will be the Doomsday Book, the Golden Book, of Yoknapatawpha County. Then I shall break the pencil and I'll have to stop."[4]

Magny's conception of Faulkner and Balzac is suitably headed "Competition with God the Father." Like Jehovah in Genesis, Faulkner peopled the world of his imagination with his own creations. This is the central fact, the essential truth of the creative process in Faulkner's work. He was too busy "trying to create flesh-and-blood, living, suffering, anguishing human beings" to be able to construct a conceptual, schematized plan. In his universe, there was neither the predestination of the Calvinistic God nor the foreknowledge of Milton's God: convinced that "any writer worth his salt . . . can create much better people than God can," Faulkner claimed no omniscient foreknowledge of, much less control over, what his characters would do (*Faulkner in the University*, pp. 47, 118). The characters live and move and have their being independently. They stand on their "hind legs and cast a shadow" and walk out of the book and "take off and so the writer is going at a dead run behind them trying to put down what they say and do in time" (*Faulkner in the University*, pp. 118, 120). His characters name themselves—usually with names characteristic of the actual region—and develop their own personality (*Faulkner in the University*, pp. 206, 96). As Dominique Aury observed, Faulkner is "no more merciful to his people than the Creator to the race of Cain and Abel."[5] His doomed characters are doomed by circumstances and their own natures, not by being used as pawns to demonstrate a concept of fatality.

[4] Jean Stein, "William Faulkner," in *Writers at Work: The Paris Review Interviews*, Malcolm Cowley, ed. (New York: Viking, 1958), p. 141.

[5] Quoted by Coindreau, p. 33. The rest of the quotation, however, suggests puppet-like characters, in contrast to Faulkner's own sense of the vitality and unpredictability of his creations.

Faulkner's account of the dynamic quality of his characters and his consequent compulsion to keep up with them and tell their stories is reinforced by John Faulkner's comment: "I think that if a man's characters didn't force him to write he would not do it at all."[6] The use of recurrent characters would greatly increase the creative urge. Faulkner's accounts of the creative process are limited but valuable in presenting the truth so far as he was conscious of it. Gay Wilson Allen notes the limitations of Faulkner's awareness:

But artistic creation takes place in solitude, with intense concentration and self-forgetfulness; and it involves all the realms of the author's being and experience to such an extent that the creation may seem alien to him in his more normal and relaxed hours.[7]

Once the creation, the work of art rather than the character, was completed, Faulkner did not like to go back to it or hear comments on it.[8] This characteristic is responsible for many of the discrepancies between accounts of the same events and characters in different stories, for numerous inaccurate statements about his works in the published interviews, and for his reluctance to revise his works for new editions. Faulkner was so busy trying to improve, so dissatisfied with what he had already done, that it was always the work in progress or in prospect that engaged his energies. An artist driven by demons is not driven backwards. Despite Faulkner's description of himself as a countryman, one may conjecture that writing was his most vital and personal activity, that creation was his life.

[6] John Faulkner, *My Brother Bill* (New York: Trident Press, 1963), p. 149. Unfortunately this account of William Faulkner gives little information about him as a writer except as factual information suggests fictional parallels.
[7] Gay Wilson Allen, "With William Faulkner in Japan," *American Scholar*, XXXI (Autumn, 1962), 571.
[8] John Faulkner, p. 172. But in a conversation with his editor, "Faulkner might ask, 'By the way, did you hear what happened to Sarty Snopes?'" ("The Curse and the Hope," *Time*, LXXXIV [July 17, 1964], 45).

The likeness of the author to God has been dealt with by Flaubert and James Joyce, two authors whom Faulkner admired, though he said that Joyce was "electrocuted by the divine fire" and that he could not, like Flaubert, "try to tell the truth in a chalice" (*Faulkner in the University,* pp. 280, 56). William York Tindall quotes a letter in which Flaubert says that the artist must "be in his work like God in creation, present everywhere and visible nowhere. Since art is a second world, its creator must act by analogous methods."[9] James Joyce, in a better known passage, says much the same thing:

The personality of the artist . . . finally refines itself out of existence, impersonalizes itself, so to speak. . . . The artist, like the God of the creation, remains within or behind or beyond or above his handiwork, invisible, refined out of existence, indifferent, paring his fingernails.[10]

Between *Sartoris* and *The Sound and the Fury,* Faulkner as the artist disappeared; his reappearances have been sporadic, the only sustained one being the prologues in *Requiem for a Nun* which represent Joyce's epical stage, preceding the final disappearance of the author: "the artist prolongs and broods upon himself as the centre of an epical event and this form progresses until the centre of emotional gravity is equidistant from the artist himself and from others."[11] Faulkner's creative genius also seems to explain his technique.

Given Faulkner's creative genius, the impossibility of long-range planning is apparent. Faulkner had both talent and genius, in the senses in which Malcolm Cowley uses the terms: " 'Genius' . . . would stand for everything that is essentially the gift of the subconscious mind—inspiration, imagination, the creative vision—while 'talent' would stand for conscious ingenuity, calculation, acquired skill, and the critical judgment that an author displays when revising his own work." If some-

[9] *The Literary Symbol* (Bloomington: University of Indiana Press, Midland Book Edition, 1955), p. 76.
[10] *A Portrait of the Artist as a Young Man* (New York: Viking, 1962), p. 215.
[11] *Ibid.,* p. 214.

times, as Cowley believes, Faulkner sacrificed his talent to his genius, being more interested in what "the voices" of his unconscious said to him than in technique,[12] perhaps he approached as near to God-like power as we should require. The comparative weakness of parts of *Snopes* is no doubt due to its origin in an inspiration that demanded trilogy development and that thus forced Faulkner to choose between delaying the completion of the trilogy or putting aside other intervening inspirations that were more urgent. When the compulsion seized him, Faulkner seemed to do best by yielding to it and letting his demon drive him until the work was completed.

Unpredictability was increased by another vital quality in Faulkner. He grew, he said, with his characters and learned from them:

. . . the writer is learning all the time he writes and he learns from his own people, once he has conceived them truthfully and has stuck to the verities of human conduct, human behavior, human aspirations, then he learns—yes, they teach him, they surprise him, they teach him things that he didn't know, they do things and suddenly he says to himself, Why yes, that is true, that is so [*Faulkner in the University,* p. 96].

In this respect also the creator of Yoknapatawpha County was like God—the God of *The Green Pastures.* This characteristic of Faulkner's would explain some of the apparent inconsistencies in characters who recur in the fiction over a long period, a conjecture confirmed in Faulkner's prefatory note to *The Mansion*:

[12] Malcolm Cowley, *The Faulkner-Cowley File: Letters and Memories, 1944–1962* (New York: Viking Press, 1966), pp. 158–159. Faulkner's bold experimentation and inexhaustible variety suggest that he was vitally interested in technique in the sense in which Mark Schorer uses the term: "the means by which a writer gets his initial impulse to create a work out into the open and over to his readers . . . ; the means by which the writer himself first finds out what he is really trying to say, from all those inarticulate impulses that impel him to say it, and then to say it, that is, to make it a created object" ("Notes on the Creative Act and Its Function," in *The World We Imagine* [New York: Farrar, Straus and Giroux, 1968], p. 395).

. . . the author has learned, he believes, more about the human heart and its dilemma than he knew thirty-four years ago; and is sure that, having lived with them that long time, he knows the characters in his chronicle better than he did then.

As Coindreau said of Faulkner's inconsistencies which were due to his power to restore his characters to life and give new roles to them: "A creator is not bound to be a courthouse clerk as well."[13] The very vitality of his characters and his own deep involvement with them were in conflict with the logical and reasonable consistency to be expected in a coherent and realistic society: the resuscitated and rejuvenated Nancy in *Requiem for a Nun,* whose death had seemed imminent in "That Evening Sun," is only one of several extreme examples, amid a host of minor ones.

The criticism that William Faulkner was not a great thinker and that the Yoknapatawpha fiction shows no clear consistent theory and plan is irrelevant. The Yoknapatawpha novels and stories as a dynamic, organic body of fiction would have defied planning by the author, who could not control creative imagination by an act of will or a process of reasoning. Northrop Frye's description of the poetic process applies equally well to Faulkner's fiction:

It could be said, of course, that poetry is the product, not only of a deliberate and voluntary act of consciousness, like discursive writing, but of processes which are subconscious or preconscious or half-conscious or unconscious as well. . . . It takes a great deal of will power to write poetry, but part of that will power must be employed in trying to relax the will, so making a great part of one's writing involuntary . . . ; it ssems now almost impossible to avoid the term "creative," when speaking of the arts. And creation, whether of God, man, or nature, seems to be an activity whose only intention is to abolish intention, to eliminate final dependence on or relation to something else, to destroy the shadow that falls between itself and its conception.[14]

[13] Coindreau, p. 34.
[14] *Anatomy of Criticism* (Princeton: Princeton University Press, 1957), pp. 88–89. For an analysis dealing with intention and uncon-

Faulkner's disregard of criticism of his work was wise, lest "Between the conception / And the creation" the Shadow fall and his characters become Hollow Men. In a later passage (p. 98) Frye pursues his biological analogy:

. . . the poet, who writes creatively rather than deliberately, is not the father of his poem; he is at best a midwife, or, more accurately still, the womb of Mother Nature herself. . . .

Carl Gustav Jung's account of the poet confirms Frye's:

The artist is not a person endowed with free will who seeks his own ends, but one who allows art to realize its purposes through him. . . .
   It makes no difference whether the poet knows that his work is begotten, grows and matures with him, or whether he supposes that by taking thought he produces it out of the void. His opinion of the matter does not change that fact that his own work outgrows him as a child its mother. The creative process has feminine quality, and the creative work arises from unconscious depths. . . . Whenever the creative force predominates, human life is ruled and moulded by the unconscious as against the active will, and the conscious ego is swept along on a subterranean current, being nothing more than a helpless observer of events. The work in process becomes the poet's fate and determines his psychic development.[15]

Perhaps that last statement is similar to what Coindreau had in mind when he said that Jefferson made Faulkner her slave: "She imposed attitudes, opinions, and ideas which transformed *him* into a citizen of Jefferson. The people, the animals, the buildings he loved were part of the landscape of

---

scious creation in the novel which throws light on how Faulkner must have written his fiction, see Brewster Ghiselin, "Automatism, Intention, and Autonomy in the Novelist's Production," *Daedalus,* XCII (Spring, 1963), 297–311.
   [15] "Psychology and Literature," in *The Creative Process,* Brewster Ghiselin, ed. (New York: New American Library, Mentor Ed., 1955), pp. 221, 222.

Yoknapatawpha."[16] It is obviously futile for an author or critic to attempt to predict the creative process by which a world like Yoknapatawpha comes into being.

The Doomsday Book of Yoknapatawpha County, *The Reivers,* is indeed the Golden Book that ends Faulkner's work. Of all the narrators, Grandfather Lucius Priest, speaking to his grandson, is closest to Faulkner at the time of writing, not only in age and circumstances but perhaps in mood.[17] The mellow tone, the emphasis on the old verities as discovered by a boy in his initiation into the adult world and confirmed by his elderly self, the combination of hilarious comedy with the truths of the heart—all may well reveal Faulkner the man. The wealth of characters and scenes, both familiar and new, makes *The Reivers* a substantial contribution to the world of Yoknapatawpha and an appropriate, though perhaps unpremeditated, conclusion.[18] The "world of William Faulkner" is now complete.

The basic parallels between that world and the geographical, historical, and social facts of Lafayette County are significant and impressive. There seem to be no major characteristics of society or of personal behavior which are not substantiated by facts, local or regional. Therefore the changes, omissions, and modifications assume a significance increased by the fidelity to fact in other respects. The changes noted which make Jefferson more typical than Oxford, the omission of such favorable aspects of reality as the exceptional citizens and leaders, the large and hospitable families, and education as an institution, and the modifications of less favorable aspects of reality in Mississippi as represented in the legal system, politics, and violence —all combine to show Faulkner to be neither a chauvinistic

[16] Coindreau, p. 34.

[17] One of the last portrait photographs of Faulkner shows him looking down and smiling, as he rarely did in photographs. His wife expressed a preference for that picture among a number taken at that time and remarked that he looked as if he were smiling at one of his grandchildren. See frontispiece.

[18] This idea is developed at length in my article, "*The Reivers*: The Golden Book of Yoknapatawpha County," *Modern Fiction Studies,* XIII (Spring, 1967), 95–113. Blotner cites an unfinished biography of John Sartoris, dated 1932 and titled "The Golden Book of Jefferson & Yoknapatawpha County in Mississippi as compiled by William Faulkner of Rowanoak" (p. 791). Blotner also quotes a letter to Malcolm Cowley, in regard to Cowley's plan for the Portable Library

glorifier nor a scathing critic of his land and people. The reality is no doubt better and worse than the fiction. William Faulkner himself is the most impressive evidence of what is vital and noble in the traditions of his society. If he suffered the tragedy of becoming a "pariah," as Hodding Carter said, to many white Mississippians, "whom he knew better than they knew themselves and pitied and loved," he "is all but forgiven" because he is better understood.[19] The dimensions of his world should be considered as reflecting what he was concerned with having his readers understand. Aspects of reality which lie outside the fictional world are outside the scope of this study, which does not pretend to cover the world of Oxford and Lafayette County. But Faulkner was faithful to one principle in his vision of the human world of Yoknapatawpha County, a principle which one may be sure applied equally to Lafayette County: its only despicable citizens are those who lack compassion for human needs and griefs.

The prevailing realism in the Yoknapatawpha fiction may, for artistic reasons, be distorted or obscured in separate works, but the distortions are minimized by viewing Yoknapatawpha as a whole. In the separate works or in the entire body of fiction, however, realism is only one aspect; it is helpful to know what is based on fact and what should be ascribed to imagination or moral purpose, but for interpretation of the whole mythology, realism is too narrow a criterion. Faulkner's "scrupulously faithful report of the real world" noted by Robert Penn Warren, and his "'thick' conception of fiction in which history, sociology, sexual psychology, moral analysis, and the religious sense kaleidoscopically interpenetrate in the presentation of an image of reality,"[20] beginning with *Sartoris,* are not adequate to explain the literary qualities of Yoknapatawpha fiction. The matter of the land and the people is transmuted by the alchemy of spirit, working through tech-

series collection: "By all means let us make a Golden Book of my apocryphal county" (p. 1187). For his last work, Faulkner returned to an idea he outlined in a letter to Robert Haas in 1940 (Blotner, pp. 1044–1055), rather than to the genealogical "Golden Book" he had essayed and abandoned.

[19] Hodding Carter, "The Forgiven Faulkner," *Journal of Inter-American Studies,* VII (1965), 143, 147.

[20] Robert Penn Warren, "The South, the Negro, and Time," in *Faulkner: A Collection of Critical Essays,* Robert Penn Warren, ed. (Englewood Cliffs, N.J.: Prentice-Hall, Inc., 1966), pp. 255, 252.

nique and style, into comedy and tragedy. Yoknapatawpha County becomes a microcosm not only of the South and of the United States but of the human world. The American dilemma and the human predicament are dramatized in the characters and families of Yoknapatawpha County. Even as the South produced its own myth, so, as the world of Yoknapatawpha was built up, a new legend was created and a mythology grew up in which the truths of the heart were revealed. The aspects of the Yoknapatawpha fiction with which this study has been concerned are those in which Faulkner's creative genius is most apparent. A study of the literary qualities which are achieved by talent and genius combined, whereby technique serves as a means to both discovery and revelation of meaning, is the critical goal for which this study of the world of Yoknapatawpha is a necessary first step.

APPENDICES

APPENDICES

A. THE COURTHOUSE

The story of the building of the courthouse in Yoknapatawpha adds picturesque and symbolic details to bare facts which are roughly parallel to the fiction. According to the history of the courthouse written by Annendal Harrison, an Oxford high school boy, and published in the Oxford *Eagle,* the room which was the first courthouse was attached to the trading post and served from 1836 to 1839. Faulkner has the room attached to the jail, in order that, for symbolic significance, the jail might be "older even than the town itself" (*Requiem for a Nun,* p. 213). The Jefferson courthouse was built from 1833 to 1836. The original Oxford courthouse was begun in 1839, of brick with wood trim, at a cost of $23,600 for both courthouse and jail, the latter in use until 1962. The courthouse was fifty-two feet by forty (Oxford *Eagle,* February 21, 1963). A photograph taken during Grant's occupation of the town shows a fence around the courthouse and inside the fence the tents of an Illinois regiment which was guarding Confederate prisoners in the courthouse. A photograph taken after the burning of the Square shows the walls and four chimneys still standing. The present courthouse was built in 1871, using only the foundation of the old one, and adding the cupola with its four clocks. It was enlarged by wings in 1952. The description

quoted from *Requiem for a Nun* raises the courthouse to mythic
proportions by exaggerating its size but has a factual basis, even
to the sparrows and pigeons, which, Mr. Harrison explains,
moved in before the rebuilt courthouse was complete and were a
hazard to the townspeople who frequented the courtyard. John
Faulkner described the Square as it was in his childhood, the activities there, and the changes since then (pp. 108–109). He
explained why Faulkner's symbolic pigeons are no longer in
evidence, both they and the sparrows having been dependent on
the age of horses. The original fence now surrounds a house in
which there was an idiot son whom the townspeople compare
with Benjy Compson. (John Faulkner's account of boy, house, and
fence [pp. 271–272] differs from the more popular version in
referring to the boy as an epileptic.) A. Wigfall Green's account
of the Square and town is excellent: "William Faulkner at
Home," reprinted in *William Faulkner: Two Decades of Criticism,* Frederick J. Hoffman and Olga W. Vickery, eds. (East
Lansing: Michigan State University Press, 1951), pp. 33–47.

B. RUINED MANSIONS

The prevalence of ruined mansions in Mississippi, in fact or fiction, is not necessarily a mark of the ravages of war and the consequent decline of ante-bellum plantations. As early as 1828 and 1832, "the consuming hunger with which the land had been used up, the irresponsible manner in which the soil had been exhausted and then abandoned" had produced in the southeastern states the scenes of "desolation that baffles description" which caused the South to be called "the Ireland of America." In the debates on the slavery problem in the Virginia Convention of 1832, Charles James Faulkner gave the cause for the change from virgin soil to a land "barren, desolate, and seared": "the withering, blasting effects of slavery" (J. W. Schulte Nordholt, *The People that Walk in Darkness* [New York: Ballentine Books, 1960], pp. 44–46). The exploitation of the land in Mississippi which constitutes one of the main themes of the Yoknapatawpha fiction was due in part to men whose planter forefathers had been guilty of the same "land-killing" and who found it easier to despoil a new area than to restore an old one. Howard Odum remarks that in the modern South, Frederick Law Olmsted would see in "mile after mile, area upon area, pictures of the same limited and sordid conditions of which he complained" (*The Way of the South* [New York: Macmillan, 1947], p. 133).

One ruin near Oxford, inhabited by a Negro family, has a spring like that on the Old Frenchman's Place and a family graveyard in which the names *Jones* and *Bond* recall the Sutpen story. The earliest date of birth noted was 1802; of death, 1871. Du Bois describes similar ruins inhabited by descendants of slaves, with "phantom gates and falling homes" (*The Souls of Black Folk* [Greenwich, Conn.: Fawcett Publications, 1961], p. 97). In an area first settled well after 1800, the Beauchamp house was falling into ruin in 1859 ("Was," *Go Down, Moses,* pp. 9, 10). Another Lafayette County ruin, uninhabited, was that of a house finished in 1857. It was a two-storey, ten-room house of typical architecture with four columns at the front, much like Faulkner's house. The bricks in the chimneys were made on the place, as was customary. Plastered throughout, it had one ceiling which was

a replica of one at the Hermitage in Nashville. The family graveyard, at a little distance from the house, is still in use. One grave
has the birthplace and date, Abbeville, South Carolina, 1780, and
the death date 1857. The original owner of the house, Dr. Felix
Grundy Shipp, came to the area in 1833 with a family of sixty-
five, including slaves, and bought land in Lafayette County in
1839. In the road, the cedars, and the grounds, the Old Frenchman's Place resembles the Shipp house, but these are all typical
features. The Shipp house is used to illustrate Faulkner scenes
in *Literary America* ([New York: Dodd, Mead, 1952], p. 149),
in "Faulkner County" (*Life,* LV [August 2, 1963], 48–49), and
in Martin Dain's *Faulkner's County: Yoknapatawpha* ([New
York: Random House, 1964], p. 84); Dain's book also pictures
the first house described above (p. 101): it is now abandoned and
is rapidly disintegrating.

C. THE CAVALIER TRADITION

In the myth of the South, one of the most attractive and persistent traditions, popular as a theme in literature, is that the Southern gentry were descended from the aristocratic Cavalier supporters of the Stuarts in seventeenth- and eighteenth-century England and Scotland. Faulkner's founding families illustrate Cash's denial of the Cavalier thesis, and Faulkner's fiction gives the Cavalier tradition a turn toward less romantic truth: the Compsons, the only family associated with the Jacobite cause, were descended from a Glasgow printer, not from gentlemen or aristocrats. William R. Taylor, in his study of the development of the Cavalier tradition in literature, *Cavalier and Yankee: The Old South and American National Character* (Garden City, N.Y.: Doubleday Anchor Books, 1961), compares Wilbur Cash and Faulkner as men with "ardent but tortured Southern loyalties" who "possessed the vision required to look into the deepest recesses of Southern character and, if only fleetingly, see it in all of its complexity. They, not the critical outsiders, have spied the Snopeses lurking in the plantation portico, and not only spied them, but understood them, feared and respected them, and known they belonged" (p. 303). Contrary to the legend, the origin of most of the planters was not aristocratic but yeoman or even poor white, two or three generations removed (Du Bois, p. 34; Myrdal, pp. 460, 1209). The legend of Cavalier origin developed during the 1830s and 1840s and was established by the time of the Civil War: "In the final stages of the tradition, Southerners in all states became descendants of the Cavaliers," according to Jay B. Hubbell, in *Southern Life in Fiction* ([Athens: University of Georgia Press, 1960], p. 334). Taylor agrees on the origin of the legend in the 1830s, identifies the first period of its flourishing as from 1832 to the mid-fifties and the second period from 1880 to 1900. He notes that the creation of the legend was due to "aspiring men seeking to understand the values of the society in which they made their way" (pp. 126, 43).

D. MISSISSIPPI PLANTATIONS AND PLANTERS

The size of Sutpen's Hundred not only is unrealistic in relation
to its geographical location but would be exceptional in Mississippi even in the period of expansion before the Civil War. John
Hathorn cites only two men in Lafayette County who in 1850
owned 5,000 acres or more; one owned 5,000 acres and the other
7,500. In 1860, only A. H. Pegues owned as much as 5,000 acres
(p. 99). Thomas Dabney of Hinds County, "a distinguished example of the gentry who moved to the Southwest" from Tidewater Virginia, expanded his holdings to 4,000 acres and after
twelve years was still living in "the old house with the leaky
roof" built when he first settled. The six Mississippi plantations
of Wade Hampton III totaled 10,409 acres (Eaton, *The Growth
of Southern Civilization,* pp. 39, 40, 43). A "first-rate cotton plantation" in the fertile lower Mississippi Valley is described by Frederick Law Olmsted as having a "large and handsome mansion,"
unoccupied because its owner had not visited it for several years,
and covering "several square miles," with 1,300 to 1,400 acres
under cultivation and 135 slaves. Plantation houses in another
area were "of a cottage class." The overseer on the first-rate plantation represents a plantation figure completely absent from
Yoknapatawpha County but typical elsewhere and sometimes successful enough to become a plantation owner. Sutpen's career in
the West Indies suggests a possible parallel to such success. Olmsted also notes that "among the rich planters of Mississippi" the
number of men of refinement and cultivation ". . . is smaller in
proportion to that of the immoral, vulgar, and ignorant newly-
rich than in any other part of the United States" (*The Slave
States before the Civil War* [New York: Capricorn Books, 1959],
pp. 200–201, 177, 186). In *The Southern Plantation: A Study in
the Development and the Accuracy of a Tradition* (Gloucester,
Mass.: Peter Smith, 1962), Francis Pendleton Gaines remarks on
the general tendency in fiction illustrated by the accounts of the
Grenier, Sutpen, and Compson plantations before the war: "The
scale of life was steadily enlarged, the colors were made increasingly vivid. Estates swelled in size and mansions grew proportionately great" (p. 64). The imaginative recreation of the Sutpen

story, long after the events, allows ample scope for much magnification, whether through the local legend and the twice-told Compson tales or through Miss Rosa's childhood memories of the demon, the ogre, and his estate before it was devastated by the Civil War.

E. COLONEL WILLIAM C. FALKNER

In the character of Colonel John Sartoris, William Faulkner made use of some parts of the Mississippi legend about his great-grandfather, Colonel William C. Falkner. Since he was not trying to present historical facts or even to preserve in the fictitious character all of the essential aspects of his ancestor's character and personality, Faulkner used details which were commonly regarded as factual but which within recent years have been revealed as legendary; many parts of the legend he did not use at all. The most complete and fully documented account of the life of W. C. Falkner is an unpublished Ph.D. thesis by Donald Duclos, "Son of Sorrow" (University of Michigan, 1962). This thesis was a main source of Thomas F. Hickerson's pamphlet, *The Falkner Feuds,* which purports to distinguish between fact and legend and sometimes does so. Hickerson, who is related to Thurmond, the slayer of Colonel Falkner, was motivated by desire to disprove not only the legend, which favored Falkner, but also the fiction about Colonel Sartoris; in this respect, Hickerson unjustifiably attacks Faulkner for departing from the facts about Colonel Falkner's life in writing about a fictitious character whose resemblance to Colonel Falkner is very limited.

Although Faulkner's source was the legend, he makes Colonel Sartoris a much less versatile person than Colonel Falkner and shows, even though the point of view is that of young Bayard in *The Unvanquished,* the arrogance that caused Sartoris to have "no friends: only enemies and frantic admirers" (*Requiem for a Nun,* p. 238). A comparison between Colonel Sartoris and Leroy and William Percy, aristocrats prominent in Mississippi, shows how far short of a living ideal the Sartorises fall. V. O. Key says of the Percys, in *Southern Politics:* "Bound by a tradition of honor, of dignity, of fair-dealing, the family has typified the best of the old Southern aristocracy" (p. 238). William Percy's comments on the hubristic sense of superiority of Southern leaders as perhaps one cause of the Civil War and on manners as essentially morals further reveal the significance of the weakness of Colonel John Sartoris (*Lanterns on the Levee* [New York: Knopf, 1953], pp.

69, 120). His bad manners, his disregard for the self-esteem and dignity of others, caused his death. Colonel Sartoris's too belated renunciation of violence ("An Odor of Verbena," p. 175) has a basis in the legend that Colonel Falkner was unarmed when Thurmond shot him. Hickerson quotes an interview between Robert Cantwell and Faulkner in which Faulkner stressed Colonel Falkner's overbearing nature but said that the Colonel grew tired of killing and was unarmed when shot (pp. 2–3). Hickerson disproved parts of the legend as given by John Faulkner in *My Brother Bill,* notably the statement that Colonel Falkner was shot on the street between the depot and the square. Hickerson quotes a statement by Andrew Brown that Falkner spoke to Thurmond through the open window of Thurmond's office and "moved his hand toward his hip pocket," whereupon Thurmond, thinking Falkner might be reaching for a gun, fired a pistol which was lying on his desk. That the shooting occurred at Thurmond's office is confirmed by papers discovered in the demolition of an old freight depot at New Albany and quoted in the New Albany *Gazette,* November 5, 1964. A news dispatch by J. Brown to the Memphis *Avalanche,* the night of the shooting, says: "The difficulty occurred in front of Thurmond's office and was the result, we learn, of demonstrations made by Falkner, he being intoxicated." (Falkner was then thought not fatally injured.) A dispatch from Charles Douglass on November 7 described Falkner as a self-made man who "had accumulated a fortune of nearly half a million dollars" and who "was noted for his noble nature and generous deeds." Thurmond was indicted for manslaughter and acquitted. All court papers concerning the trial disappeared from the file. The New Albany *Gazette* article also disproved the legend, used by William Faulkner, of political rivalry as a motive in the killing: Falkner was elected to the state legislature without opposition.

Had Faulkner wished to romanticize and glorify Colonel Falkner, he need only have endowed Colonel Sartoris with all of Colonel Falkner's talents and interests and presented his actions in the favorably exaggerated light of the legend according to which Colonel Falkner was remembered in Mississippi as a great railroad builder for having carried through a project, originated by others in 1856, and constructed twenty-six miles of narrow-gauge railroad in 1872. (Duclos gives a detailed account of the whole railroad enterprise, pp. 195–198.) In comparison with either facts or legend, Colonel Sartoris is a diminished version of Colonel Falkner as a military leader and railroad builder, a man of violence who met a violent end.

BIBLIOGRAPHY

BIBLIOGRAPHY

Agee, James and Walker Evans. *Let Us Now Praise Famous Men*. Boston: Houghton Mifflin Company, 1960.

Allen, Gay Wilson. "With William Faulkner in Japan." *American Scholar,* XXXI (Autumn 1962), 571.

Bailey, Kenneth K. *Southern White Protestantism in the Twentieth Century*. New York: Harper & Row, 1964.

Baker, Carlos. "William Faulkner: The Doomed and the Damned." In *The Young Rebel in American Literature,* Carl Bode, ed. London: Heinemann, 1959.

Baldwin, James. *Notes of a Native Son*. Boston: The Beacon Press, 1957.

Barrett, Russell H. *Integration at Ole Miss*. Chicago: Quadrangle Books, 1965.

Beck, Warren. "Faulkner and the South." *Antioch Review,* I (Spring 1941), 82–94.

Berland, Alwyn. *"Light in August*: The Calvinism of William Faulkner." *Modern Fiction Studies,* VIII (Summer 1962), 159–170.

Bertault, Philippe. *Balzac and the Human Comedy*. English version by Richard Monges. New York: New York University Press, 1963.

Bouvard, Loïc. "Conversation with William Faulkner," trans. Henry Dan Piper. *Modern Fiction Studies,* V (Winter 1959–1960), 361–364.

Boyle, Sarah Patton. *The Desegregated Heart*. New York: William Morrow & Company, 1962.

Brooks, Cleanth. *William Faulkner: The Yoknapatawpha Country*. New Haven: Yale University Press, 1963.

Brooks, Peter. "The Laboratory of the Novel." *Daedalus,* XCII (Spring 1963), 265–280.

Brown, Calvin S. "Faulkner's Manhunts: Fact into Fiction." *Georgia Review,* XX (Winter 1966), 388–395.

——. "Faulkner's Geography and Topography." *PMLA,* LXXVII (December 1962), 652–659.

Brown, Sterling A. "A Century of Negro Portraiture in American Literature." *Massachusetts Review,* VII (Winter 1966), 73–96.

Burgum, Edwin Berry. *The Novel and the World's Dilemma.* New York: Oxford University Press, 1947.

Burrows, Robert N. "Institutional Christianity as Reflected in the Works of William Faulkner." *Mississippi Quarterly,* XIV (Summer 1961), 138–147.

Cable, George W. *The Negro Question: A Selection of Writings on Civil Rights in the South,* Arlin Turner, ed. Garden City, N.Y.: Doubleday Anchor Books, 1958.

Caldwell, Erskine. *Deep South: Memory and Observation.* New York: Weybright and Talley, 1968.

Calhoun, Arthur W. *A Social History of the American Family,* Vols. II, III. New York: Barnes and Noble, 1960.

Canzoneri, Robert. *"I Do So Politely": A Voice from the South.* Boston: Houghton Mifflin Company, 1965.

Carter, Hodding. "The Forgiven Faulkner." *Journal of Inter-American Studies,* VII (1965), 137–147.

——. *The Winds of Fear.* New York: Award Books, 1964.

Cash, Wilbur J. *The Mind of the South.* New York: Vintage Books, 1960.

Chesnut, Mary Boykin. *A Diary from Dixie.* Boston: Houghton Mifflin Company, 1961.

Church, Margaret. *Time and Reality: Studies in Contemporary Fiction.* Chapel Hill: The University of North Carolina Press, 1963.

Clark, Thomas D. *Pills, Petticoats and Plows: The Southern Country Store.* Indianapolis and New York: Bobbs-Merrill, 1944.

Coindreau, Maurice. "The Faulkner I Knew." *Shenandoah,* XVI (Winter 1965), 27–35.

Cowley, Malcolm. *The Faulkner-Cowley File: Letters and Memories, 1944–1962.* New York: Viking Press, 1966.

——. *The Portable Faulkner,* rev. ed. New York: Viking Press, 1967.

Crooks, Esther J. and Ruth W. *The Ring Tournament in the United States.* Richmond: Garrett and Massie, 1936.

Cullen, John, in collaboration with Floyd Watkins. *Old Times in the Faulkner Country.* Chapel Hill: The University of North Carolina Press, 1961.

"The Curse and the Hope." *Time,* LXXXIV (July 17, 1964), 44–48.

Daiches, David. *Critical Approaches to Literature.* Englewood Cliffs, N.J.: Prentice-Hall, Inc., 1956.

Dain, Martin. *Faulkner's County: Yoknapatawpha.* New York: Random House, 1964.

Davis, Allison, Burleigh B. Gardner and Mary R. Gardner. *Deep South: A Social Anthropological Study of Caste and Class,* abridged ed. Chicago: University of Chicago Press, Phoenix Books, 1965.

Deupree, N. D. "Greenwood LeFlore." *Publications of the Mississippi Historical Society,* VII (Oxford, 1903), 141–151.

Dollard, John. *Caste and Class in a Southern Town.* New York: Doubleday Anchor Books, 1957.

Doster, William. "William Faulkner and the Negro." Ph.D. Thesis, University of Florida, 1959.

Douglas, Harold and Robert Daniel. "Faulkner and the Puritanism of the South." *Tennessee Studies in Literature,* II (1957), 1–13.

Dowdey, Clifford. *The Great Plantation: A Profile of Berkeley Hundred and Plantation Virginia from Jamestown to Appomattox.* New York: Bonanza Books, 1957.

Doyle, Bertram Wilbur. *The Etiquette of Race Relations in the South.* Chicago: University of Chicago Press, 1937.

Du Bois, W. E. Burghardt. *Black Reconstruction in America, 1860–1880.* Cleveland and New York: The World Publishing Company, Meridian Books, 1962.

——. *The Souls of Black Folk.* Greenwich, Conn.: Fawcett Publications, Premier Americana, 1961.

Duclos, Donald P. "Son of Sorrow." Ph.D. Thesis, University of Michigan, 1962.

Eaton, Clement. *The Growth of Southern Civilization, 1790–1860*. New York: Harper & Row, Harper Torchbooks, 1963.

——. *A History of the Southern Confederacy*. New York: Collier Books, 1961.

Falkner, Murry C. *The Falkners of Mississippi*. Baton Rouge: Louisiana State University Press, 1967.

Faulkner, John. *My Brother Bill*. New York: Trident Press. 1963.

Faulkner, William. *Absalom, Absalom!* New York: Modern Library, 1951.

——. *As I Lay Dying*. New York: Vintage Books, 1964.

——. *Collected Stories of William Faulkner*. New York: Random House, 1950.

——. *Go Down, Moses*. New York: Modern Library, 1942.

——. *Intruder in the Dust*. New York: Random House, 1948.

——. *Knight's Gambit*. New York: Random House, 1949.

——. *Light in August*. New York: Modern Library, 1950.

——. *The Reivers*. New York: Random House, 1962.

——. *Requiem for a Nun*. New York: Random House, 1951.

——. *Sanctuary*. New York: Random House, 1958.

——. *Sartoris*. New York: Random House, 1956.

——. *Snopes: The Hamlet, The Town, The Mansion*. New York: Random House, 1964.

——. *The Sound and the Fury*. New York: Vintage Books, c1956.

——. *The Unvanquished*. New York: Random House, 1965.

——. *Essays, Speeches, and Public Letters*, James B. Meriwether, ed. New York: Random House, 1965.

——. *Faulkner at Nagano*, Robert A. Jelliffe, ed. Tokyo: Kenkyusha, 1958.

——. *Faulkner in the University*, Frederick L. Gwynn and Joseph L. Blotner, eds. Charlottesville: University of Virginia Press, 1959.

——. *Faulkner at West Point*, Joseph L. Fant III and Robert Ashley, eds. New York: Random House, 1964.

Frye, Northrop. *Anatomy of Criticism*. Princeton: Princeton University Press, 1957.

Gaines, Francis Pendleton. *The Southern Plantation: A Study in the Development and the Accuracy of a Tradition.* Gloucester, Mass.: Peter Smith, 1962.

Ghiselin, Brewster. "Automatism, Intention and Autonomy in the Novelist's Production." *Daedalus,* XCII (Spring 1963), 297–311.

Grenier, Cynthia. "The Art of Fiction: An Interview with William Faulkner—September, 1955." *Accent,* XVI (Summer 1956), 167–177.

Griffin, John Howard. *Black Like Me.* New York: New American Library, Signet Books, 1962.

Guerard, Albert J. *Conrad the Novelist.* Cambridge: Harvard University Press, 1958.

——. Introduction to "Perspectives on the Novel." *Daedalus,* XCII (Spring 1963), 199–205.

Guerard, Albert Jr. *"Requiem for a Nun:* An Examination." *Harvard Advocate,* CXXXV (1951), 1–9, 41–42.

Hathorn, John Cooper. "A Period Study of Lafayette County from 1836 to 1860 with Emphasis on Population Groups." M.A. Thesis, University of Mississippi, 1938.

Hawkins, E. O. "Jane Cook and Cecilia Farmer." *Mississippi Quarterly,* XVIII (Fall 1965), 248–251.

Hickerson, Thomas Felix. *Echoes of Happy Valley.* Chapel Hill: T. H. Hickerson, 1962.

——. *The Falkner Feuds.* Chapel Hill: The Colonial Press, 1964.

Hoffman, Frederick J. and Olga Vickery. *William Faulkner: Three Decades of Criticism.* East Lansing: Michigan State University Press, 1960.

Howe, Russell Warren. "Prejudice, Superstition, and Economics." *Phylon,* XVII (3rd quarter, 1956), 215–226.

Howell, Elmo. "William Faulkner and the Andrews Raid in Georgia, 1862." *Georgia Historical Quarterly,* XLIX (1965), 187–192.

——. "William Faulkner's Caledonia: A Note on *Intruder in the Dust." Studies in Scottish Literature,* III (1966), 248–252.

——. "William Faulkner and the Chickasaw Funeral." *American Literature,* XXXVI (January 1965), 523-525.

Hubbell, Jay B. *Southern Life in Fiction.* Athens: University of Georgia Press, 1960.

Jamison, Lena Mitchell. "The Natchez Trace: A Federal Highway of the Old Southwest," *Journal of Mississippi History,* I (April 1939), 82–89.

Jenks, Christopher. "Mississippi: When Law Collides with Custom." *The New Republic,* CLI (July 25, 1964), 15–18.

Johnson, Charles S. *Shadow of the Plantation.* Chicago: University of Chicago Press, Phoenix Books, 1966.

Joyce, James. *A Portrait of the Artist as a Young Man.* New York: Viking Press, 1962.

Jung, Carl Gustav. "Psychology and Literature." In *The Creative Process,* Brewster Ghiselin, ed. New York: New American Library, Mentor Edition, 1955.

Kardiner, Abram and Lionel Ovesey. *The Mark of Oppression: Explorations in the Personality of the American Negro.* Cleveland and New York: The World Publishing Company, Meridian Books, 1962.

Kaufman, Harold F. "Mississippi Churches: A Half Century of Change." *Mississippi Quarterly,* XII (Summer 1959), 105–135.

Kennedy, John F. *Profiles in Courage.* New York: Pocket Books, 1963.

Kerr, Elizabeth M. "*The Reivers*: The Golden Book of Yoknapatawpha County." *Modern Fiction Studies,* XIII (Spring 1967), 95–114.

——. "William Faulkner and the Southern Concept of Woman." *Mississippi Quarterly,* XV (Winter 1961–1962), 1–16.

Key, V. O., Jr. *Southern Politics in State and Nation.* New York: Vintage Books, Caravelle Edition, 1949.

Kirwan, Albert D. *Revolt of the Rednecks: Mississippi Politics, 1876–1925.* Lexington: University of Kentucky Press, 1951.

Kullman, Frederick S. "A Comparison of Yoknapatawpha and Lafayette Counties." M.A. Thesis, Harvard University, 1958.

Lee, Harper. *To Kill a Mocking Bird.* Philadelphia and New York: J. B. Lippincott Company, 1960.

Leonard, George. "A Southerner Appeals to the North." *Look*, XXVIII (August 11, 1964), 15–16.

Lord, Walter. *The Past That Would Not Die*. New York: Harper & Row, 1965.

Lumpkin, Katharine Du Pre. *The Making of a Southerner*. New York: Alfred A. Knopf, 1947.

Lytle, Andrew. *The Velvet Horn*. New York: McDowell, Obolensky, 1957.

——. "The Working Novelist and the Mythmaking Process." *Daedalus*, LXXXVIII (Spring 1959), 326–338.

McGill, Ralph. *The South and the Southerner*. Boston: Little, Brown and Company, 1963.

McIlwaine, Shields. *The Southern Poor-White from Lubberland to Tobacco Road*. Norman: University of Oklahoma Press, 1939.

Maclachlan, John M. "No Faulkner in Metropolis." In *Southern Renascence: The Literature of the Modern South*, Louis D. Rubin, Jr. and Robert D. Jacobs, eds. Baltimore: Johns Hopkins Press, 1953. Pp. 101–111.

Magny, Claude-Edmonde. *L'Age du roman Américain*. Paris: Éditions du Seuil, 1948. Pp. 196–243.

Malinowski, Bronislaw. *Sex, Culture, and Myth*. New York: Harcourt, Brace and World, 1962.

Meredith, James. *Three Years in Mississippi*. Bloomington: Indiana University Press, 1966.

Meriwether, James B. "Faulkner and the South." In *Southern Writers: Appraisals in Our Time*, R. C. Simonini, ed. Charlottesville: University of Virginia Press, 1964. Pp. 142–161.

Miller, Douglas T. "Faulkner and the Civil War: Myth and Reality." *American Quarterly*, XV (Summer 1963), 200–209.

Miller, J. Hillis. *Charles Dickens: The World of his Novels*. Cambridge: Harvard University Press, 1959.

Miner, Ward. *The World of William Faulkner*. New York: Grove Press, c1952.

Morris, Wright. "The Violent Land: Some Observations on the Faulkner Country." *Magazine of Art*, XLV (March 1952), 99–104.

Mumford, Louis. *The Golden Day*. Boston: Beacon Press, 1957.

Myrdal, Gunnar. *An American Dilemma*. New York and Evanston: Harper & Row, 1962.

Nilon, Charles H. *Faulkner and the Negro*. New York: The Citadel Press, 1965.

Nordholt, J. W. Schulte. *The People That Walk in Darkness,* trans. M. B. Wijngaarden. New York: Ballentine Books, 1960.

O'Connor, William Van. "Protestantism in Yoknapatawpha County." In *Southern Renascence: The Literature of the Modern South,* Louis D. Rubin, Jr. and Robert D. Jacobs, eds. Baltimore: Johns Hopkins Press, 1953. Pp. 153–169.

Odum, Howard. "On Southern Literature and Southern Culture." In *Southern Renascence: The Literature of the Modern South,* Louis D. Rubin, Jr. and Robert D. Jacobs, eds. Baltimore: Johns Hopkins Press, 1953. Pp. 84–100.

——. *The Way of the South*. New York: Macmillan Company, 1947.

Olmsted, Frederick Law. *A Journey in the Seaboard Slave States in the Years 1853–1854 With Remarks on their Economy*. New York: G. P. Putnam's Sons, 1904.

——. *The Slave States before the Civil War,* Harvey Wish, ed. New York: G. P. Putnam's Sons, Capricorn Books, 1959.

Oxford *Eagle*: July 19, 1906; August 30, 1928; December 13, 1928; April 3, 1930; April 18, 1930; February 2, 1933; December 12, 1935; December 10, 1936; May 13, 1937; September 8, 1950; October 11, 1962; February 21, 1963.

Parsons, Malcolm B. "Violence and Caste in Southern Justice." *South Atlantic Quarterly,* LX (Autumn 1961), 458–468.

Percy, William Alexander. *Lanterns on the Levee*. New York: Alfred A. Knopf, 1953.

Peters, William. *The Southern Temper*. Garden City, N.Y.: Doubleday and Company, 1959.

Phillips, Ulrich. *Life and Labor in the Old South*. Boston: Little, Brown and Company, 1963.

Pollitt, Daniel G. "Timid Lawyers and Neglected Clients." *Harper's Magazine,* CCXXIX (August 1964), 81–86.

Powdermaker, Hortense. *After Freedom: A Cultural Study in the Deep South.* New York: Viking Press, 1939.

Rank, Otto. *The Myth of the Birth of the Hero and Other Writings,* Philip Freund, ed. New York: Vintage Books, 1959.

Richardson, H. Edward. "The Ways that Faulkner Walked: A Pilgrimage." *Arizona Quarterly,* XXI (Summer 1965), 133–145.

Robertson, Ben. *Red Hills and Cotton: An Upcountry Memory.* New York: Alfred A. Knopf, 1942.

Rougemont, Denis de. *Love in the Western World,* trans. Montgomery Belgion. New York: Pantheon Books, 1956.

Rowan, Carl T. *South of Freedom.* New York: Alfred A. Knopf, 1952.

Rubin, Louis D., Jr. *The Faraway Country: Writers of the Modern South.* Seattle: University of Washington Press, 1963.

Rubin, Louis D., Jr. and Robert D. Jacobs, eds. *South: Modern Southern Literature in its Cultural Setting.* Garden City, N.Y.: Doubleday and Company, Dolphin Books, 1961.

——. *Southern Renascence: The Literature of the Modern South.* Baltimore: Johns Hopkins Press, 1953.

Schorer, Mark. *The World We Imagine: Selected Essays.* New York: Farrar, Straus and Giroux, 1968.

Shaw, Joe C. "Sociological Aspects of Faulkner's Writing." *Mississippi Quarterly,* XIV (Summer 1961), 148–152.

Silberman, Charles E. *Crisis in Black and White.* New York: Random House, 1964.

Silver, James. Review of *An American Dilemma. Bookweek,* paperback issue, January 10, 1965.

——. *Mississippi: The Closed Society.* New York: Harcourt, Brace and World, 1964.

Simkins, Francis Butler. *The South Old and New.* New York: Alfred A. Knopf, 1948.

Smith, Lillian. *Killers of the Dream.* Garden City, N.Y.: Doubleday and Company, Anchor Books, 1963.

Stampp, Kenneth M. *The Peculiar Institution: Slavery in the Ante-Bellum South.* New York: Vintage Books, 1964.

Stein, Jean. "William Faulkner." In *Writers at Work: The*

Paris Review Interviews, Malcolm Cowley, ed. New York: Viking Press, 1958. Pp. 119–141.

Stone, Phil. "William Faulkner: The Man and his Work." *Mississippi Quarterly,* XVII (Summer 1964), 148–164.

Stone, Philip Alston. *No Place to Run.* New York: Viking Press, 1959.

Taylor, William R. *Cavalier and Yankee.* Garden City, N.Y.: Doubleday and Company, Anchor Books, 1963.

Tindall, William York. *The Literary Symbol.* Bloomington: Indiana University Press, Midland Book, 1955.

Turnell, Martin. *The Novel in France.* New York: Vintage Books, 1958.

Turner, Arlin. "William Faulkner, Southern Novelist." *Mississippi Quarterly,* XIV (Summer 1961), 117–130.

Vahanian, Gabriel. *Wait Without Idols.* New York: George Braziller, 1964.

Vickery, Olga. *The Novels of William Faulkner, A Critical Interpretation,* revised ed. Baton Rouge: Louisiana State University Press, 1964.

Volpe, Edmond. *A Reader's Guide to William Faulkner.* New York: The Noonday Press, 1964.

Warren, Robert Penn. "Faulkner: The South, the Negro, and Time." In *Faulkner: A Collection of Critical Essays,* R. P. Warren, ed. Englewood Cliffs, N.J.: Prentice-Hall, Inc., 1966. Pp. 251–271.

——. "William Faulkner." In *William Faulkner: Three Decades of Criticism,* Frederick J. Hoffman and Olga Vickery, eds. East Lansing: Michigan State University Press, 1960. Pp. 109–124.

Wasserstrom, William. *Heiress of All the Ages.* Minneapolis: University of Minnesota Press, 1959.

Webb, James W. and A. Wigfall Green, eds. *William Faulkner of Oxford.* Baton Rouge: Louisiana State University Press, 1965.

Wellek, René. *Concepts of Criticism,* Stephen G. Nichols Jr., ed. New Haven: Yale University Press, 1963.

Welter, Barbara. "The Cult of True Womanhood: 1820–1860." *American Quarterly,* XVIII (Summer 1966), 151–174.

Wharton, Vernon Lane. *The Negro in Mississippi, 1865–1890.* New York: Harper Torchbooks, 1965.

Wolfe, Thomas. *The Story of a Novel.* New York: Charles Scribner's Sons, 1936.

Woodward, C. Vann. "The Irony of Southern History." In *Southern Renascence: The Literature of the Modern South.* Louis D. Rubin, Jr. and Robert D. Jacobs, eds. Baltimore: Johns Hopkins Press, 1953.

——. *The Strange Career of Jim Crow.* New York: Oxford University Press, Galaxy Books, 1957.

Zweig, Stefan. *Balzac,* trans. William and Dorothy Rose. New York: Viking Press, 1946.

INDEX

INDEX

212; courthouse, county seat, 44, 45, 46-48, 86—destruction of, 92, 93n; elevation, 34; establishment and history of, 9, 13, 83n, 84-92, 93n; federal courthouse, 45; Freedman Town, 43; geography of, 24; golf course, 39; and Hortense Powdermaker's "Cottonville," 119n; hotels, 48n, 85; hub and spoke pattern, 30, 32, 34-35, 43-44, 68; identification of buildings in, 70-71; industry in, 67n; jail, 48-49, 205; mansions in, 42-43 (see also names of estates); map, 43; museum, 45, 93n; Negro Hollow, 43; Negroes in, 130-136; newspaper in, 29-30; "Oxford" location and, 35-37; planing mill, 154; political liberals in, 194; poor whites, 127, 130; pride of past in, 118; railroad in, 36, 49; roads in, 68n; social undesirables in, 132-133; the Square, 27, 36n, 39, 40n, 42n, 43, 44, 45-46, 48, 49, 50, 225—burning of, 47, 92, 93n; twentieth-century society in, 117-136; University and, 35-38, 96, 126n, 194; violence in, 212-213; water tower, 45

Jenks, Christopher, "Mississippi: When Law Collides with Custom," 197n

Jesus, see Manigault, Nancy

Jim Crow laws, 109-110

Job Uncle, 114, 132

Johnson, Charles, Shadow of the Plantation, 67n, 112n, 145n, 149n, 150n, 152n, 153n, 184n, 210n

Johnson, Paul B., 225

Joliet, Ill., 206

Jones, Wash, 56, 95, 134, 152, 188, 215; Milly, granddaughter of, 98; killing of Sutpen and Milly, 215; Sutpen and, 97-98

Journeys, significance of, 68-70

Joyce, James, A Portrait of the Artist as a Young Man, 232

Jung, Carl Gustav, "Psychology and Literature" (The Creative Process), 235

"Justice, A," see Collected Stories

Ka concept, 16

Kardiner, Abram, and Ovesey, Lionel, The Mark of Oppression: Explorations in the Personality of the American Negro, 112, 113n

Kaufman, Harold F., "Mississippi Churches: A Half Century of Change," 178n, 179

Kennedy, John F., Profiles in Courage, 104n, 105n

Kentucky, 85n

Kerr, Elizabeth M., Bibliography of the Sequence Novel, 5n; "The Reivers: The Golden Book of Yoknapatawpha County," 236n; "William Faulkner and the Southern Concept of Woman," 159n

Key, V. O., Jr., Southern Politics in State and Nation, 125, 137, 182n, 185, 186, 190n, 197n, 248

Kirwan, Albert D., The Revolt of the Rednecks: Mississippi Politics, 1876-1925, 119n, 161n, 190n

Knight's Gambit (Faulkner), 36n, 45, 65, 69, 122n, 123, 195; "An Error in Chemistry," 216n; "Hand upon the Waters," 86; "Knight's Gambit," 45; "Monk," 58, 73; "Tomorrow," 62n, 153, 154

Ku Klux Klan, 93n, 100, 101n, 141n, 188n, 191, 207, 220

Kullman, Frederick S., "A Comparison of Yoknapatawpha and Lafayette Counties," 80n, 100n

Lafayette County, see Yoknapatawpha County

Lafayette Springs, Miss., 62

Lamar, Lucius Quintus Cincinnatus, 85n, 103-104, 187

Lamar, Ruby, 103, 177

Land: exploitation of, 21-22; man's relationship to, 84

Lawlessness, see Violence

Lee, Harper, To Kill a Mockingbird, 172n, 184n, 196, 201n, 202n, 203n

Lee, Gen. Robert E., 94

Leflore, Greenwood, 82, 83n

Legal system, double standard of jus-

Rivers: in Garden of Eden, 31; Mississippi, 18, 57, 59; Oceanus, 31; Okatoba, 67; Otuckalofa, 67; Tallahatchie, 31, 32, 34, 54, 55n, 57, 60, 94; Yazoo, 57; Yoknapatawpha (Yocona), 31, 32, 34, 63, 65, 100
Rivers, Miss Reba, 70, 132, 140, 198
Roads: in Jefferson, 40n; Natchez Trace, 85n; "Old 6," 63n, 65n; in Yoknapatawpha Co., 35, 40n, 57-58, 68-71
Robertson, Ben, *Red Hills and Cotton: An Upcountry Memory,* 39n, 41-42, 43n, 51, 59n
Rogers, Will, 182
Roosevelt, Franklin D., 155n
Rose, Arnold, 145n, 186
"Rose for Emily, A, " see *Collected Stories*
Roskus, 90; *see* McCaslin
Rowan, Carl, 110; *South of Freedom,* 110n, 116, 156, 188, 197, 204
Rowan Oak (Faulkner's home), 42
Rubin, Louis D., Jr., *The Faraway Country: Writers of the Modern South,* 37, 209
Rubin, Louis D., Jr., and Jacobs, Robert D., *South: Modern Southern Literature in its Cultural Setting,* 105n; *Southern Renascence: The Literature of the Modern South,* 25n, 30n, 118n, 174n

Saint-Hilaire, 5; *see* Geoffroy Saint-Hilaire
Sanctuary (Faulkner), 18, 28, 29, 36n, 47, 64, 66, 70, 122, 132, 159, 172, 177, 178, 190, 204, 206, 214, 222; violence in, 207
Sardis, Miss., 88n
Sardis Dam, 64
Sardis Lake, 56
Sardis Reservoir, 36n, 54, 57
Sartoris, Algernon, 88n
Sartoris, Col. Bayard ("Old Bayard"), 38, 48n, 49, 60, 95, 96, 97, 100, 101, 108, 121, 122, 123, 130, 131, 150, 172, 180, 210
Sartoris, Young Bayard, 25, 36n, 49, 53, 60, 69, 98-99, 123, 131, 140,

173n, 180, 213-214, 248; "rebel without cause" type, 121
Sartoris, Benbow, 122
Sartoris, Brenda, 88
Sartoris, Col. John, 38, 49, 53, 88, 92, 93, 94, 95, 96, 99, 121, 122, 130, 167n, 223; killing of carpetbaggers, 101, 102, 211; monument, 50-51; model for, 94n, 248-250; shooting of, 96, 210
Sartoris, John (son of Old Bayard), 121
Sartoris, John (twin of Young Bayard), 121, 173n, 212n
Sartoris, Narcissa (Benbow), 40, 122, 123, 159, 172, 177, 212n
Sartoris family, 38, 49, 118, 119, 122, 123, 137, 167n, 180; "moral weakness" of, 121; and the railroad, 52-53; servants of, 114, 130-132; *see also* Strother
Sartoris plantation, 36n, 38-39, 61, 88, 95
Sartoris (Faulkner), 8, 18, 36n, 37, 38, 39, 40, 50-51, 52, 60, 71n, 92, 101, 102n, 114, 122, 129, 131, 140, 159, 172, 210n, 227, 232, 237
Sawmill, Quick's, 154
Schorer, Mark, *The World We Imagine,* 233n
Scott, Sir Walter, 5, 156
Segregation, 176; slavery vs. caste system, 109-111; *see also* Education
Seminary (College) Hill, 32, 33, 35, 179
Sentinel (Yazoo newspaper), 210n
Sequence novel: and Faulkner, 6-7, 10, 15-16, 20; social history sequence novel, 5, 6; and Thomas Wolfe, 13-16
Sex, Sex relations: apartheid and, 160n; obsession with, 210; white-Negro, 157-158, 160, 163n; *see also* Homosexuality; Incest; Miscegenation; Rape
"Shall Not Perish," see *Collected Stories*
Sharecropping system, 130, 144-147, 148, 149, 150n, 152, 154n
Shaw, Joe, "Sociological Aspects of Faulkner's Writing," 160n, 162

John Sartoris' Railroad

T A L L A H A T C H I E

Fishing Camp
where Wash Jones
killed Sutpen, later bought and
restored by Major Cassius de Spain

Sutpen's Hundred
12 mi.

#314

Sartoris
Plantation
E. Gin. 4 mi.

Church which Thomas
Sutpen rode fast to

Reverend Hightowers,
where Christmas was killed

Miss Joanna Burden's, where
Christmas killed Miss Burden, & where
Lena Grove's child was born

Courthouse where Temple Drake testified, and
Confederate Monument which Benjy had to
pass on his LEFT side

#6

Holston House

Sawmill where Byron Bunch first saw Lena Grove

FAULKNER'S MISSISSIPPI

JEFFERSON & YOKNAPATAWPHA COUNTY

Roads
Railroads
Rivers

OXFORD & LAFAYETTE COUNTY

Roads
Railroads
Rivers

Miss Rosa
Coldfield's

Compson
mile

To Mottstown,
where Jason
Compson lost his
niece's trail, and where
Anse Bundren and
his boys had to go in
order to reach
Jefferson

Y O C O N A

#7

Y O K N A P A T A W P H A

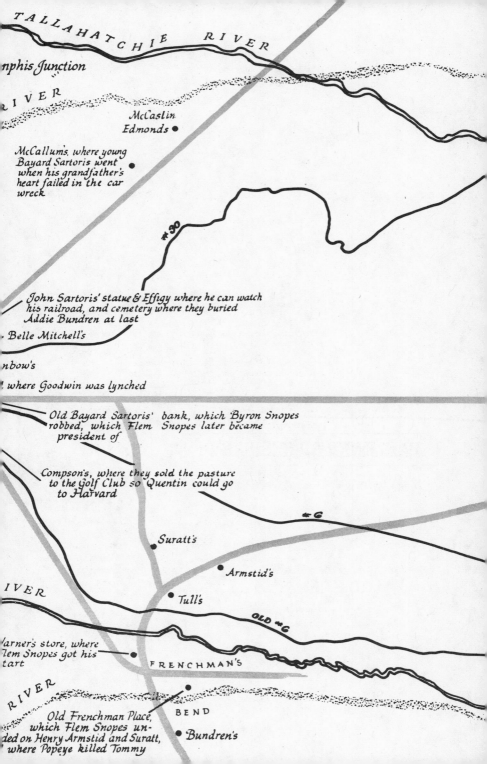

TALLAHATCHIE RIVER

...nphis Junction

...RIVER

McCaslin
Edmonds •

McCallum's, where young
Bayard Sartoris went
when his grandfather's
heart failed in the car
wreck •

#30

John Sartoris' statue & Effigy where he can watch
his railroad, and cemetery where they buried
Addie Bundren at last

Belle Mitchell's

...nbow's

...where Goodwin was lynched

Old Bayard Sartoris' bank, which Byron Snopes
robbed, which Flem Snopes later became
president of

Compson's, where they sold the pasture
to the Golf Club so Quentin could go
to Harvard

#6

Suratt's •

Armstid's •

Tull's •

...IVER

OLD #6

...arner's store, where
...lem Snopes got his
...tart •

FRENCHMAN'S

...RIVER

BEND

Bundren's •

Old Frenchman Place,
which Flem Snopes un-
...ded on Henry Armstid and Suratt,
where Popeye killed Tommy